Have a very

Happy Birthday

Gillian

Lots of Love

Jill & Steve

David L. Gosling was principal of Edwardes College in the University of Peshawar from 2006-2010. He trained as a nuclear physicist and has held positions in the universities of Hull and Delhi (St Stephen's College), the East-West Center in Hawaii, and at the World Council of Churches in Geneva where he was director of Church and Society. More recently he taught in the Faculty of Education at Cambridge University. He was also Spalding Fellow at Clare Hall. He has published on ecological and scientific issues in south Asia, and on nuclear power.

'This very personal history of a great institution now facing an uncertain future raises some hard questions about Western responses to the political crises of Pakistan and its neighbours, not least a clear statement of why drone warfare is so gravely counterproductive. As one man's perspective on a complex and painful situation, it needs careful reading and pondering, especially by those who shape Western strategy in the region.' **– Professor Rowan Williams, Master of Magdalene College, Cambridge, Former Archbishop of Canterbury**

'A fascinating, informative but disturbing read with its descriptions of the rise of the Taliban, escalating violence in the political scene and corruption in unexpected places. What shines through is the founding commitment of Edwardes College to excellence in education and service as well as the author's own commitment, as principal in threatening times, to continue this with his own passionate resolution to ensure equal opportunities for women. No wonder he quotes Mandela, "Education is the most powerful weapon you can have to change the world".' **– Dame Mary Tanner, Former President for Europe, World Council of Churches**

'Having visited Peshawar and Edwardes College many times I can confirm the authenticity of David Gosling's portrayal of events. He deserves great credit for his unrelenting commitment to maintaining and developing the College's academic standards and for his stand against the corruption and nepotism which infected even the Church of Pakistan. Despite a death threat and many disappointments the author always maintains a deep empathy with the people in and around Edwardes College. He also gives important pointers towards a better understanding of the manifold problems faced by Christians and Muslims in this region.' **– Dr Gunter Mulack, Former German Ambassador to Pakistan and first German Commissioner for Dialogue with the Muslim World**

'David Gosling's courageous and vivid account of his four years as principal of the distinguished Edwardes College in Pakistan's ancient frontier city of Peshawar, adjoining Afghanistan, provides so much more than just a personal memoir accompanied by insightful comments and attractive photographs. His wide knowledge of the Indian subcontinent, its rich history and culture, and his own scientific and educational expertise enable him to bring into view wide vistas of tribal and global politics, unravelling some of the complex tapestry of political machinations in an essentially still feudal frontier society. Gosling retraces the major lines of radicalisation and describes in some detail the unprecedented levels of violence in Peshawar, much of it connected with years of using destructive drones by Western powers. It is a provocative, hard-hitting account full of amazing local, national and international detail. But ultimately it is also a clarion call for the radically transformative power of education, linked to a vision of hope that positive collaboration and peace must be possible.—**Professor Ursula King, Institute of Advanced Studies, University of Bristol**

Readers on the North American continent would certainly benefit from this account of the historical background of the Pak/Afghan region, as well as from knowing that quality education is available to students of all ethnic backgrounds. As principal of Edwardes College Gosling deftly met the numerous challenges of a Christian college whose students were mainly Muslim. He describes the political and social problems of the area, yet offers hope for an educational institution many of whose alumni have gone on to become leaders in all walks of life. – **Thomas J. Lindell PhD, Emeritus Professor, University of Arizona**

'Every page reminds me of those dark days in Peshawar when the terrorists seemed to be moving closer and closer, and how our principal led the college. At the same time he was able to increase academic standards all round, especially among the women students and teachers. An important feature of the book is its portrayal of Sufi-inspired Islam which is much closer to our hearts than imported versions; there are also references to the inspiring science-based legacy of Muhammad Iqbāl.'– **Muhammad Jehangir, Professor of English, Edwardes College, Peshawar**

Frontier of Fear

Confronting the Taliban on Pakistan's Border

David L. Gosling

◆

The Radcliffe Press
LONDON • NEW YORK

An imprint of I.B. Tauris

Published in 2016 by The Radcliffe Press
An imprint of I.B.Tauris & Co. Ltd
London • New York
Reprinted 2016
www.ibtauris.com

ISBN: 978 1 78453 468 4
eISBN: 978 0 85772 993 4

A full CIP record for this book is available from the British Library
A full CIP record is available from the Library of Congress

Library of Congress Catalog Card Number: available

Typeset by Saxon Graphics Ltd, Derby
Printed and bound by CPI Group (UK) Ltd, Croydon, CR0 4YY

This book is dedicated to the teaching and administrative staff and the students of Edwardes College, Peshawar, and the younger members of St John's Cathedral and All Saints' Church, Peshawar. I am grateful to all of them for their wisdom, friendship and affection.

* * * * *

Humanity is all one body,
To torture another is simply to wound yourself.
When you don't look for faults in others,
They will conceal your weakness in return.
Make your path straight now, by the bright light of day;
For pitch darkness will come without warning . . .
The heart that is safe in the storm
Is the one which carries others' burdens like a boat.

Abdur Rahman (seventeenth-century Pashto poet)

Contents

CONTENTS

List of Illustrations and Tables

(Please note that all images are copyright of the author with the exception of those numbered 13 and 21.)

Tables

Introduction

In a country that has five million children out of school (three million of them girls) it may seem incongruous to prioritise higher education. But prestigious secondary and higher education institutions such as Edwardes College – to be the focus of much of what follows – are capable of producing the calibre of leaders able to address wider educational issues at the appropriate levels – national, regional and local.

For more than a hundred years Edwardes College in Peshawar, close to the Afghan border, has provided quality education to young people in Khyber-Pakhtunkhwa (formerly known as the North-West Frontier Province). It was the first college in the province to become co-educational and has consistently maintained high academic standards, especially in the sciences.

The following account describes the events in and around the college during the period 2006-10, interspersing them with the political changes that partially shaped them. It carries the reader from a prosaic and nostalgic beginning into the furious backlash of Taliban violence against 'soft' targets, which claimed innumerable lives; the author also received a death threat. These incidents are listed in Chapter 5, but two subsequent atrocities in particular aroused international condemnation; the bombing of All Saints' Church in September 2013 and the terrorist attack on the Army Public School in December 2014, killing 132 children.

In spite of the dramatic – though tragically inevitable – title of this volume, several chapters offer credible alternatives to the fundamentalist versions of Islam which fuel violence. These are notably in Chapters 6 and 7, which consider the Sufi-inspired Islam of the border region and the more recent educationally-based thinking of Iqbāl and his associates.

There are three appendices to the main narrative. The first contains details of the investigation into the embezzlement of half a million pounds from college funds. The second appendix is the principal's final report to the College Board of Governors in May 2010. This usefully supplements the early chapters and provides concrete evidence of all-round academic improvement, especially among the women students. The tables contain geographical information about the home location of students, especially in the Afghan border areas.

The third appendix consists of a report by the author commissioned for the US Defense Secretary. It is an estimate of Pakistan's potential role in bringing about peace in Afghanistan and stresses the need for education at all levels throughout the region. In the words of Nelson Mandela, 'Education is the most powerful weapon you can use to change the world.'

I should like to thank Sir Nicholas Barrington, former British High Commissioner in Pakistan, for encouraging me to take up the position of principal of Edwardes College and for helpful suggestions about this text. I should also like to thank former principal Dr Ron Pont, Canon Dr Dan O'Connor, and Professor Muhammad Jehangir for reading through parts of it. I am grateful to my former secretary, Shahzad Ashraf, for taking so many excellent photographs, and to Matthew Wright for processing them. Most of all, I should like to thank Mrs Rosemary Smith for her meticulous typing of the manuscript and helpful stylistic suggestions.

David L. Gosling
frontieroffear@gmail.com

Maps of Khyber-Pakhtunkhwa and Peshawar

District map of Pakistan's North-West Frontier Province (NWFP, since renamed Khyber-Pakhtunkhwa) and Federally Administered Tribal Areas (FATA).

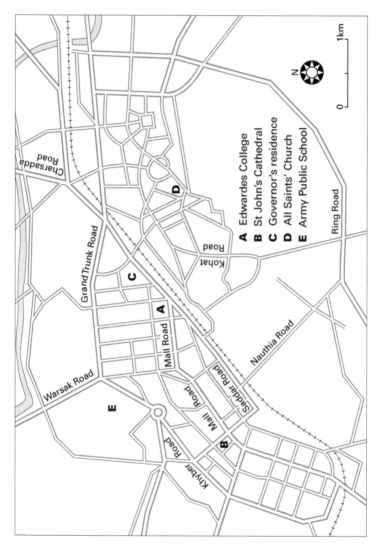

Map of Peshawar showing important locations mentioned in the text

A Edwardes College
B St John's Cathedral
C Governor's residence
D All Saints' Church
E Army Public School

1

The Prince Who Never Came

'It's good that you're a scientist,' remarked my predecessor as principal of Edwardes College, Peshawar, as we sat together in the college car, and shook hands before parting. It was evening, and the shadows were lengthening. The youthful voice of the *muezzin* at the nearby Darwish Masjid on Mall Road began to chant the *maghrib* prayer, robustly competing with a cacophony of birdsong.[1]

Huw Thomas had been principal for five years before my arrival at the beginning of September 2006. He was an Oxford history graduate, and had held clergy posts in Addis Ababa and Cairo in addition to becoming a canon of Liverpool Cathedral. Many of the college students addressed him as 'Canon' without any idea of what it meant. He possessed a warm and genial personality, which won him friends among staff and students alike. On this last evening he would drive himself back to the college, prior to his departure the next day.

'And by the way,' Huw remarked, almost as an afterthought, 'the Prince of Wales will be coming to the college as soon as Ramazan is over.'[2]

I was more than a little taken aback by this unexpected announcement. Ramazan was due to start fairly soon, and would last for a month, so I had little more than six weeks to find my feet and prepare for a visit by Prince Charles and his wife Camilla as part of their official visit to Pakistan. How would I cope?

The voice of the *muezzin* had been joined by several others, and it was getting dark. A dignified wave from Huw, and away he drove into the night, his last in the huge colonial-style 'bungalow', which served as the principal's residence. He flew from Islamabad to Heathrow, where no chauffeured car awaited him, and I imagined him standing at the inter-city bus station guarding such luggage as the airline had allowed on the flight.

* * * * *

For a substantial part of my time in Peshawar, the provincial Governor, Chief Minister, Chief Secretary, and the Vice-Chancellor of the university were all graduates of Edwardes College – Edwardians. So was the Pakistani High Commissioner in Delhi. Much the same could be said for the products of the comparable St Stephen's College in Delhi, where I had previously worked for a number of years – thus, until recently, the Indian High Commissioner in London was a Stephanian, as still are several senior members of the Indian government. The daughter of India's former prime minister headed the history department at St Stephen's. For such and other reasons that should become apparent, alumni of these and a few similar colleges are much more likely than others to find their way into European and other Western centres. This adds significance to these particular educational institutions, their histories and often paradoxical characteristics.

Edwardes College was established as a higher education institution in 1900. It grew out of a high school founded by the Church Missionary Society (CMS) in 1855, and was named after Sir Herbert Edwardes (1819–68) – soldier turned administrator – who was a CMS vice-president. Degrees were originally awarded by the University of Punjab based in Lahore; this was also the case for St Stephen's College in Delhi, which had been founded earlier. It is interesting that although these colleges have been described as Western and dubbed elitist, both initially adopted local vernacular languages as their medium of instruction, rather than English. In

Figure 1. The oldest Edwardes College buildings display Mughal architectural features

1952, Edwardes College transferred for degree-awarding purposes to the University of Peshawar.

In 1973/74, the Federal Government led by Prime Minister Z. A. Bhutto instituted a thoroughgoing policy of nationalisation in which church foundations such as Kinnaird, Forman Christian, Gordon, Murray and Edwardes colleges were targeted. All succumbed except Edwardes, and this on account of the tenacity of the college community and its robust Australian principal Phil Edmunds, and the opposition of the local Pashtun-dominated provincial government to policies emanating from Islamabad. This resulted in a compromise whereby the provincial Governor became chair of a Board on which the local government, the church, the university and the college were all represented, the two vice-chairs being the Bishop of Lahore and the provincial Minister for Higher Education. This arrangement has worked well for most of the subsequent years.

The college remains a Christian foundation (United Church of Pakistan) belonging to the provincial government and the Lahore Diocesan Trust Association, in which the CMS vested the ownership of many of its former properties following

Independence. It is also important to note that the college was the first in the province to introduce co-education, a progressive move in an extremely conservative region.

During its more than a hundred years as the premier higher education institution in the then North-West Frontier Province, Edwardes College has received many distinguished visitors. These have included Mahatma Gandhi in 1933 and 1938. Muhammad Ali Jinnah visited three times – the third in the dark days of 1947, when the division between India and Pakistan led to appalling bloodshed on both sides of the border. The Archbishop of Canterbury, Rowan Williams, had come more recently. In view of the college's patronage by such luminaries it was not surprising that the Prince of Wales should have been encouraged to pay the college a visit.

There were six weeks before the arrival of Their Royal Highnesses, and I had not yet begun to take stock of my new responsibilities. Principal Huw had walked me briefly around the campus; en route to the science block he waved his hand towards the former cafeteria on the other side of the sports field: 'Don't let that fellow back,' he urged, explaining how he had terminated an unsatisfactory caterer without realising the extent to which a barrage of court orders could prevent the building from being used for any other purpose. When I left four years later the case was still being batted between the upper and lower courts – but at least lectures were taking place in the building.

Vice-principal Naveed Attaullah was busy in the chemistry laboratories, which were sparsely though adequately stocked. He was smartly dressed in an immaculate suit, and distinguished by a smart moustache. The bursar, Kanwal Isaacs, had come to meet me at the airport. His moustache was military and very large – so much so that when former principal Ron Pont came back on a visit, he commented on its prominence. Both vice-principal and bursar were Punjabis and senior members of the Cathedral Church of St John, where the headquarters of the Peshawar Diocese of the Church of Pakistan are located.

An athletic-looking younger man was shouting at a group of students, wanting to know why they were not in their classrooms.

That was Kalimullah – or more usually just Kalim – the chief proctor and head of the English Department, who hails from an area close to the Swat valley. In the staff room I met other staff – Muhammad Jehangir, also from the English Department, Nasim Haider and Donald Joseph, both biologists, Naveed Ali, head of Computer Science, and Shah Mehmoud, who was initially to be my secretary. I also met Mrs Nasira Manzoor, lecturer in physics, whom I was to appoint as the college's first women's officer – everybody called her Madame Nasira.

College admissions were almost complete, and the most popular courses such as Pre-Medical, Pre-Engineering and Computer Science had their full quota. But there were some stragglers, and Huw sat me in on an interview with three such, who had arrived unexpectedly and late, together with their school principal. John, Israer and Saijit were from Landikotal, a small village overlooking the Khyber Pass. All were church members, and were late on account of the many security problems arising from the war across the border in Afghanistan, compounded by the activities of a warlord called Mangal Bagh, who had risen to prominence from humble origins as a bus conductor.

The three spoke good English and their marks were just below the Pre-Engineering cut-off. They had no money to pay their fees, but Huw gave them a kindly smile and waved them towards the admissions office. I subsequently solved their financial problems with a tuition fee concession and put them up free of charge in the recesses at the back of my spacious new house.

Two years after I left Pakistan all three of these students were still in regular contact, and had passed their exams. They were back in the Khyber Agency, where John had a job with Vodafone, Israer was working for Immigration and Customs at the border crossing of Torkham, and Saijit was applying for scholarships – with the help of myself and Huw Thomas he got one to the USA. Armed with mobile phones and laptops, Saijit and Israer were probably able to tell me more about exchanges between NATO convoys crossing the Khyber Pass and the Taliban than any regular media source.

* * * * *

Among the small group that had come to meet me at Peshawar airport were Sarah Safdar, Professor of Social Work at Peshawar University, and Benita Rumalshah, wife of the bishop. Sarah was a member of the College Board of Governors, representing the Diocese, and had informally interviewed me for the job of principal during her research project at Durham University. Benita had had a distinguished career as a school principal in India prior to marriage, and almost became head of Auckland House in Shimla – which is north India's equivalent to Roedean in Britain. But as a result of skulduggery between the Bishop of Amritsar (who chaired the school Board) and St Stephen's College in Delhi, she didn't get the job, and returned with her husband to Peshawar, where he became bishop. Both these eminent women offered me breakfast, and as I sensed tension between them, I ended up eating breakfast twice.

The provincial Governor, who chaired the College Board, wanted to meet me the following day. He was Lt General Jan Muhammad Aurakzai, appointed by General Pervez Musharraf, at that time President, and still in uniform, having ousted Nawaz Sharif some years earlier in a coup. General Aurakzai was an appropriate choice because his family was local and hailed from the Aurakzai district, which is part of the Federally Administered Tribal Areas (FATA) and close to the Afghan border.

In spite of his military bearing, General Aurakzai possessed a warm and kindly personality, and took an immense interest in the college – even though he himself was a graduate of Islamia College, our main rival situated near the university campus on the far side of town. Our first meeting was brief, and he indicated to me that my channel of communication to him was to be through his military secretary, a smart and good-looking colonel whose uniform could have been tailored in Savile Row. He was aware of the forthcoming visit by the Prince of Wales – 'You will be told,' he commented reassuringly.

The bishop duly materialised from his latest foreign travels, and in his capacity as a vice-chair of the Governing Body, introduced me formally to the teaching staff. 'I am a simple man' were my first words – which I repeated at my final farewell dinner four years later. I apologised for the fact that I had taught for some years at a rival college in India (St Stephen's), but they brightened when I stated my credentials as a physicist. Not knowing what else to say, I seized on some knowledge I had of their most famous philosopher-poet, Muhammad Iqbāl, explaining how much he appreciated Einstein's 'new vision of the universe'.[3] Their looks became blank again, so I stopped.

It was customary to begin each academic year with an assembly in the Canterbury Hall, which had been dedicated by Archbishop Rowan Williams. The hall was packed with as many as 800 students at a time according to year, all wearing college uniform, the young women sitting together on one side. The teaching staff were in a group and I sat on a raised platform wearing academic robes, as advised by the vice-principal. The bishop read the college prayer – carefully crafted by a former principal to be equally acceptable to Christians and Muslims – introduced me and welcomed me on behalf of the college and the Board.

I stood and moved towards the microphone. But then a strange thing happened. Another person – whom later I discovered to be the diocesan director of education – tried to get there first. I smiled at him and looked at the bishop, who motioned me forwards with his eyes. I stood before the microphone and greeted everybody confidently with the words '*assalam-ualaikum*' ('peace be upon you'), to which everybody replied '*wa-alaikum-salam*' ('peace be upon you also').

* * * * *

Details of the Royal visit finally arrived, not, as I had anticipated, from the British High Commission, but from the Ministry of Foreign Affairs via the Governor's Military Secretary. The covering letter read as follows:

Government of NWFP

No. D/PW/Admn: Deptt:/1-30/2005-11/310

Dated Peshawar, the 19.10.06

The Military Secretary to

Governor, NWPF

Subject:- OFFICIAL VISIT OF HRH THE PRINCE OF WALES

Dear Sir,

I am directed to refer to the subject noted above and to enclose herewith the visit programme of HRH The Prince Wales to Peshawar on 31.10.2006 by Special Aircraft at 1110 hours for further necessary arrangements please.

Yours faithfully

[signature illegible]

Assistant Protocol Officer

I was impressed by the procedurally correct capitalisation of the definite article.

The accompanying document gave more details:

SECRET

Ministry of Foreign Affairs

(Protocol Division)

PS. Secy: Administrative Dept

Diary No 5137 Dated 18.10.06

Subject: Official Visit of HRH The Prince of Wales

HRH the Prince of Wales shall undertake an official visit to Pakistan at the invitation of the Prime Minister from 29 Oct–03 Nov 2006. The dignitary and spouse shall be VVIP State Guests.

A copy of the tentative visit program is enclosed. It is requested that necessary action as indicated below may please be taken:-

(a) *Security* The VVIP security is to be provided to the Royal couple at all places [...]

(b) *Full Red Carpet* to be spread on first arrival and final departure at each destination.

(c) *03X Helicopters* to be provided by the Cabinet Division for the trip [...] Flights would commence and terminate at Islamabad Heliport [...]

(e) *Inland Air Travel* will take place by special flight Boeing 737 using [...] Lahore, Peshawar [...]

(h) *Media Coverage* As it is essentially a goodwill visit and the first trip to Pakistan by the Heir to the British Throne, full media coverage of the engagements may be arranged at all locations [...]

(o) *02X bullet-proof/armored cars* to be made available for the VVIPs at Islamabad, Lahore and Peshawar by MFA and Provincial Governments respectively.

Forwarded for information and necessary action as requested

[signature illegible]

Deputy Chief of Protocol (V-1)

My mind was racing. Did we have a red carpet? I called the vice-principal.

'Red carpet?' he queried, and called the hostel manager.

'Red carpet?' he repeated.

'Did anybody see a red carpet when the Archbishop of Canterbury came?' I asked. There was silence. Meanwhile my secretary was phoning the Governor's residence to see if they had a spare red carpet.

The Governor's staff had access to two red carpets, but one would be at the airport, while the other would be covering the vast staircase leading up to His Excellency's residence. By this time I had called a college officers' meeting to discuss the problem.

'Would it be possible,' I speculated, 'to take one of the red carpets from the airport and drive it to college while the Prince is with the Governor?'

'What if there is a traffic hold up?' asked the vice-principal. The prospect of a red carpet arriving by road after the Prince and his entourage had arrived was too dreadful to contemplate. What were we to do?

Suddenly the bursar appeared in my office doorway, his huge moustaches twitching with excitement.

'There is a red carpet in a cupboard underneath the Arts building,' he declared triumphantly. And so there was. It was old and dusty, so we immediately commissioned all the *malis* (gardeners) and sweepers to line up along its length and brush it clean.

'And what about the line-up?' queried Nasim Haider, the meticulous director of studies. I assumed this to be the college representatives first to greet the Prince.

'What line-up?' intruded a new voice. The bishop had appeared in the doorway and wanted to join in our discussions.

'As vice-chair of the Governing Body, you must be there, Bishop Sahib,' I pronounced deferentially.

'And the Old Edwardians' Board representative,' urged Kalimullah, the chief proctor.

'And Professor Sarah, who is also on the Board,' I urged, thinking it would be good to have at least one woman present to match the Prince's wife.

'No,' interrupted the bishop. 'Our director of education, Humphrey Peters, must be there.'

'But,' I argued, 'he will meet the Prince at the British Council reception later.' But the bishop was emphatic, and nobody else was prepared to disagree with him.

Normally the bishop was accommodating towards my suggestions, but not this time. Whether I liked it or not, Their Highnesses would be greeted by a line-up of none-too-youthful men.

* * * * *

I had met the Prince of Wales at a British High Commission function in Delhi, and liked his downbeat humour. The occasion was in honour of his mother's birthday, and the England cricket team were also there. He made no bones about the fact that most people were probably more interested in meeting the cricketers than him, and was probably right. Indians and Pakistanis adore cricket.

What might the Prince be interested in talking about at Edwardes College? In Delhi I had had a brief discussion with him about environmental issues, in particular the death of vultures as a result of the use of a tranquilliser given to cattle.

'Ah, the vultures,' he mused, knowingly. But he was interested when I told him that Saddam Hussein had become India's latest supplier of these birds, and was a frequent visitor.

A phone call from the British High Commission informed me that the Prince would give his longest speech during his visit in our college.

'What about?'

'Dialogue.' Oh, and did we have a red carpet?

Dialogue, I wondered; presumably between religious traditions. But why do we need that? I had already been in college long enough to sense that neither Muslims nor most of the Christian minority wanted to be identified according to their religion. We all strictly observed Ramazan, and were careful to end Friday classes in time for the *jum'a* prayers – because Pakistan is an Islamic Republic. But in other respects, the college prided itself on non-factional solidarity among its members. I decided that in my speech of welcome to the Prince I would quote the words of a former principal, the Revd R. H. Noble, as follows:

> We are people of different communities, faiths and races, living in harmony and friendship. We work together and try to learn the secret of fellowship and peace. We hope our lives may be more useful and this spirit of helpfulness will enrich the province in which we live to the greater glory of God.

All four of the previous principals of the college still alive endorsed these sentiments, and I felt certain that the Prince would appreciate them also. Had he not, I reminded myself, once stated that on becoming monarch he wanted to be known as the defender of all faiths, not of any particular one? All the same, I would have preferred him to speak about the environment.

But there was other work to be done. I was miffed by the bishop's insistence on an all-male line-up for Their Royal Highnesses, and wanted to brighten up this aspect of their visit. Once they had shaken hands with our top brass and entered the main college campus, I would ask two personable and youthful college members to lead them around. I had already grown to like the newly appointed economics lecturer, Aqsa, who came to my office to genuinely ask after my wellbeing, rather than to make polite conversation. She was also very beautiful, and the cameras would like that.

Then there was Khayam, who introduced himself to me because his uncle was a Cambridge University graduate, and he wanted to read architecture there himself. Khayam occasionally took me shopping; he would arrive driving a family car, with a gunman sitting behind him.

'Khayam,' I asked him once, 'your family must be well off to let you have a gunman wherever you go?'

'Oh no, Sir, we are very middle class,' he explained. 'The gunman doubles as a cook at home.'

I called my own cook, Emmanuel, a Roman Catholic.

'Emmanuel,' I asked him, 'do you want a gun in the kitchen?'

'Oh no, Sir,' said Emmanuel. 'I believe in Jesus – he will look after us.'

Both Aqsa and Khayam were happy to conduct the Prince and his wife around the campus, and I would take a back seat. It was checkmate to the bishop.

What about security? Various routine traditions were explained. Whenever a VVIP such as the Governor came to the principal's residence somebody must accompany him to taste any food on offer. A doctor should also be available. In the case of the Prince, the official ministerial letter had stated that a military/civil flying squad ambulance should 'accompany the cavalcade of the dignitary at all places of visit'.

As I discovered later, whenever the Governor arrived to chair a Board meeting, the first vehicles to enter the gates of the principal's residence were security cars that would back into a space at the

Figure 2 Khayam Hassan with his gunman's weapon in the principal's garden

front of the house. A posh Mercedes would glide up to the waiting principal, who would step forward to greet the VVIP. But this was a decoy car, which backed round the corner. So if at this point a bomber rushed out of the bushes, the car would be blown up together with the principal, but the Governor would be safe in the car behind. I noted that if the marksman on the roof of the Canterbury Hall took a shot at a bomber, then I would also be in the line of fire. Clearly I was expendable.

A posse of Intelligence agents arrived from Islamabad. Two were from the Intelligence Bureau (IB), both with small moustaches and dapper suits. There was a nondescript ministerial official, also smartly dressed. Our MI6 man in Islamabad was there, and there was a Special Branch officer specifically allocated to the Prince – both in pinstriped suits. Together we walked around the campus, and it was explained that on the morning of the Royal Visit a group of Intelligence personnel would inspect just about everywhere.

'And what about the foreigner standing before you?' I asked one of the IB officers, pointing to myself.

'Oh, we know all about you,' he responded.

'But I spent several years working for your Indian enemies in Delhi, for example.'

'And Bangalore,' he replied with a knowing smile.

They had done their homework. I had spent two years at the Indian Institute of Science in Bangalore.

Inter-Services Intelligence (ISI) were conspicuous by their absence at this meeting. This is the powerful organisation related to the military and expanded by General Zia-ul-Haq to counter the Russian intervention in Afghanistan in 1979. When I eventually met my ISI minder he explained that the ISI did not attend meetings.

'We don't need to, because we are everywhere,' he explained.

I encountered the third major Pakistani intelligence agency, Military Intelligence, just before I left. They are the smartest, and wear uniform. The ISI never seem to wear suits.

The Great Day was almost upon us. Before I went to bed I inspected the red carpet for a final time. A *chowkidar* (night watchman) had been designated to sit over it all night, and I made certain he was not asleep. It was still autumn, and the smell of *frangipani* wafted across the verandah. Above my head two white owls engaged in a raucous duet.

* * * * *

The next morning I wondered if the vice-principal had slept in his three-piece suit to be outside my bedroom door at 5am.

'There was an incident in Bajaur last night. The Prince is not coming,' he announced simply.

The general atmosphere when I went outside told me that everybody already knew. The red carpet was being rolled up.

Accounts of the Bajaur incident varied, but basically an artillery shell fired by the Pakistani military had reportedly hit a *madrasa* and killed 85 students. No weapons had been found anywhere near the *madrasa*, and there was no indication that anything untoward was happening there. But 85 teenage boys were now dead, and the province was seething with anger. The Federal Government had requested the Prince to cancel his visit to Peshawar, and I later learned that two death threats were delivered to him in London.

When major incidents involving many deaths occurred, groups went on the rampage and randomly vented their rage on whoever came within their purview. An additional problem for Edwardes College was that whenever the protesters wanted to lobby the authorities by marching to their offices, they inevitably passed our gates – this applied in relation to the Governor, the Chief Minister and the Press Club. Principal Huw Thomas had already told me how he once failed to close the college early enough to prevent busloads of teenagers from surrounding villages, armed with clubs and crowbars, from smashing everything they could break (though they did not attack college personnel). I therefore sent everybody home, and ordered the gates to be closed. The great day that should have electrified the world with glowing tributes and photographs of Royalty gracing our humble educational achievements – and our red carpet – had ended in disaster.

I phoned Aqsa and Khayam, and apologised for what had happened. Aqsa was philosophical; she never really expected the Prince to come.

'Only in fairy tales,' she added reassuringly.

'Oh fuck,' said Khayam, and laughed.

The British High Commission sent a consoling letter from Islamabad:

British High Commission

Islamabad

Chancery

26 November 2006

Dear Dr Gosling,

Visit to Pakistan of Their Royal Highnesses The Prince of Wales and Duchess of Cornwall

We were all so disappointed when the visit to Peshawar of Their Royal Highnesses The Prince of Wales and Duchess of Cornwall was cancelled at the request of the Government of Pakistan.

We are most grateful to you and your staff for working so closely with the [...] British High Commission[...] The staff of Clarence House was [sic] really impressed with the work of the College and chose Edwardes as the location for the Prince of Wales to deliver his one set piece in Pakistan on education.

We look forward to continuing the close friendship we have with Edwardes College [...]

Yours sincerely,

[signature]

Peter Wilson
Political Counsellor

A later letter from Clarence House echoed these sentiments:

The Prince of Wales and the Duchess of Cornwall were very disappointed that in the event it was not possible to come to the College during their visit to Pakistan and to see the marvellous work you are doing with their own eyes.

It was indeed disappointing, but at least we had been spared a long lecture about religious dialogue!

College reopened and classes resumed. One evening, a student from Bajaur in the FATA area came to see me about a request for leave. This was Majid Ullah Khan, a tall tribal who had spent much of his pre-college education in Peshawar.

'Sir,' he said as he left, 'those *madrasa* students in Bajaur were not killed accidentally by a Pakistani artillery shell; it was a USA drone.'

This was later confirmed by General Musharraf in a personal conversation at his London residence in the autumn of 2011. The Bureau of Investigative Journalism notes the same incident and claims that it was caused by a drone, though this has never been admitted by the USA.[4]

2

Brave New World

In a spacious garden adjoining the provincial government's Secretariat in Peshawar's Cantonment area, there is a marble slab inscribed with the following tribute to the city by the Pashtun poet Ejaz Rahim:

> My heart sprawls out
> like the environs
> of Peshawar, seen
> from the sky, in portions, Jamrud brown
> in places, Cantonment green.
> The heart is a city
> of contrasts,
> held together like a dream.

Not only the Cantonment, but much of the adjacent part of the city, is green with vegetation and bazaars full of fruit and vegetables for most of the year. The colour of the Afghan border town, Jamrud, however, remained unknown to me following its takeover by Taliban militants.

Peshawar is the provincial capital of Khyber-Pakhtunkhwa, which currently boasts a population of just under one and a half million. Its proximity to the Khyber Pass has made it an important centre for trade with Afghanistan and beyond. But although the

Pass registers a neat geographical separation between the two countries (the actual border being just over the top at Torkham), ethnic differences are essentially non-existent because the Pashtun tribal belt stretches from deep inside Khyber-Pakhtunkhwa across the Pass well into Afghanistan.

The regional language on both sides of the border is Pashto, which is one of two official Afghan languages, the other being Dari (i.e. Persian). But the main language for Pakistan as a whole is Urdu, which means that students in Peshawar must know both Pashto and Urdu in addition to English, the medium of instruction for most of their education. This is quite an undertaking, and it is not surprising that pupils from disadvantaged schools struggle to pass their exams.

The education system in Pakistan is divided into five levels: primary, middle and high (grades 1-10), leading to the Secondary School Certificate (SSC); intermediate (grades 11-12), leading to the Higher Secondary (School) Certificate (usually abbreviated to HSC, without the additional 'S'); and university courses leading to degrees. Article 25-A of the Constitution of Pakistan commits the state to 'free and compulsory education to all children of the age of

Figure 3 The gateway from Peshawar to the Khyber Pass

five to 16 years in such a manner as may be determined by law'. The whole process is overseen jointly by the Ministry of Education of the federal government (which deals, for example, with curriculum development and accreditation) and the various provincial governments, each of which has its own department of education.

Peshawar boasts a variety of secondary schools that enable their pupils to matriculate or pass O-levels. Many, such as the Beaconhouse schools, charge high fees and can attract capable teachers – their Model and Grammar schools supply Edwardes College with a significant proportion of day scholars. The same is true for Warsak Model School, another private institution. Four government high schools produce consistently capable matriculates, as does Peshawar Public School and College, which although not a private institution, appeals to an elite constituency and charges high fees.

The Army Public School on Warsak Road became known internationally in December 2014 when a group of Taliban gunmen entered the buildings and killed 141 people, mostly children. This horrendous attack was stated by the assailants to be in response to military action in Waziristan. The school was founded in 1992 and is one of approximately 150 schools and colleges associated with the Pakistani army, though many of the boys and girls are not from military families. It contains about 1,100 pupils, and the fees are very reasonable; some pupils admitted to Edwardes College prove to be extremely capable and obtain high grades.

Madrasa schools tend to be populated with poorer pupils; their science laboratory facilities and pupils' command of English are sometimes inadequate. Christian schools include the historic Edwardes High School (Church of Pakistan) in the inner city and St Mary's School (Roman Catholic), which occupies a fine campus on the Khyber Road. Both these and comparable Christian foundations such as the Church of Pakistan Pennell Memorial High School in Bannu attract capable staff and students.

Further afield, the brighter students to enter Edwardes College often come from Swabi or Parachinar – occasionally from Islamabad or Lahore, though the majority of Edwardes inmates are from inside the province. And no such summary would be complete without mention of pupils from the school in Chitral named after its charismatic principal, Geoffrey D. Langlands, one-time British Army major, who continued to administer it until the age of 95!

* * * * *

'Are you threatening me?'

Surprised at my own temerity, I stood to face an assertive parent who was insisting on his son's admission to our college. He was taller than I, and dressed in full military attire.

'I was merely pointing out […],' he backtracked.

To my irritation the vice-principal sitting next to me had left our table and dived into a corner clutching his mobile phone.

'That damned wife again,' I said to myself.

'He's a brigadier,' the bursar intervened, as the vice-principal reappeared.

'I've checked with the Station Commander – he's retired.'

'And not allowed to wear uniform,' declared the bursar, moustaches twitching.

'So please wait outside until your name is called,' I proffered, as the uniformed parent and his son beat a hasty retreat.

This particular incident occurred when General Musharraf was still President and 'in uniform', as his detractors constantly pointed out, though nobody seemed to know the implications of this in terms of the entitlements of military personnel.

The college's admissions are the most important annual event and require the presence of the principal. There we sat, hour after hour, in the sweltering heat of August aggravated by endless power cuts, and some years made additionally unbearable by the prohibition of even a glass of water on account of Ramazan. Tables were arranged in hierarchical order around the Canterbury Hall, some occupied by administrative minions otherwise seldom noticed. The top table was reserved for me, the vice-principal, the bursar and the director of studies. By my second year I had appointed another vice-principal and a women's officer, to whom

I allocated a table of her own at which she could personally interview all the incoming women students.

Admissions usually began with the most competitive courses. These were Pre-Medical, Pre-Engineering and, to a lesser extent, Computer Science. We began as soon as administratively feasible after the declaration of the secondary school matriculation results. According to the number of places available, a cut-off aggregate mark was established in each course, and only those above it were initially called for interview – which usually meant that their admission was automatic. Some, however, who had applied might have dropped out to accept places elsewhere, or simply didn't turn up, in which case their places could go to those below the cut-off who were waiting hopefully outside. And this was where some attempts at 'negotiation' often began.

The three most prestigious subjects were known collectively as Faculty of Science or FSc. The Pre-Medical and Pre-Engineering courses lasted for two years; the brightest students might then sit exams for the even more prestigious medical and engineering universities while less able ones could continue as candidates for the BSc degree in the University of Peshawar. For the computer scientists there was also a four-year bachelor's degree conducted through the college – the first in the province, and also the first course in college to admit women students.

All in all the FSc admissions might take a week. Then came those for the Faculty of Arts, or FA, which were less competitive. Later came the A-levels, and interviews for special categories, which included women and minorities, such as Christians or the Kalash, a small but talented tribal group occupying three valleys in Chitral, according to some legends left behind by Alexander the Macedonian, and still worshipping multiple gods. When I first arrived, special status was also assigned to some whose parents were Old Edwardians or who had attended the adjacent diocesan-administered Edwardes College School – I abolished both categories. We were also obliged by law to admit a small quota of candidates as *hafiz-e-Qur'ān*, young men qualified to intone from the Qur'ān at the beginning of public occasions. Sons and daughters of the teaching and some other staff were automatically admitted.

These special categories for admission only applied to those who did not have sufficient marks to qualify in the earlier part of the process. Many women students were admitted to the Pre-Medical FSc course during the first three days, and many students classed in the minority category had sufficient marks to gain admission without reference to their special status.

* * * * *

Admissions provided an opportunity to meet parents. Those from Peshawar tended to be from the professional and business classes. The fathers might be local and provincial administrators (some very senior), academics, school teachers, military or police. Tradespeople and the finance and transport sectors were all represented. Some mothers were teachers, but most let their husbands do the talking; a few wore full *burqa* (or *niqab*), though *hijab* was much more common. Not all the women I met in Peshawar were so modest. I was full of admiration for the head of the local National Bank who occupied a central office consisting of a glass cage surrounded by a huge open-plan network of desks, each containing a male occupant. The manager herself seemed to relish a role that reminded me of the manner in which a former Speaker of Britain's House of Commons, Betty Boothroyd, functioned in relation to a chamber of unruly, and largely male, MPs.

Some parents had travelled considerable distances to accompany their wards for admission. I was impressed by the patience that most displayed with our often inevitably clumsy procedures, and their confidence that we would respond appropriately to their trust. Applicants without parents had to find local guardians.

'How old is your local guardian?' barked the bursar at one candidate.

'Sir, he is my twin brother,' came the reply.

'And who will pay your fees?' demanded the bursar, unrelenting.

The bursar sat on my right and handed out forms to some applicants who might be eligible for fee concessions. The initial payment had to be made in full, but subsequent reductions could be negotiated according to need. Most of the needy were minority students, especially Christians, and the funds required to cover the concessions came from an account known as the Mission Fund, of which I was one of two signatories, the other being the bursar.

One early morning during admissions two young men looking like waifs turned up at my office. Their village had been destroyed in the huge earthquake of October 2005, and most of their school had sunk into the ground. They had no matriculation results, and no money. A brief interview convinced us that they seemed capable and could speak good English, so we admitted them, and to cover their fees I used some earthquake relief money given to the college.

The admissions process included the allocation of accommodation in the small number of hostel rooms available on campus. There were essentially three designated hostel buildings: for first-years, second-years, and third- and fourth-years combined. Most rooms were shared; a new block was constructed during my time as principal in which three second-years shared each room. There was no hostel provision for women students, all of whom lived with parents or local guardians. A women's hostel on campus would have been an open invitation for extremist violence.

Accommodation was offered almost entirely to students living outside Peshawar; exceptions being two or three disabled students, and an occasional one who successfully concealed the fact that his parents had recently moved from some far-flung tribal area into the city. College hostel life was spartan, but those who experienced it later maintained that to be a genuine Edwardian you had to have lived 'in residence'. Each of the main hostels possessed a common room adorned with faded photographs of sports activities from earlier years. There was provision for billiards and table tennis, and a full-size sports field in the centre of the accommodation area and the mess.

Incoming students said very little in the presence of their parents, but my questions sometimes elicited interesting replies. I often asked them what they wanted to do when they left college. One young woman blinked at me from inside her partial *hijab*.

'I want to be a pilot with Pakistan International Airways,' she exclaimed enthusiastically.

Figure 4 A student reads from the Holy Qur'ān

I knew that Pakistan already had at least one woman pilot, and that she was a member of the Chitral Kalash. We discussed her ambitious plans, and I congratulated her; meanwhile her *burqa*-clad mother remained completely silent.

It was important for us to follow very strictly the printed admission guidelines in the college prospectus and our cut-off procedures in relation to matriculation aggregate marks, otherwise we knew that some unsuccessful parents might take out court orders against us. I never had to go to court myself, and the college lawyer – a law graduate from Cambridge University – always fielded for us very well. Once all our available places had been filled, though there were prospects that some of those who had been offered places would drop out, then the really difficult horse-trading began. We illustrate this in some detail because it mirrors many features of regional society as a whole.

* * * * *

Generally speaking, the most senior members of the local hierarchy were diplomatic and cautious in their requests for admission favours. Lt General Jan Muhammad Aurakzai, the first Governor during my tenure who chaired our Board, once phoned to ask if we could admit a student whose marks were above our cut-off but whose application was too late because his father had unexpectedly been moved from Islamabad to Peshawar. We agreed. The wife of the next Governor, Owais Ahmed Ghani, made a request on behalf of a student who had misbehaved in his first year and had been denied a place in the second on the recommendation of the chief proctor. His misdemeanour seemed slight, so we fined him and let him continue. The third of the vice-chancellors of Peshawar University whom I encountered phoned to ask for admission on behalf of a nephew; once I told him our cut-off level, he immediately withdrew his request.

Chief ministers were less diplomatic. My first Chief Minister was Akram Khan Durrani, who represented the religiously conservative Muttahida Majlis-e-Amal (MMA) party, which was dominating provincial politics when I arrived. During his tenure, we received strongly worded letters prohibiting music, dancing and almost every kind of entertainment on campus. He phoned our vice-principal late one night and told him (in Urdu) that the next day he must admit a certain person to the college. The next day I decided that we wouldn't. In some ways the request seemed strange; Durrani already had a son in college who had been admitted on the basis of good marks, and never tried to pull rank on anyone on account of his father's job. The Chief Minister followed up his phone call with a letter dated 29 August 2007 to the vice-principal; studiously ignoring me as principal, he wrote:

Kindly refer to my telephone talk, I am sending Mr Waqas Nawaz s/o Noor Nawaz Khan for admission. I shall be grateful if you could kindly look into the matter and allow him admission in Pre-Engineering.

Yours sincerely

Akram Khan Durrani

We ignored both the phone call and the letter; the Chief Minister's protégé never turned up, and there were no repercussions.

25

Similar pressures from on high appeared in relation to students proceeding into their next year, and those whose attendance record at lectures fell short of the required level. The following is a request (date unclear) from the Minister for Higher Education, who was also a member of the College Board:

Dear Principal,

As discussed on the telephone I am writing to strongly recommend readmission to continue for a student of Edwardes College in favour of Farman Ullah s/o Manawar Khan, 3rd Year FA, whose attendance is below the minimum required 25% which was basically due to the law and order situation in the province especially in Peshawar. And being the son of a member of the provincial assembly he was unable to attend the college as per normal routine in face of death and kidnapping threats. I assure that he would attend the college regularly and follow all the rules and regulations of the college in future.

Warmest regards,

Qazi Mohammad Asad

We acceded to his request. During my time as principal I developed a liking for this youthful but rather shy minister from Abbottabad. At the bottom of his letter he added: 'Sir, it was raised in the assembly and I had given assurance that I'd resolve it. I'd be very grateful for this favour.'

The Speaker of the provincial assembly wrote to the Governor on behalf of his nephew's admission. In a letter dated 7 September 2009 (well after our admissions had closed), he wrote:

Respected Governor,

May I have the honour to bother you for my tiny personal task and to submit that as your highness is aware that my native village Chaghar Matti is located at a risky and unsafe skirts [sic] of Peshawar District [...] We have a joint family system, three children of my family are already getting education in Edwardes College but unfortunately the fourth one Mr Saadullah Khan s/o Nazirullah Khan, my nephew

*who has attained 851 marks in his SSC Examinations, is
deprived of admission in the said institute.*

*Being constrained by the present precarious situations at my
native village, I personally request to kindly ask the authority
of the above institute to give admission to my above named
nephew in 1st year (Pre-Eng), enabling him to pick up and
drop together with his other brothers through one van/vehicle
[...]*

With profound regards and best wishes

Yours faithfully

Kiramatullah Khan

The Governor's office sent the letter on to me, and I composed a
careful reply explaining that, although this applicant was only very
slightly below the cut-off of 857, there were 45 students with better
marks, any one of whom could win a court case against the college
for non-admission. Not only that, I added, but in a case against us
the plaintiff could have maintained in open court that we were
favouring a candidate because he was the nephew of the Speaker of
the provincial assembly. This could have been picked up in the
local press, especially *Mashrik*, which loves to name and shame
local politicians and institutions. Nothing further was said, but
when I met the Speaker some weeks later at a social function, he
said that he understood perfectly, and that his nephew was
extremely happy in another college.

   On account of the university attendance rules, court cases over
admissions could only be effective if they were completed before it
was too late to satisfy them. If not, then we could legally remove a
candidate for inadequate attendance at the end of December. A
successful Stay Order against us meant that lecture attendance
could be notched up; it then became in the plaintiff's interests to
procrastinate so that a judge might ultimately argue that since the
candidate was effectively in the college he or she might as well
continue. There was nothing malicious in our stance; once the
science laboratories, for example, had their quota of students we
simply had no room for any more. Once any applicant had found

a loophole in our procedures, others could drive a legal coach and horses through our entire system. Then the press could ridicule us.

After three years of presiding over admissions, I thought I had become adept at plugging all loopholes. Then came the tortuous case of Muhammad Jamdad Khan s/o Dost Muhammad Khan. Jamdad had applied for Faculty of Arts (FA) admission with marks above the cut-off, but when his name was posted for interview on the notice board near the college gate, he did not turn up. It was naturally assumed that he had gone elsewhere, and his place went to the next on the list.

Nothing happened for some time, and then communications began to arrive demanding admission. College was by this time overfull, and lectures had started. A Stay Order suddenly arrived, effectively forcing us to admit him, so our college lawyer rushed to the court and successfully had it 'vacated' (to use the legal terminology). The following day, 21 October 2008, a six-page foolscap document arrived appealing against the 'vacation' on nine grounds, the main one being that 'the plaintiff/appellant was not called for interview and was deprived of admission'. Other grounds included 'that appellant was shown successful in merit list but even then the appellant was not called for interview and was ignored', and that the prospectus contained no affirmation 'that a seat shall be given to next candidate in case default is made'.

Furthermore, 'no notice of interview has been served upon the appellant and his admission was canceled [*sic*] without notice, hence the principle of *audi alterium partim* is completed [*sic*] violated'. The document concluded:

> *It is, therefore, most humbly prayed that on acceptance of this appeal, the impugned order of the learned Civil Judge dated 20.10.2008 may kindly be set aside and an order of interim injunction, directing the respondents [...] to provisionally allow admission to appellant in FA (Arts Group) till final disposal of the suit, may kindly be passed.*
>
> *Appellant, through*
>
> *Iftikar Elahi*
>
> *Advocate, Peshawar*

The request was only for an interim injunction, presumably because the attendance rule clock was ticking and Jamdad and his lawyer realised that within a week a forced admission would fall foul of it. Also, a careless district judge might have found the document too lengthy to assimilate, and decided that an interim ruling would merely serve to pass the buck onto someone else. But this didn't happen, and Jamdad lost his appeal.

Had Jamdad won, then not only would the college have been forced to admit him, but every college in Pakistan might have felt obliged to revise its admission rules. No longer would it have been sufficient to post notices on a specified day on a notice board, but it could have become necessary to publish them in newspapers or email them to families, many of which have no computers. Jamdad probably didn't turn up because he preferred initially to go somewhere else, but when that fell through he tried us once again. It was all very exasperating, but we couldn't afford to ignore any of the legal challenges.

A second problematic case was on behalf of Muhammad Nauman Sher s/o Subhan Sher. The basic issue was that although this applicant's marks were well below the cut-off for FSc admission, the son of the then vice-principal had even lower marks but had been admitted because it was the college's stated policy in the prospectus to automatically admit the sons and daughters of staff. The irony of the situation was aggravated by the fact that the young men had been in the same class at Edwardes College School. The real problem for me and my colleagues was not this apparent unfairness, but the fact that the father of the applicant was a judge, and another judge, a friend of his, was apparently working with him.

This other judge was Justice Afsar Ali Shah, judge of the Peshawar Accountability Court; he approached the vice-principal, who told him that, irrespective of the marks, the application for admission was too late. The judge threatened to have the case taken up in court if I did not meet him personally. I agreed, but he came to my office in the company of the Superintendent of Police for the Police Lines, Masood Khan. Although the police superintendent said nothing, I felt that his presence was intimidating, so I simply re-stated our college policy. At one point the vice-principal whose son was the focus of the perceived injustice became so embarrassed that he left my office and sat in the living room. The judge threatened court proceedings, and became extremely abrasive before leaving with the police superintendent.

I made an appointment to meet the Chief Justice, Ejaz Afzal Khan, to complain about intimidation. On 26 October 2009 I sat in his tiny book-lined office tucked away in a remote corner of the High Court, enjoying green tea and cakes. He was a diminutive figure from a local village; he paid careful attention to my complaint and promised to investigate.

The college lawyer was away on the Hajj pilgrimage so I went with the vice-principal to meet a senior advocate who discovered that the two judges seemed to be working in tandem. To save time they had somehow avoided the lower court where complaints are conventionally registered and had managed to gain direct access to a higher one, from which it might prove far harder for us to remove a Stay Order. The clock was ticking; we reckoned we had a week before the university attendance rule would kick in and render the admission pointless. Our new lawyer would do his best for us, but could not be certain of victory. I went to bed envisaging humiliation at the hands of *Mashrik* and the rest of the Urdu press.

The next morning my secretary, Shahzad, came to my room with a broad grin on his face.

'Sir,' he announced, 'the college is saved. Taliban extremists have blown up the High Court.'

For some strange reason all I could think of was a recollection by my grandfather that following the Battle of Mons during World War I, angels appeared in the sky above him and his fellow soldiers. The vice-principal went home that evening to enjoy rather more than his usual tot of whisky!

* * * * *

I took advantage of my meeting with the Chief Justice to ask if there was any way of disposing of the legal proceedings over the college cafeteria to which my predecessor had alluded on my arrival. The basic problem was that the small snacks facility run by a local entrepreneur had been closed without due notice and a Stay Order had been served on the college preventing that part of the building from being used by anyone else. Ably assisted by our college law lecturer, Shujaat Ali Khan, I had deftly manoeuvred the case between the lower and upper courts; the case was against my predecessor by name and not against me, so did that give me a possible loophole?

The Chief Justice thumbed through some files on his desk.

'The case is currently in the court of Civil Judge Ms Lubna Zaman,' he explained.

There was a pause, then he lowered his pince-nez slightly, and peered at me over the top.

'You know,' he observed solemnly, 'these legal processes were inherited by us from your predecessors. I'm afraid I cannot help you.'

There was only one other significant legal issue during my initial period, and it concerned an elderly lecturer, Dr Rashida Mazhar, who disputed the terms of her pensions settlement. This was in two parts, a cash sum followed by monthly payments, and was calculated by actuaries based in Lahore whose reliability we had no reason to dispute. In addition to questioning her pension, Dr Rashida wanted her services as lecturer to be extended for two more years, but both her colleagues and her students – especially the women – were adamant that she was incompetent. Her consequent legal case against us was intimated by no less than an advocate of the Supreme Court:

15 November 2007

Dear Sir

With reference to my Notice dated 22 May, 2007, it may be stated that you have not responded to the request made therein.

Dr Rashida Mazhar, my client, is determined to get the matter sorted out through court, in case your reluctance to

solve it amicably persists. It is now for you to determine the
manner in which you would like to settle the matter. So far I
have been avoiding to drag an educational institution into
litigation, but I cannot restrain my client any more. For the
time being I have told her to wait for another week or so.

[signed] Atiq-ur-Rahman Qazi

Advocate, Supreme Court

We did nothing, and I never heard anything further. I felt sorry for
Dr Mazhar, but members of her department were emphatic that
she should leave. A group of her female students came to my office
to underline their determination.

Such legal sparring turned out to be a useful introduction to
more daunting problems towards the end of my tenure as principal,
involving the embezzlement of huge sums of college funds.

* * * * *

On the one hand, Edwardes College is a private and independent
college, inherited by Pakistani Christians from a pre-Independence
foreign mission, the CMS. But on the other – as we have seen – the
college is subject to decisions by the courts and normative civil and
criminal law processes. It is also part of a provincial and national
educational system – with additional foreign inputs via the
Cambridge O- and A-level examination system.

The requirements of the Board of Intermediate and Secondary
Education (BISE) and the University of Peshawar rules about
attendance at lectures constrain the college (and can sometimes be
used to the college's advantage to resolve a tricky legal situation!).
But although the college is technically bound by these rules, it does
not always adhere to them. At the end of the first term of every
academic year, a proportion of students who were short of
attendance would come – often with their parents – to plead to be
allowed to continue on the grounds that they could make up their
attendance during the second, and longer, semester (which ran
from January to May, depending on course).

If both their attendance and their marks in monthly tests were poor, then it was in their interests, and the college's, for them to leave and sit the summer exams privately. But few were prepared to do this, preferring to exert pressure on us to let them continue. Those who continued and failed to meet their total annual attendance requirements by the end of March were prohibited from registering for the exams. In both situations I tended to be as accommodating as possible. At least the end-of-first-term crisis alerted parents and local guardians to the fact that their wards were cutting classes. At the end of the second session we even sometimes laid on extra classes to enable students to 'make up' their attendance. Then, at least, they could sit their exams and, if they failed, had only themselves to blame. Our overall aggregate marks for the year might suffer, but no parent could argue that if we had not held back a student then he or she might have passed into the next year.

In all of this I was conscious of the fact that, while a few students were 'winging it', others faced genuine hardship regarding finance, transport, or a poor command of English. After I had left, a first-year student, Hamza Khan, killed himself because he was expelled for shortage of attendance at the end of the first term.

The BISE and A-level exams were invigilated by college teaching staff. For the BSc and BA exams, lecturers from the university were drafted in. There were hardly any cases of irregularities on the part of students.

There were some problems, however, in relation to the scheduling of science practicals on Fridays, especially with regard to the Cambridge A-levels. We tried very hard to end these exams before the *jum 'a* prayers at lunchtime. If we started them too early and tried to fit two practicals into the morning, then some students would have difficulty getting in on time. But it would also be a problem for them to travel in on a Saturday morning, and there were additional problems if we tried to hold an exam after the Friday prayers.

My policy, as previously, was to 'bend with the wind' and avoid any overlapping with the prayers. I was therefore extremely put out during my second year to receive a death threat, according to which one of my major sins was specified as refusing to let students out of college for the *jum'a* prayers.[1] In fact we leaned over backwards to accommodate all such practices; we should do so, I felt, because we were living in the Islamic Republic of Pakistan. Fortunately, I was never required to justify such actions in correspondence with the Cambridge A-level examination board!

* * * * *

The determination of parents that their offspring must at all costs be admitted to the college was matched by their expectation that all other college students should comply with what they perceived to be Edwardian values and behaviour. The following example illustrates an occasion on which such parental hopes were not fulfilled.

One evening soon after I arrived, the senior warden of the student hostel, Francis Karamat, asked me to accompany him to a nearby hospital. A student (we shall call him Adil) had been seriously injured by another (Abbas) following an argument in the third-year hostel common room. Apparently Abbas had picked up a small but heavy marble-topped table and smashed it into Adil's face, breaking his nose in three places.

We rushed to the Combined Military Hospital to find Adil semi-conscious on a bed, with three fellow-students in attendance. The parents had been notified, and were on their way from Kohat, just over an hour's drive from Peshawar. A junior doctor appeared and gave us a preliminary assessment of the injuries.

In spite of an injection, Adil was throbbing with pain, but gripped my hand firmly until his parents arrived.

'How did this happen?' his father demanded. Karamat began to explain, but the angry parent cut him short.

'When I chose Edwardes for my son, I never expected him to meet anyone who could do this.'

The anger was directed more towards Karamat than against me. We expressed our deep regret, and left with two of the three students. The third, Munaf, whom I came to know well, said that he would borrow a mattress and sleep on the floor beside his friend.

In these situations, which were mercifully very infrequent, it was the college's policy to pay the initial hospital fees in full, recovering the money at a later date. The Combined Military Hospital was conveniently located, and reported to be the best – so much so, the junior doctor explained enthusiastically to me, that when Osama bin Laden lived in Peshawar and worked for the Americans, he had visited the hospital several times as an outpatient.

Adil convalesced at home, and his nose was operated on several times. After a few months I visited the family in Kohat and was pleased to see that there was no permanent disfigurement to Adil's face. His father's anger had gone, but he repeated his question as to how his son's assailant had ever been admitted to the college.

Abbas was a third-year student and had displayed no signs of violent behaviour prior to this incident. The argument with Adil had been about a young woman student whom both admired. After a few days, Abbas's father came to my office with his son to apologise. Abbas said nothing and never once looked at me. It was a foregone conclusion that I would not see either again, but that the two families would wrangle in the courts over compensation. In spite of what Abbas had done, I felt sad for him, and even more so for his father. But it was Adil's father's repeated criticism of the college for admitting Abbas that remained with me. Clearly, he understood Edwardians to be a special category of individuals incapable of physical violence to others.

* * * * *

In addition to external constraints, such as the courts and various education authorities, we also had to take account of the intelligence agencies, which wield considerable power in Pakistan. Following Independence in 1947, two new intelligence agencies were created: the Intelligence Bureau (IB) and Military Intelligence (MI). However, during the 1948 war between Pakistan and India, MI was felt to have failed to coordinate intelligence between the three forces, and as a result the Directorate for Inter-Services Intelligence (ISI) was set up the following year. It was expanded and gained in influence following the seizure of power by General Zia-ul-Haq in July 1977 and the declaration of martial law.

I had encountered representatives of the Intelligence Bureau prior to the anticipated visit of the Prince of Wales, and subsequently met the local one when my visa needed extending. My ISI minder, Inspector Qasim Zafar, periodically passed messages via college security staff or through my secretary saying that he wanted to meet me. The bursar, ex-military himself, did not like this. At first he told me that Inspector Qasim worked for MI but after the vice-principal had checked and found that this was not the case, he advised me not to meet him.

Inspector Qasim turned out to have a Masters degree in my own academic subject, physics, so this gave us a bond that eased communication. Part of his job was to 'spy' on me and submit reports about my activities. But he would tell me who he had been talking to:

'The gardeners (*malis*) say you get up early to feed your cranes (*koonj*).'

'The library staff say you have donated books to the library.'

And so on. He asked Elias, the faithful *chowkidar* who guarded my bungalow at night, if I was getting any foreign visitors. The answer to that question was always very easy. I didn't get any foreign visitors because they had all left Peshawar after 9/11.

The claim that the ISI were 'everywhere' was evidenced by the fact that when I took my evening constitutional walk several times through Aree Bazaar[2] – a short but vibrant commercial street close to the college – Inspector Qasim came round to advise me to vary my route in case I was waylaid. Clearly, he had his informers among the local tradespeople. On one occasion he gave me a lift back to the college on his motor scooter. Dropping me off at the gate, he explained that in a few days he would be getting a new Royal Enfield motorcycle; would I like a ride around town? I told him I'd like to see the original home of Shah Rukh Khan, the Bollywood heartthrob, whom I knew to be from Peshawar.

At first he seemed puzzled.

'But you are from Pakistan's premier intelligence agency,' I chided him. 'Surely you know everything.'

A few days later he arrived on his new acquisition and transported me into the Qissa Khwani Bazaar area to the house where Shah Rukh had grown up.[3] In a street nearby was the original home of another Bollywood favourite, Dilip Kumar – apparently the two were acquainted. Moving through Ander Shahar – the jewellers' bazaar – we passed Mahabat Khan Masjid, built in 1630 by the governors of Peshawar under Mughal emperor Shah Jahan. Under Sikh rule, my guide explained, the emperor had stamped his authority over the region by having his men begin each day by catching hold of any group of luckless pedestrians and flinging them to their deaths from the minarets.

Inspector Qasim occasionally asked me political questions, to which I gave cautious replies.

'Why,' he asked once, 'do the Americans target their drones on Waziristan, but never on the Swat valley?'

He asked this at a time when it was apparent that the Taliban were the dominant influence in the valley. I said I didn't know, though I always made it clear to him and to others that I was opposed to the use of drones inside Pakistan's borders.

From time to time Inspector Qasim made requests for favours relating to college admissions, but they were never too unreasonable. Once he wanted a particular first-year student from Parachinar admitted to the hostel, which was no great problem because we tried to give hostel priority to students from outside Peshawar. There was a bearer in the mess who had been in a fight with a cook and had been sacked – could I get him reinstated? I tried, but didn't succeed. One year, the son of the local ISI colonel wanted admission, but his marks were low. This was probably because the family had moved around a lot, and this could have affected his performance. I processed the application routinely; he glanced at me gratefully as I passed his form to the bursar.

* * * * *

One of the most enjoyable events of the year was the first-year hostel outing to Bara Gali, a small residential complex in the Nathiagali area of the Murree hills. We stayed there across a long weekend, taking as many cooks and other staff as needed to provide for just under a hundred students.

I had been to the Indian part of Kashmir twice. The first visit was with my fellow lecturer from St Stephen's College, William Crawley, on his motor scooter. We had tried to drive, and then climb, above Pahalgam, to reach the Amarnath cave famous for its stalagmites, but bad weather forced us to turn back. So we visited Gulmarg, a military ski training centre a few miles from the line of control between India and Pakistan, and tried our hand at pony trekking.

By the time of my second visit to Indian Kashmir in the mid-nineties the security situation had totally changed. Flying into Srinagar airport from Delhi I was placed in a bulletproof vehicle escorted by two security vehicles, one of which sported a light machine gun on top. These provisions were arranged by the father of one of my Stephanian students, a senior officer with the Reserve Police. But once I reached my accommodation at the Tyndale Biscoe School I was looked after by junior teaching staff and senior students, who took me around the city on their motorcycles on the back of which, they claimed, I would be less likely to attract the attention of militants than with a police escort. Some of the students were sympathetic to anti-government elements, which had also been the case during my earlier period of teaching at St Stephen's College (a few had been Naxalites).

Now I was firmly on the other side of the line of control – 8,000 feet up in the Galyat mountain range – and an hour's drive from both Murree and Abbottabad. An exhausting trek with our group brought me to within sight of the Jhelum River, a silver strip bordered by clusters of buildings, which must have been Srinagar. In another direction we could just make out the Nanga Parbat range – which aroused poignant memories because it was there that the inspirational founder of the Scargill community centre in West Yorkshire, Dick Marsh, met his death in a mountaineering accident. Below the snow-capped peaks were forests of oak, cedar and pine. Nathiagali boasts an attractive church, St Matthew's, made of wood – a legacy from the colonial period.

We occupied our three days with a mountain trek, a long leisurely walk through the woods – carefully avoiding armies of Rhesus monkeys – and a chairlift ride to a lush picnic area. Initially we hired buses, but after a couple of years our mess and hostel in charge, Francis Karamat, acquired a fine college bus. At first it was grandly labelled with the college's name, but after using it in Peshawar to provide a regular daily service to and from the college it was felt that this might render it too easy a target for militants, so we had it repainted.

Sometimes I left the main party and went with Fayyaz and Shahzad to explore Murree, occasionally stopping to buy jars of honey at the roadside. We visited Lawrence College, a short distance from Murree, and were impressed by its high standards and the commitment of the staff. I had a particular interest in this school because there were several of its alumni in Edwardes College, and Dr Robin Brooke-Smith had grown up there. (His stepfather, Michael L. Charlesworth, was principal from 1961 to 1966.)

Our annual trips to Bara Gali gave me a good opportunity to get to know the new intake of hostel first-years, several of whom have subsequently kept in touch. We ate together, and at night there was dancing around a huge bonfire, usually organised by Changez Khan. One young cook had a particularly erotic style of dancing, which everybody seemed to enjoy except for the bursar, during the only time he went with us; the following year he prevented the cook from coming along, but I got him back subsequently. On these night-time occasions I sometimes gave short talks, one year about the planet Mars, suspended above our heads from the Milky Way as a majestic red orb. The Himalayan skies on a clear night can rival just about any other astronomical event.

3

The Daily Round

One day, shortly after a chemistry practical examination had ended, the vice-principals and chief proctor came to my office looking very grim.

'There has been an incident,' declared Kalimullah, the chief proctor. I asked them to elaborate. Apparently two women students had reported to the senior vice-principal that they had seen a female friend enter a room in one of the men's hostels. This was forbidden, but as it was in the afternoon I couldn't see why the senior college officers were so concerned.

'We shall bring the girl and her local guardian to your office tomorrow,' announced Kalimullah.

'And the young man whose room she entered?' I enquired.

'He has run away to his home in Chitral,' I was informed.

The next morning the same three trooped into my office accompanied by the young woman and her aunt, who lived in Peshawar. The senior vice-principal sonorously explained that the girl had gone into the young man's room, and they had closed the door. Alerted by the girl's friends (I thought that strange), the vice-principals had knocked on the door and demanded entry.

The young man opened the door, but his friend was nowhere to be seen.

'She was hiding under the bed,' explained the chief proctor, without a flicker of a smile.

'And were they fully dressed?' enquired the aunt.

I had taken a liking to the aunt, a popular and energetic primary school teacher in the city. The chief proctor looked shocked at even the possibility that either of the miscreants was not fully dressed in college uniform.

My mind was racing, and I had no idea of what to do. The girl said nothing. Sensing my confusion, the aunt leaned across the corner of the table towards me.

'Look,' she said, 'the problem is basically that if my niece's father finds out what has happened, then he may kill her.'

This dramatic observation focused my mind decisively.

'She must leave the college,' stated the senior vice-principal, emphatically.

It was the end of the academic year, and in all probability the young woman would pass her exams.

'Can she move to a college exclusively for women?' I offered.

Nobody seemed to object, so the next day I contacted the principal of an all-women's college, carefully explaining the

Figure 5 College members arrive at Bara Gali in the Murree Hills in the newly acquired bus

Figure 6 Looking after the plants at the newly opened women's centre

situation. To my immense relief she agreed. Before the student left with her aunt I advised her that if her father asked why she was changing colleges she might say that we were overcrowded and the library and laboratory facilities were poor. I added that we needed a proper women's centre – which was very true at that time.

'And the young man who has run off home?' I later asked the senior staff, who seemed to have lost interest in the whole issue. 'If she has to be punished by leaving the college, then shouldn't he go as well?' I argued.

But Kalimullah owned land in Chitral and showed a marked reluctance to expel this particular student, and so in the end I let the matter drop. But the incident as a whole was a salutary reminder of the difference between our oasis-like college existence and the harsh realities of some of the surrounding areas.

* * * * *

There are considerable differences between the social situations of women in different parts of the region. Benazir Bhutto, from a rich landowning family in Sindh, was not only prime minister of Pakistan twice but as an undergraduate at Oxford University was voted president of the Oxford Union Society. A combination of her background and education gave her an immense self-confidence. She once said: 'I had faith in myself. I had always felt that I could become prime minister if I wanted.'

In Pashtun society, on both sides of the Pakistan/Afghan border, women are unlikely to achieve such distinction, though there is still considerable variety in their roles and backgrounds. At the national level in Afghanistan Zeenat Karzai, wife of former president Hamid Karzai, has been prominent in representing women at national and international forums, and there have been significant historical figures such as the seventeenth-century Pashto poet Nazo Tokhi, who played an important role in uniting the Pashtun tribes against the Persians.

At the village level the role of women's leader covers a variety of functions, ranging from religious activities, such as preparing the dead for burial, to arranging marriages and conflict resolution. The Afghan wars and the rise of the Taliban have curtailed the traditional roles of women to some extent. Some Taliban leaders, such as Sufi Muhammad and Jalaluddin Haqqani (allied with the Taliban), are fairly liberal about women's education (though not co-education) compared with, say, Fazlullah (Sufi Muhammad's son-in-law), who is believed to have been behind the attempted killing of Malala Yousafzai, and could well have been responsible for the deaths of more than 140 people, mostly children, at the Army Public School in Peshawar in December 2014.

The literacy rate for Pashtun women is considerably lower than for men. Women are abused and discriminated against, though this is increasingly being challenged by women's rights organisations. But these in turn are opposed by conservative religious groups – not just the Taliban – and government officials in both Afghanistan and Pakistan. In Afghanistan during the 1970s there was a sustained campaign for women's rights led by Meena Keshwar Kamal, who founded the Revolutionary Association of the Women of Afghanistan in 1977. In 2003, Vida Samadzai was chosen as Miss Afghanistan!

Although women can vote in both Afghanistan and Pakistan, they may be prevented from doing so by their menfolk and local public opinion. Child marriage was made illegal in Pakistan in 2000 but continues in some places. There are organisations in Pakistan that help women who are victims of domestic violence. But in spite of these continuing problems – which are also to be found in comparable societies such as in India – many Pashtun women are beginning to better their social situations, and in the province of Khyber-Pakhtunkhwa as a whole the tradition of poetry, music and culture has encouraged many Pashtun women to improve their education. And at Edwardes College, the first higher education institution in the province to become co-educational, we were committed to doing everything we could to facilitate such objectives.

* * * * *

A typical day for an Edwardes College principal illustrates some of the many-faceted features of college life.

A combination of hot weather stretching from April to September – plus lengthy power cuts – argued for an early start to the day. My five chickens announced their latest presentation of eggs and the dawn, which I greeted over a mug of coffee. I would unlock the chapel, which was attached to the principal's bungalow, and collect a bowl of naan bread pieces from the night watchman to give to the chickens and various other garden birds.

Two of my four demoiselle cranes were gifts from two students from Swabi; the other two had been netted in Bannu, where many stopped during their vast migratory journeys between Siberia and the western coast of India. Their wings had been clipped to prevent them from flying away, but the garden was spacious, and they were regularly fed. I also had two peacocks, which spent much of their time in a small paddock at the far end of the garden.

My cook, Emmanuel, arrived on his bicycle soon after 7am, and prepared breakfast. He had been acquired by my predecessor from working in a British Council guest house; it took me some time to persuade him that I would rather have good Pakistani-style food than his pseudo-Western concoctions, and I learned in the process that his earlier job was as a housekeeper rather than as a cook. It showed!

Fayyaz, who drove the principal's car, arrived shortly after Emmanuel, followed by Rahat, my daytime house assistant, and Shahzad, who did my secretarial work. The household team were usually all on the premises by 9am, by which time teaching was well under way in the main college buildings. A few Christian students would drop into the college chapel before their classes, but the only organised services took place at Friday lunchtime when the college closed on account of the *jum 'a* prayers.

I met with the college senior staff every morning at 9am to discuss important matters. Those usually present were the vice-principals, the bursar (or finance officer), the director of studies and the chief proctor. I had wanted to include Mrs Nasira Manzoor, the women's officer, but she needed to complete her physics lectures in good time to leave early, so I usually saw her on her own. On occasions when I had a meeting with the teaching staff as a whole, I stressed that my daily meetings with the senior staff did not constitute a clique or a mafia, and I made sure that whenever we discussed an issue relating to a particular section of the college the relevant personnel were invited to join us. In retrospect, I believe that this worked well.

At the end of our daily staff meetings – which sometimes lasted for no more than ten minutes – I went with a member of the senior staff around the lecture rooms. At first I thought that this would be intrusive, but I knew that my predecessors had done it and that it was expected of me. These encounters were important; I kept them brief and light-hearted. Occasionally, I tried to pick up on what was on the blackboard and sometimes the students would ask questions. I taught only one formal class in the college, and that was for the Higher National Diploma students, some of whom had already graduated.

On the way back to my office I often stopped at the mess for a cup of tea and a samosa. Try as I might by suggesting recipes, I was never able to get the cook to produce samosas up to anything like the standard of those available at St Stephen's College in Delhi. Sukhia's samosas, sold beneath a sign that assured us that 'the samosas is hot' [*sic*], were so delicious and famous that even Rajiv Gandhi went back to his old college to sample them after he became prime minister! But quoting precedents from India was never a good idea in Pakistan.

Unless I needed to visit anyone outside the college, I usually sat in my office in the principal's bungalow from mid-morning until lunchtime. My predecessor had positioned himself in an inner library there, with his faithful secretary Shah Mehmoud fielding visitors via the larger so-called board room, but I preferred to sit in the larger room where I could see who was outside the door. Most college members could speak English; otherwise, Shahzad could come in from a smaller office near the kitchen, and interpret for me. VIPs could be taken into the living room adjacent to the boardroom, and ensconced in armchairs. The living room led into my bedroom – the coolest part of the house – and I had a small desk in there.

Breakfast and lunch always included bowls of fruit and salad, diligently prepared by Rahat with produce obtained from Aree Bazaar. I tried to rest after lunch, leaving Shahzad to deal with phone calls, but the first of my vice-principals, Naveed Attaullah, invariably turned up just as my head touched the pillow. A shower and tea in the early evening might be followed by more visitors, after which I either went for a lengthy walk or took a lift from Fayyaz to the Garrison Services Club, where I would walk several times briskly round their athletics track. To gain membership of this club, which was open only to the military and Pakistani citizens with military connections, I had written to the Corps Commander, Lt General Masood Aslam. He didn't reply, but when I went to see the club secretary, Major M. Hassan Shah Afridi, it was clear that permission had been granted. Both of them came to my assistance during my final weeks at Edwardes College, when I came up against strong opposition after the discovery of embezzlement in college funds.

Following my club admission, my ISI minder, Inspector Qasim Zafar, came round to tell me that it was much preferable for me to take my evening constitutional there than around town. He had already told me never to take the same route in case kidnappers were in wait. Occasionally, when I was walking, a student would draw up alongside and offer a lift: 'It's not safe for you to walk alone, Sir.'

The hostel students ate their evening meals in three sittings; I often turned up between the first- and second-year sessions, or later when the third and fourth years were in the dining room. I sometimes ate with the students, but more often I drank tea made by Bashir who presided over the small canteen attached to the mess. After dinner, groups of students often came to the house and we would talk informally about a range of topics. Initially some were shy, more than anything because they were self-conscious about their English. I went to bed after they had gone, sometimes quite late.

I arranged for a local doctor and a female nurse to come into the hostel on alternate days to give medical assistance to resident and day scholars. I also did my best to improve the nutritional quality of hostel meals, though this wasn't easy within budgetary constraints – an additional plate of onions or a banana was sometimes all that was possible. I also put up notices discouraging the consumption of Pepsi and Coca Cola. Smoking and the use of mobile phones were prohibited on the college premises.

* * * * *

The allegation in my death threat that we didn't close the college on Fridays early enough to permit Muslim students to attend the *jum'a* prayers rankled, because nothing could have been further from the truth. Whether or not they went to their local mosques when they left was not our problem.

Christian students took advantage of the Friday lunchtime break to attend a chapel service. The chapel was of a simple Anglican style with plain white walls bearing a plaque stating that it had been built by the Church Missionary Society. When I arrived there were two large and very lavish portraits of saints behind the altar; one night I loaded them into the car boot and deposited them at St Michael's Roman Catholic cathedral, where I thought their ornate style would be appreciated.

Although English was the lingua franca throughout the college, I decided that chapel services should be in Urdu, which was essentially the mother tongue of Christian students, the majority of whom were of Punjabi origin. Service books in Pashto existed, but were never used. I preached from time to time in English, but otherwise services were conducted in Urdu by Mr Taj, lecturer in Urdu, or the senior priest at the cathedral. Vice-Principal Naveed Attaullah gave occasional talks under the auspices of the Student Christian Movement (SCM), and every year we organised an SCM coach trip into the Murree Hills. Some of our Muslim students were envious of these outings, because we allowed men and women to travel, and even sit, together.

Services were open to members of all churches, and quite a number of those who attended were Roman Catholic. The chapel was cleaned and maintained by the Roman Catholic students who lived at the back of my house. Attendance increased until we had to accommodate an overflow of worshippers outside the door. At one point I tried holding the entire service on the front lawns, but on the third occasion our worship was disrupted by a huge bomb in the neighbourhood, so we moved back inside the chapel. For reasons that were never clear to me, the extremists often let off their bombs to coincide with Friday prayers.

After dinner on Fridays I introduced film nights for the hostel students. Sometimes we sat in the Memorial Hall in the arts building; occasionally, and weather permitting, we occupied the steps of the first-year hostel facing a large screen on the edge of the sports field. The technology was expertly handled by Changez Khan and Naveed Ali, both from the computer science department.

Many of the films that were shown were obtained from local DVD shops where it was possible to buy an extraordinary range of material. On account of their lurid film covers these shops were periodically set on fire, or were bombed. On one occasion, I spotted an early Dracula horror movie starring Bela Lugosi, who was shown on the cover carrying a scantily dressed woman out of her bedroom. It was in black and white, and unsuitable for the students, so I thought I'd take it home as a souvenir. But at the airport, a customs official took it out of my bag and solemnly reprimanded me for carrying such pornographic material!

Whenever a film was to be shown, I put up announcements around the college noticeboards giving a brief account of its content. Of *One Flew Over the Cuckoo's Nest* I observed: 'Aren't all societies a bit like this?' The students agreed. I started *The Deer Hunter* at the point where the young Americans arrived in Vietnam. Our students saw the film as anti-war, but not anti-USA. We watched Bollywood films, such as *Rang De Basanti*, and anything we could find starring Shah Rukh Khan, our neighbourhood hero.

I knew that the Pakistan film *Khuda Kay Liye* ('In the name of God') was controversial and had been banned on account of a dialogue between two mullahs about women's rights, but we decided to show it. One of our *hafiz-e-Qur'ān* students told me that he didn't like it, but I felt that his objection was token and represented only a small minority view. For the most part, students watched these films attentively; occasionally they cheered, but I couldn't help being surprised when, during a Bollywood film about a terrorist attack on the New York subway, a huge cheer went up from the viewers.

'Why did you all get so excited about such a terrible event?' I asked Mudasir, a second-year from Waziristan, later.

'Because that is what the Americans are doing to us at home,' he explained. 'So when we see them being paid back in the film, we cheer,' he added.

* * * * *

Board meetings and encounters with Board members were not regular events, but they kept me in touch with sections of the provincial government and the University of Peshawar.

The province of Khyber-Pakhtunkhwa (replacing the former North-West Frontier Province in 2010) consists of 25 districts including Peshawar, which is both a district and the provincial capital. Administration is achieved by an elected assembly of 124, of which three (2 per cent) are reserved for non-Muslims and 22 (17 per cent) for women. The President of Pakistan appoints a governor as head of the entire provincial government and the assembly elects a chief minister as the chief executive, assisted by a cabinet of ministers.

Because successive provincial governors chaired the College Board, I encountered them fairly frequently. Lt General Aurakzai, my first Board chair, took a keen interest in every aspect of the college; he would wander around chatting informally to students, and if any of the young men appeared shabbily dressed, he would reprimand them. Governor Owais Ahmed Ghani came to the province in January 2008 from the governorship of Balochistan, where he held office at the time of the controversial murder of Nawab Bugti. It seemed ironic that Ghani, an Edwardian, appeared to take less interest in college affairs than his predecessor, who was a graduate of our rival Islamia College.

I met neither of the chief ministers who held office during my principalship, and we did not invite them to college functions. This was partly because the provincial government leaders were political targets for the militant groups, which might have breached our poor security to attack them. But we did invite the chair of the provincial assembly and the Minister for Higher Education, who was a Board member.

The vice-chancellor of Peshawar University was an ex officio member of our Board of Governors, and for a time the director of the Institute of Management Sciences was the Old Edwardians' representative. Vice-chancellors seemed to come and go fairly rapidly – one was sacked very publicly by General Aurakzai in his ex officio capacity as Chancellor of Peshawar University. All in all, I always felt that the combination of constituency representatives which made up our Board – the government, the university, the Church of Pakistan, the college, and the Old Edwardians – worked extremely well, and I was sad when it fell apart shortly after my departure.

*　*　*　*　*

We observed seasonal occasions, such as Ramazan and Christmas, and there were important annual college events, such as plays and a work camp for degree students, usually held in the hills above Abbottabad.

For three of my four years, Ramazan came between the beginning of the academic year and the admissions period, moving forward each year. Muslim students in the hostel – the vast majority – observed it strictly, and we made provision for Christians and other minorities to have food and drink at lunchtime, provided they were discreet. For the first half of the month, the Qur'ān was recited by an invited *kharee* (reciter), assisted on some occasions by one of our *hafiz-e-Qur'ān* students. The recitation began around 8pm in a *shamiana* (tent) set up on the lawns of Shalimar Court and lasted for approximately an hour. I attended several of these, sitting on the grass at the back.

On the final night of the recitation, known as *khatam-ul-Qur'ān*, the principal is traditionally called to the front to thank the *kharee* and his assistant, and speak briefly to those present, including Shi'i (or Shia – variously spelled) Muslims, who attended on this final night. I was not aware of Christian students on these occasions, though Donald Joseph from the teaching staff was usually there. I was deeply impressed by the devotion and commitment of the students who participated in these gatherings.

There was an annual Na'at evening when students recited poems in praise of the prophet Muhammad, and a more secular day-long *mushaira* when distinguished Pashto poets from all over the province came to the college to read their poems. This occasion was presided over by Dr Yar Muhammad, head of the Pashto department and the author of several Pashto books.

The college closed for a short vacation across the Christmas period, but before it did so there was a carol service, which was put on by the Christian students, and attended by their parents and a number of Muslims. The Bishop of Peshawar was usually invited. The second term began shortly after the New Year, and ran on until May or even early June, with the university final exams coming at the end. By this time the weather was extremely hot, and the monsoon rains with their refreshing breezes rarely appeared before early July. Admissions began in late July or early August, and ran on for three to four weeks.

Other significant annual events were English-language plays organised by lecturers from the English department, and several special dinners when important guests were invited. There were two plays during my time as principal, *Macbeth* and Christopher

Figure 7 Students hard at work in the chemistry laboratory under the watchful eye of Javed Hyatt

Marlowe's *Doctor Faustus. Macbeth*'s witches were represented, utterly convincingly, by male students, but a woman student played Lady Macbeth – as she explained – only because the college hall where the performances took place was well away from the road, and 'Edwardians are not like some of those *goonda* students (and others) in the main university campus'. *Faustus* also involved women actors, but their parts were nothing like as sustained as that of Lady Macbeth.

As I participated in these varied college activities I sometimes wondered what I, as a foreigner, could offer as principal that could not be better carried out by a Pakistani national. Although I never really resolved this question in my mind, there was one bizarre incident that illustrated how in an essentially feudal society an outsider such as myself can sometimes usefully cross social boundaries.

Although I did my best to get to know some of the 'class 4' college employees – *malis*, mess staff, *chowkidars*, etc., my ignorance of Pashto made this difficult, and I constantly needed to ask others to interpret. I was particularly fond of Bashir, who made tea for me and was disabled, and Elias, my most reliable night

Figure 8 Students play basketball in front of the first-year hostel

watchman, the only one who, according to Inspector Qasim Zafar, 'will not climb up a tree if the Taliban come for you'.

One night I received a phone call from Vice-Principal Naveed to say that there had been an incident at the main gate involving Elias, who had been on duty. By the time I got there Elias had gone – I was told – to his village. Changez Khan was there to explain. The story was complicated, but began with the Cantonment water engineer whose daughter, aged about sixteen, had become the object of affection of a student who had recently left the college.

The girl had left her car – I mentally noted that she was too young to drive – outside the Khyber College, opposite our main gates. When she came back, her admirer and a friend had boxed her car in with their own vehicle. So she called her father, the engineer, and he contacted his friend the Station Commander, who was off duty and wearing civilian clothes. They arrived with two Military Police just as the students were teasing the girl about her car. When they saw her father they ran across the road and into our college.

Elias may not have seen the students enter the gate, but by the time the engineer and the Station Commander had crossed the road he had closed the gate and refused them admission. At this point, the Commander ordered the police to climb the gate and open it, which they did. Accounts differ about what happened next; apparently Elias slapped the Station Commander, but on being told of his identity ran off. Vice-Principal Naveed appeared on the scene and assured the angry visitors that Elias would be handed over to them as soon as he reappeared.

'They will torture him,' the bursar, a former military major himself, observed when he heard of the incident.

I therefore decided to visit the Station Commander early the next morning and I sent a message to Elias to remain in his village for some time. Although the Commander had calmed down by the time I met him, a colonel who shared his office was extremely indignant. The Station Commander had been publicly humiliated and the culprit must be severely punished. When I left, the Station Commander thanked me for coming, but the colonel refused to shake hands.

I thought the Governor as a retired general would be the ideal person to resolve this issue, and I made an appointment to see him (Pakistan was still under military rule with General Musharraf as President). General Aurakzai listened carefully as I described the sequence of events leading to my inconclusive meeting with the Station Commander.

'And so Elias was merely doing his duty, and the Station Commander was dressed as a civilian,' I concluded rather lamely.

'So what are the essential facts of the matter?' queried His Excellency.

'Boy meets girl, the adults disapprove, and there is *panga* (anger),' I offered.

'Eve teasing,' said the Governor, citing a topical phrase for sexist behaviour, and picked up the phone. 'I'll talk to the Station Commander.'

They spoke in Urdu for some time.

'Your *chowkidar* will not be harmed,' he said, simply.

I thanked him, and left.

I think the Governor was pleased by my initiative. Certainly Kalimullah was:

'Your credit rating has gone up,' he remarked.

Figure 9 The principal with Governor Owais A.Ghani

Figure 10 Recital of the Holy Qur'ān during Ramazan

Although Elias was never formally arrested, the authorities kept summoning him to attend court, but never sent anyone to press charges against him. This continued for several months. A few weeks later at a social gathering following a college dinner, I called Elias into the Memorial Hall and onto the platform beside me. Briefly, I told the students what had happened, and raised Elias's arm as a sign of victory. They all cheered.

* * * * *

We spent Saturday mornings in the local prison. This was the formidable Central Prison, Peshawar, a few minutes' drive from the college. Constructed by the colonial rulers in 1854 for fewer than 600 prisoners, it now contained 3000. Although the college had several social work programmes, I felt that one based on the prison would encourage students to interact with members of society – especially young ones – that they would otherwise not encounter.

The importance of prison visiting had been impressed on me during my academic research visits to Thailand and during a longer, more recent, period as a physics lecturer at Delhi University. Family members of a British prisoner in a Thai jail had asked me to contact him, and at the same time I was able to set up a scheme whereby members of my home church in Cambridge supported two Nigerian women with babies inside the adjacent women's prison.

In Delhi, I had tried to set up a programme between Tihar Jail and St Stephen's College. The principal agreed, but then took leave, and the acting principal was less than sympathetic:

'You are good people, so why do you want to go to the prison where they are bad people? What if you go to the prison one day, and the next they riot. Everybody will blame you, and the college will get a bad name.'

The Tihar prison governor, Kiran Bedi, had been very much in favour of an educational link between the college and the prison, but she was too progressive for the local politicians, and was transferred soon after I met her. But she arranged conducted tours

Figure 11 The prison visiting team with the deputy superintendent

of the prison for our group, during which I came into close contact with two of the most notorious inmates; one was Sushil Sharma, who 'tandooried' his wife at a Delhi hotel, the other was one of the killers of Jessica Lal, the late-night bar hostess who was elevated by the press to near sainthood for refusing to serve a group of rich young men after hours. I was never aware of any such 'celebrities' in Pakistan's prisons.

Our main contact at the Central Prison was the deputy superintendent, Maqsood Ur Rehman, a burly and seasoned prison officer who took us under his wing from our first arrival. There were seldom more than half a dozen of us – myself, Shahzad, Changez Khan, and three or four students – usually including Shahan Shahzad and Romail Iqbal, who had been close friends at St Mary's School. Muhammad Jehangir sometimes came, as did Mrs Nasira Manzoor when our visit included the women's section. Officially, we were not allowed to go there unless accompanied by a woman. Sajid Masih (one of the students who lived in my house), Waliullah and Ahmad Mustafa also came.

Initially, we spent most of our time in the foreign men's section of the prison, which housed about twenty or thirty inmates. Many were English- and French-speaking Africans who were serving long sentences for drug-related offences. The only prisoner in this section with whom I had any detailed conversations was Hendrik from South Africa. I made a few phone calls on his behalf to his relatives, and we visited him once when he was transferred to Haripur Central Prison.

In addition to talking with foreign inmates, we gave them books, including Bibles, which one of them requested, and sports equipment. There was some controversy when they asked for a table tennis table; apparently the chief superintendent thought that it could all too easily be leaned against a wall as a means of escape. Maqsood arranged for the table legs to be cemented into the ground, and the objection disappeared. The only two foreign women we met in the women's section asked us for instant coffee, which we purchased for them, and they made some for us in the common area outside their cells. We also left medical items with the nurse responsible for the women, several of whom had babies with them.

Superintendent Maqsood took me to 'death row', where just under a hundred prisoners awaited execution. At the time of my visit all death sentences had been suspended.

'At one time,' explained Maqsood, 'once their appeal to the President had failed, all we could do was hang them.' After I had left Pakistan the new government of Nawaz Sharif ended the amnesty.

Many of those who had received the death penalty were surprisingly well educated and personable. Two doctors from Islamabad shared a cell, and I met a police superintendent, a water engineer, and several other 'white-collar' professionals. There were usually similarities between the circumstances of their arrest and prosecution. Thus, for example, when a murder took place in a locality everyone initially remained totally silent; the police did their best to investigate, but lacking proper resources could accomplish very little. Then some influential local individual would accuse anyone they had a dispute with, and that person was arrested. From then on it was up to him or her to prove their innocence.

'That's how it works if you are poor and the police are ineffective,' commented Maqsood. 'It is not, as the Christians complain, that our blasphemy laws are used to discriminate against them; all laws can be used any time to discriminate against anyone without money or political backing. Now you see why some people prefer sharia law to our system!' Maqsood was nothing if not phlegmatic; he offered to show me the execution chamber, but I declined.

I asked the death row engineer about his legal representation. His lawyer, Latif Afridi, was a well-known barrister who was at that time the chair of the Bar Council and who had once lobbied me about the admission of a student with poor marks. I wondered whether or not such an eminent lawyer would pay much attention to any prisoner on death row. So I called him, and was reassured to find that he knew every detail of the case, and felt that he could get an acquittal within a few weeks.

Following an unsuccessful scam over passports involving one particular foreign prisoner about to be released, the foreign group as a whole were dispersed around the prison as a punishment. Even before this happened, Maqsood had encouraged us to have regular meetings with the prison boys who attended a makeshift school on Saturday mornings. An outside organisation was responsible for this educational programme, but everyone seemed very happy to give us an hour before lunch.

Initially, we sat facing the seventy or so boys distributed on floor mats. We introduced ourselves and shared some topical conversation, and then we broke up into small groups with one or two of us joining each. One of our Afghan students, Ahmad Mustafa, took the Afghan boys into a special group, noting their names and home villages. He later took this list to the Afghan Consulate, a stone's throw from the college, where the consular staff tried to contact the boys' families. I was interested to discover that although Mustafa was free to do this as part of our college programme, the Afghan Consul and his staff were effectively prohibited from entering the prison by the vast amount of red tape required for permission.

The boys spoke Pashto so I could only speak to them with Shahzad interpreting. We always asked them where they came from, which could be helpful because some were shy and withdrawn, and might not otherwise know that other boys came from the same home area. We never asked them directly why they were in prison, but some told us. Most were there for petty offences such as stealing mobile phones or illegal entry into Pakistan. The latter was especially true of the Afghans and a group of Nepalese we came to know well. Officially, the boys were aged between 11 and 18, but we came across seven-year-olds and some who had no idea of their age ('I have an older sister and a younger brother').

One particular boy was very happy to tell us why he was in prison.

'I stole three cows and two sheep,' he announced cheerfully, and then, amid laughter, 'but I got away with five chickens, and they never caught me for that!'

An 11-year-old was accused of murder – I was told that some adult murderers try to shift the blame onto children who are too young to hang, but nonetheless must remain for many years in prison. During our conversations, Maqsood often waited outside the building to meet boys whom we discovered to have problems of which the prison authorities were unaware. Apparently his position made it otherwise inappropriate for him to make direct contact with individual boys.

At the beginning of one session we noticed a group of boys pushing a friend to the front. Shahzad explained:

'They think that we consider them all as little more than stealers of mobile phones and petty thieves. But today they have a big-time criminal – a Taliban bomber!'

The boy – probably in his early teens – looked embarrassed. Another boy explained that he felt a failure because he had been stopped before his bomb went off.

'Better alive?' queried Mustafa.

'And how about a nice shag with a girlfriend?' commented somebody else.

The boy gave a bit of a smile. The therapy was working.

Figure 12 Inside the prison on World Aids Day

Another Taliban bomber was more assertive. He remonstrated with Shahzad about his association with me, an obvious foreigner. Shahzad offered an explanation, but the anger remained, and when I handed the boy a packet of biscuits as our usual parting gift, he flung it on the floor. This embarrassed some of the other boys, who gave apologies on his behalf. But when I looked at the boy again, he was crying.

I met Pakistan's most senior Taliban leader, Sufi Muhammad, during a visit to the Central Prison Peshawar. The circumstances were that I was on a routine Saturday morning visit to the prison, but was told on arrival that an administrative staff member from the college whom we had prosecuted for his involvement in embezzlement had been taken seriously ill, and was in the prison hospital wing. I decided to pay him a pastoral visit. He told me that Sufi Muhammad was a few beds along the ward with two sons who could interpret for me, so I went to meet him.

The Sufi – estimated to be about 90 years old – was propped up on his bed, his long yellowish hair down to his shoulders.

61

Communicating through one of his sons, I found him courteous and mildly interested in our college, which he knew about. His sons were very happy to interpret, and pleased that I addressed their father as 'sir'.

From the hospital wing, I joined our college team with the boys in their makeshift school. As soon as the boys knew that I had been with the Sufi, a buzz of excitement went round the room. Shahzad later explained that the boys, and many others, admired the Taliban leaders because they believed in Pakistan and in Islam. The Sufi had once led 10,000 *jihādis* across the mountains to fight the infidels. He was brave, and they all admired him. Who are the corresponding charismatic leaders in the West, I wondered, as the giant portcullis of the prison gate closed behind me. I am still wondering.

4

Enter the Taliban

My first encounter with a member of the Taliban was in Jerome's retail store some fifteen minutes' walk from Edwardes College. A young man, possibly in his early thirties, introduced himself as an Edwardian and a Taliban member, and asked if I was the new principal. In the ensuing conversation, he invited me to visit his *madrasa* on the outskirts of Peshawar. I expressed interest but did not go because I knew that the mullahs at certain Peshawar mosques preached vehemently anti-Western sermons after the *jum'a* prayers.

Returning to Edwardes College I was told that no Edwardian could conceivably be a Taliban member, and I must be mistaken. As time went by I came to know that several members of the college teaching staff and students were related to Taliban militants in Pakistan. With the benefit of more study of Taliban origins, it seemed perfectly reasonable that the young man I met in Jerome's was drawn from the ranks of educated urban Pashtuns connected to the Hezb-e-Islami movement.[1]

A *talib* is an Islamic student, a person who searches for knowledge in accordance with Islam. A mullah, by contrast, gives knowledge. Taliban is merely the plural of *talib*. The *Oxford Dictionary of Islam* refers to a 'group of students and religious leaders who established the Islamic Republic of Afghanistan in 1994-6 in order to end the lengthy civil war following the withdrawal of the Soviet Union from the region in 1989'.[2] Before proceeding further we must review the circumstances leading up to these events.

* * * * *

In late December 1979, thousands of troops from the Soviet Union entered Afghanistan. They intervened ostensibly in support of the Afghan communist government in its struggle against anti-communist Muslim insurgents, and they remained there until mid-February 1989. The move was to some extent unexpected, though Soviet influence had been growing in the region for many years. Since 1955, Moscow had provided military support to its neighbour; by 1973 a third of all Afghan troops had trained in the Soviet Union.

In 1973, Mohammed Daoud Khan, a former Afghan prime minister, overthrew King Zahir Shah (his cousin). Though more a nationalist than a communist he courted Soviet support and also that of the People's Democratic Party of Afghanistan (PDPA), founded in 1965 and based on Marxist ideology. But a split in the PDPA coupled with Daoud's attempts to govern the tribal regions rendered him vulnerable to the so-called 'Khalqis', mainly Pashto-speaking and rural, led by Noor Muhammad Taraki, who stormed the presidential palace and killed him. Taraki became prime minister, with the leader of the other PDPA faction, Babrak Karmal, as his deputy.

This unification of the two PDPA factions temporarily strengthened the communist base of the Kabul government, pleasing Moscow but not Jimmy Carter's government in the USA, which much preferred Daoud's middle way. They courted Taraki, hoping to limit Soviet influence as much as possible. But Babrak Karmal was implicated in a plot to overthrow him, and the resulting internal strife weakened a major programme of Taraki's to win over to communism the Islamic tribal areas beyond Kabul. By the winter of 1978 not only was this programme badly failing, but an armed national revolt was in the offing. Taraki and his new deputy, Hafizullah Amin, went to Moscow to sign a friendship treaty that would allow direct Soviet military assistance should an Islamic insurgency threaten the regime.

The Soviets believed that Taraki could not prevent a civil war and the prospect of a hostile Islamic government taking over, and so they dispatched combat troops to Bagram Airfield outside Kabul. This move prompted the US government to start supplying aid to Islamic insurgents known as *mujahideen* ('those who engage in *jihād*'). Fearing that the Soviets were favouring Taraki at his expense, Amin had him killed. The Soviets were furious and sent armed motorised divisions into Kabul; Amin was killed, and Babrak Karmal was installed as head of government.

Although there were unexpected factors in the timing of the Soviet intervention, it was essentially in line with Brezhnev's doctrine that once a country became socialist it must never be permitted to revert to capitalism. The Soviets also welcomed access via Afghanistan to southern ports, and greater contact with India, with whom they had had beneficial trade relationships since Nehru's lengthy premiership. Possibilities also existed for exploring Afghan natural resources, especially oil and gas, and minerals such as iron, copper, cobalt, gold and lithium – a key raw material in the manufacture of batteries for laptops and BlackBerrys.

For these and other reasons, Soviet tanks entered Afghanistan on the night of 24 December 1979. Ahmed Rashid, author of *Taliban*, was in Kandahar when they arrived:

> I [...] watched the first Soviet tanks roll in. Teenage Soviet soldiers had driven for two days [...] to Herat and then on to Kandahar along a metalled highway that the Soviets had themselves built in the 1960s. Many of the soldiers were of Central Asian origin. They got out of their tanks, dusted off their uniforms and ambled across to the nearest stall for a cup of sugarless green tea – a staple part of the diet in both Afghanistan and Central Asia. The Afghans in the bazaar just stood and stared.[3]

Babrak Karmal failed to retain popular support, and in 1986 was replaced by Mohammad Najibullah, who was president from 1987 until 1992, when the *mujahideen* took over Kabul. It was during his presidency that the Soviets began to withdraw from Afghanistan. With the dissolution of the Soviet Union in 1991, Najibullah was left without foreign support; he was ousted from power and forced to live in the UN compound in Kabul. When the Taliban took over Kabul in 1996, Najibullah was castrated, dragged through the streets behind a truck, and publicly hanged.

By the time of Najibullah's death, Burhanuddin Rabbani was president. He was a Persian-speaking ethnic Tajik, and an Islamic scholar. He was killed by a suicide bomber in Kabul in 2011.

There are varying theories about the motives underlying the Russian occupation of Afghanistan. Sir Nicholas Barrington, a seasoned diplomat with experience in both Afghanistan and Pakistan, cites Christopher Andrew's studies of Russia's KGB as revealed in the Mitrokhin Archive as follows:

> I wonder how much [...] was disinformation to justify Soviet actions. It emerges from Andrew's book that the KGB's main achievements in Asia were not so much killing enemies but sowing distrust through clever forgeries and other ploys. I have little doubt that they weakened Afghan resistance.[4]

Whatever rationale the Soviets had for their intervention in Afghanistan and the timing of their departure, there is no doubt that they adopted a tough and pragmatic exit strategy. Prior to their departure, an advance party would meet with village elders along the proposed route and offer them anything they wanted – money, improved roads, a school – virtually anything. These promises were carried out. But the elders were also told that if, when the tanks drove past their village, anyone fired a single shot, they would turn back, raze the village to the ground, and kill every member.[5] The Taliban accepted the deal and the Soviets made a dignified exit.

These events in Afghanistan were crucial in shaping the characteristics of the Taliban in the region. We summarise them chronologically and in a simplified form in Table 1.

Table 1 Events leading to the emergence of the Taliban in Afghanistan

1973	King Zahir Shah, leader of the Durrani dynasty, who had ruled since 1933, was deposed and sent into exile by his cousin Mohammed Daoud Khan. Afghanistan was declared a republic; Daoud was supported by leftist army officers.
1975	Leaders of Islamic opposition to Daoud fled to Peshawar where Pakistan's prime minister Zulfikar Ali Bhutto supported them. These leaders, Gulbuddin Hekmatyar, Burhanuddin Rabbani and Ahmad Shah Massoud, later led the *mujahideen*.
1978	Marxist sympathisers in the army, some of whom had helped Daoud to power, overthrew and killed him. But the Marxist PDPA was divided and out of touch with the rural mullahs and khans. The first PDPA Khalqi leader, Taraki, was killed, followed by his deputy, Hafizullah Amin.
1979	Soviets intervened and installed Babrak Karmal as president.
1986	Karmal was deposed and replaced by Najibullah, who was president from 1987 until 1992.
1989	Soviet forces withdrew from Afghanistan.
1992	*Mujahideen* took over Kabul. Rabbani became president 1992–6.
1994	The Taliban took the southern city of Kandahar.
1996	The Taliban took over Kabul and ruled Afghanistan until 2001, by which time they controlled 90 per cent of the country. During this period their leader was Mullah Omar.
2001	A US-led invasion toppled the Taliban to punish them for providing refuge to al-Qaeda. They were assisted by the Northern Alliance, composed of ethnic minority Tajiks, Uzbeks and Hazaras (Shi'is).

* * * * *

Before considering the consequences of events in Afghanistan on the rise of Pakistan's Taliban, it is important to note that the border between these two countries – the so-called Durand Line, established in 1893 – is extremely porous. This is primarily because the people on both sides are Pashtuns, and extensively tribal. There are similarities with the situation between Northern Ireland and the Irish Republic; they are Irish on both sides with a common history.

This point was brought home to me especially by the college students from Parachinar, the Shi'i enclave bordering and jutting out into Afghanistan. These students would sometimes have difficulties returning home via the shortest route inside Pakistan; they therefore crossed the Khyber Pass, travelled through Jalalabad to Kabul, then back close to Tora Bora into Parachinar. When I asked one of them, Syed Kazmi, about travel documents, he seemed quite bewildered:

'Passports?' he queried. 'We don't need passports; our homes are in those hills.'

It is important to recognise that the tribal areas are basically self-governing; collectively they are known as Federally Administered Tribal Areas or FATA. Any group of tribal elders may decide whether or not to welcome newcomers by calling a *jirga*, which is their traditional form of government, independent of both the provincial government in Peshawar and the federal government in Islamabad.

In the wake of the US-led attack, Mullah Omar and his associates escaped into Pakistan's frontier territories and constituted the Quetta Shura in the capital of Balochistan province. From there they maintained a degree of operational authority over Afghan Taliban militants, though they also delegated significant control to local leaders – a characteristic of the Taliban throughout the region.

Among those who fled with Mullah Omar was Jalaluddin Haqqani, an Afghan *mujahideen* commander, and his son Sirajuddin, who later managed the so-called Haqqani network, based near Miram Shah, the capital of North Waziristan. The Miram Shah Shura operated autonomously within the Taliban as a whole, and Sirajuddin Haqqani held a seat on the Quetta Shura. Jalaluddin and his Arab wife were close friends with Osama bin Laden, and were often seen together in Peshawar. An associated group was led by Gul Bahadur, a Wazir, and his deputy, Maulana Sadiq Noor, from the Daur tribe. They had a strong tribal base close to the Afghan border.

These groups tended to support Taliban resistance within Afghanistan. But before we consider the ones responsible for militancy inside Pakistan, it is important to summarise political events in Pakistan prior to the Afghan Taliban exodus. These concern president Zia-ul-Haq and Inter-Services Intelligence (ISI).

The personality of Zia-ul-Haq during his life was as enigmatic as were the circumstances of his death. He was educated at St Stephen's College, Delhi, with its tolerant and liberal ethos, and yet his promulgation of Islam during his ten-year presidency (1978–88) was repressive and cruel. He deposed Z. A. Bhutto's People's Party government in 1977, and declared martial law, ordering Bhutto to be hanged in prison less than two years later.

Aided by the USA and Saudi Arabia, Zia and the ISI coordinated many of the Afghan *mujahideen* against the Soviets throughout the 1980s. But the year before they left, in 1988, he was killed when a bomb exploded in his private aircraft. His assassins have never been identified. Among those who died with him was the US ambassador, which appears to rule out the involvement of the CIA. The most imaginative explanation for his death is offered by Mohammed Hanif in *A Case of Exploding Mangoes*, described by John le Carré as 'deliciously anarchic'.[6]

An important legacy of Zia's presidency was the large number of *madrasas* that he funded, many along the Afghan border. In 1971, there were only 900 *madrasas* in Pakistan, but by the end of Zia's tenure in 1988 there were 8,000 recognised *madrasas* and 25,000 unrecognised ones, educating a total of over half a million students.[7] Many of these *madrasas* based their teaching on the Sunni Deobandi tradition; they received funding from Saudi Arabia from the 1980s until about 2000, when the Saudis began to prefer movements more orientated towards the *ḥadīth*. But many mullahs were only semi-educated themselves, and more likely to be influenced by the tribal Pashtunwali. Zia's policy was to fund *madrasa*s of all sectarian persuasions. Some of the most important *madrasa* border training camps were located at Chaman (Balochistan), North Waziristan, Parachinar (Tora Bora) and Bajaur.

Between 1982 and 1992 an estimated 35,000 Muslim radicals from 43 countries were part of the Afghan *mujahideen*, and thousands more came to the new *madrasa*s funded by Zia's government and the ISI. According to Ahmed Rashid:

> Many of these radicals speculated that if the Afghan jihad had defeated one superpower, the Soviet Union, could they not also defeat the other superpower, the US, and their own regimes? The logic of their argument was based on the simple premise that the Afghan jihad alone had brought the Soviet state to its knees. The multiple internal reasons that led to the collapse of the Soviet system, of which the jihad was only one, were conveniently ignored. So while the USA saw the collapse of the Soviet state as the failure of the communist system, many Muslims saw it solely as a victory for Islam. For militants this belief was inspiring and deeply evocative of the Muslim sweep across the world in the seventh and eighth centuries. A new Islamic *Ummah*, they argued, could be forged by the sacrifices and blood of a new generation of martyrs and more such victories.[8]

Such a view may appear over-romantic, but some explanation is needed as to why one particular radical, Osama bin Laden, turned against his benefactors with such far-reaching consequences. The ISI had long wanted Saudi Intelligence to provide a capable leader, preferably with royal connections, to head the Saudi *jihādi* contingent. Bin Laden fitted the bill, and moved to Peshawar to join Abdullah Yusuf Azzam, a Jordanian Palestinian whom he had first met at university in Jeddah.

Bin Laden first travelled to Peshawar in 1980 to meet the *mujahideen* leaders, and decided to settle there two years later. In

1986, he helped with the construction of the Khost tunnel complex, funded by the CIA for the benefit of *mujahideen* fighters. He also set up his own training camp for Arab-Afghans. After Azzam was killed by a suicide bomber in 1989, bin Laden took over his organisation, which had already become known as al-Qaeda, as a service for Arab-Afghans. His promotion of ultra-orthodox Wahabism made him unpopular with many Pashtuns and Shi'i Muslims, and in 1990 he returned to Saudi Arabia. After Iraq's invasion of Kuwait, he quarrelled with the Saudi royal family over their willingness to accommodate US forces, and was obliged to leave for the Sudan in 1992.

In 1996, bin Laden travelled to Jalalabad in Afghanistan and remained there until the Taliban conquered Kabul the same year. The following year, he became friends with Mullah Omar and moved to Kandahar. By this time al-Qaeda and the Taliban had become bedfellows, bin Laden was firmly opposed to the USA, and the Clinton administration was committed to blaming him for every possible atrocity, 'desperately looking for a diversion as it wallowed through the mire of the Monica Lewinsky affair'.[9] Those who knew bin Laden in Peshawar describe him as a tall, quiet man, who lived in what at one time was the Arab quarter near University Road (close to the British Council). As a CIA collaborator he was able to use the Combined Military Hospital close to Edwardes College when necessary. 'Shy but intelligent' was one comment I picked up. He was never seen again in Peshawar following the 9/11 bombings, and nobody I knew had any idea where he was hiding when he was killed by US Seals in 2011.

* * * * *

The Quetta Shura and the Haqqani network were primarily concerned with opposing the US-led forces in Afghanistan, while other Taliban groups concentrated on events in Pakistan. In December 2007 several tribal militant bodies, and others from Kashmir and the Punjab, met in the FATA areas and created the Tehreek-e-Taliban Pakistan (TTP), or 'Movement of the Pakistan Taliban'. It was led by 35-year-old Baitullah Mehsud from South

Figure 13 Sufi Muhammad: The elder statesman of Pakistan's Taliban

Waziristan. Mehsud was a good friend of Jalaluddin Haqqani, and had fought for the Afghan Taliban. The TTP's objectives were to rule Pakistan and convert it into a sharia state.

Within the FATA areas, South Waziristan – and to a lesser extent the North – became the main centres of Taliban activity, which is why the US drone strikes were concentrated there. The countryside is wild and mountainous; the people are almost all orthodox Sunni Muslims, and mostly illiterate. The *madrasas* are connected to Jamiat Ulema-e-Islam, an Islamist party founded in the 1950s that is popular in the tribal areas.

Prior to the formation of the TTP, the first head of the Taliban in South Waziristan was Nek Muhammad, a young Wazir aged – according to reports – between 18 and 27.[10] Baitullah Mehsud supported Nek's successful resistance to the Pakistan military in

2004, but Nek was killed the same year – possibly by a US drone. Baitullah also died, and was succeeded by Hakimullah Mehsud. Hakimullah fought in Helmand province in Afghanistan, and in December 2008 was responsible for burning a large number of NATO trucks on the Peshawar ring road (I saw their burnt-out remains). The TTP eventually based itself on Miram Shah, with units spread over FATA and settled areas such as Bannu, Mardan and Swat.

The Swat valley district of the Malakand division of Khyber-Pakhtunkhwa province was not affected by the anti-Soviet *jihād* in Afghanistan to the same extent as the FATA areas. It has no border with Afghanistan, and was a princely state until 1969. Its militancy is based on the Tehreek-e-Nifaz-e-Shariat-e-Muhammadi (TNSM) or 'Movement for Implementation of the Sharia of Muhammad', led by Sufi Muhammad, a local leader of Jamaat-e-Islami since 1985.

During the early 1990s, Sufi Muhammad started a peaceful campaign in favour of implementing the sharia across the Swat valley. When they started blocking roads, the security forces confronted them, and in May 1994 11 people were killed in Buner district (Buner is historically part of princely Swat). The Sufi's popularity declined until 11 September 2001, when he led a huge tribal *lashkar* (essentially a militia) from Swat, Dir, Buner and Shangla districts, and Bajaur and Mohmand agencies across the mountains to fight US forces in Afghanistan. Large numbers died, and his popularity waned once more as many, especially in Swat and Dir, mourned their loved ones. He was imprisoned by the security forces for seven years, by which time people's anger had subsided. The TNSM was banned.

The vacuum left by Sufi Muhammad's imprisonment was filled by his son-in-law Fazle Hayat (better known as Fazlullah), who now heads the TTP, following Hakimullah Mehsud's death in 2013. Fazlullah became well known on account of his unauthorised radio channel, launched in 2004, which earned him the nickname 'Maulana Radio'. He was more extreme in his views than his father-in-law, and went so far as to oppose polio vaccination as 'a conspiracy of the Jews and Christians to stunt the population growth of Muslims'.[11] But Fazlullah also echoed Sufi Muhammad's call for social equality, more jobs, better civic facilities, and efficient justice based on the sharia rather than the cumbersome processes of civil law. According to Daud Khan Khattak:

> Fazlullah also used his brother's death in a drone strike in Damadola, Bajaur, in early January 2006, to gain supporters, and he likewise exploited the inflamed passions following the deadly storming of Islamabad's Red Mosque by security forces in the summer of 2007.[12]

Khattak may be referring to the drone strike at Chenagai in late October 2006, which led to the cancellation of the visit by the Prince of Wales to Edwardes College. There could also have been an earlier one. But certainly the storming of Lal Masjid (the Red Mosque) by security forces in 2007 on General Musharraf's instructions inflamed Taliban passions within Pakistan against the government.

The appointment of Fazlullah to succeed Hakimullah as leader of the TTP has caused sceptics to claim that this is a bad choice because he is not from Waziristan. But he is a skilled and ruthless militant with far fewer scruples than his father-in-law, and an antagonism towards minorities such as Shi'is, Jews and Christians. The suicide bombing at All Saints' Church in Peshawar in 2013, which killed more than 100 worshippers, may reflect his extremist leanings, though two subgroupings of the TTP took specific responsibility for that unexpected and shocking attack.

* * * * *

In terms of active troops, Pakistan's armed forces are the seventh largest in the world. They played a powerful and distinctive role throughout the period of Taliban growth, and their influence remains strong in spite of the country's successful transition from one democratically elected government to another.

The Pakistan Armed Forces (PAF) were formed in 1947 at Independence, when they fought their first major war with India.

By 1958, General Ayub Khan was strong enough to stage a military coup, and in 1965 led Pakistan into an inconclusive war with India, resigning under pressure in 1969 in favour of a less competent general, Yahya Khan.

I arrived in India in 1965 to teach at St Stephen's College, Delhi, on the day the second war with Pakistan ended, and was generally regarded by the senior teaching staff as the harbinger of good luck. The college principal was Satish Sircar, a talented Cambridge mathematician and a close associate of philosopher S. K. Bose, who shocked everyone with an article in the *Stephanian* describing the war between India and Pakistan as 'internecine'.

In Pakistan, General Yahya Khan resigned at the end of 1971 following the army's defeat by India, and the bloody formation of Bangladesh. Zulfikar Ali Bhutto took over as president, and set to work establishing the 1973 Constitution and a parliamentary system of government, which brought him to power as prime minister and leader of the Pakistan People's Party. But Bhutto's democratic ascendancy was terminated in 1978 by General Zia-ul-Haq, and a year later he was cruelly executed in prison. Zia ruled as military president for ten years and died under mysterious circumstances in a plane crash. Benazir Bhutto served two non-consecutive terms as prime minister, from 1988 until 1990, and 1993 until 1996. She conceded defeat in the 1997 parliamentary elections and went into self-exile for nine years.

Throughout this period and beyond the army repeatedly flexed its muscles, occasionally relaxing them sufficiently to allow a democratically elected government to run the country. Unfortunately, not everything went smoothly when the military were not in power, and the charges for corruption levelled against Benazir Bhutto and her husband Asif Ali Zardari, who became president following her untimely death in 2007, rankled with many people.

Pakistan's military have been blamed by some for what the eminent civil rights lawyer Aitzaz Ahsan has called the country's 'bonsai democracy', but opinion is sharply divided. Others attribute the failures to chronic divisions among politicians who have fatally undermined the prospects of democratic consolidation.

Those who blame the military accuse them of flouting the constitution with the intention of enhancing their own power at the expense of weakened civilian governments.

Carey Schofield has given a detailed account of Pakistan's army in *Inside the Pakistan Army*. She points out that the killing of Osama bin Laden on 2 May 2011 damaged the relationship between the army and the Pakistani public.[13] However it was the ISI Director, General Shuja Pasha, who bore the brunt of criticism in the National Assembly, while the Chief of Army Staff, General Ashfaq Parvez Kayani, himself a former ISI director general, took a back seat. This incident illustrates the closeness that exists between these two organisations.

Not everybody shares Schofield's view that the Pakistani government knew nothing about bin Laden's presence in their garrison town. According to Lt General Asad Durrani, who was ISI director general from 1990 to 1992, 'I cannot say exactly what happened but [...] it is quite possible that they [the ISI] did not know but it was more probable that they did.' It is interesting that Al Jazeera's English programme on 10 February 2015 reported this elusive and non-committal observation under the headline: 'Ex-spy chief says Pakistan likely sheltered Bin Laden.'

During and subsequent to my time in Peshawar the ISI directors general were Ashfaq Parvez Kayani (2004–7), Nadeem Taj (2001–8), Ahmad Shuja Pasha (2008–12), Zahirul Islam (2012–14) and Rizwan Akhtar (2014–). Mahmood Ahmed (1999–2001) was in post when Robin Brooke-Smith was principal of Edwardes College, and it was he who saved Robin from a conspiracy to get rid of him involving a section of the provincial government and a senior member of the local church.[14]

It was the ISI that organised opposition to the Russian intervention in Afghanistan. It did not create the Taliban and neither did the *mujahideen* become the Taliban; the Taliban emerged to fill the vacuum following the Russian withdrawal. The ISI is large, with about 25,000 current personnel on its payroll. It helped to identify those responsible for the July 2005 London bombings, but does not appear to have been given credit for this.

Carey Schofield has investigated claims that the ISI and the authorities knew that Osama bin Laden was living near the Pakistan Military Academy in Abbottabad. She concludes, somewhat enigmatically, that 'the theory that the ISI was unaware of Osama bin Laden's whereabouts is the least improbable possibility'. She maintains:

> If the ISI had known where he was they would either have protected him properly, or otherwise dealt with him. Leaving aside the successive chiefs, a string of handlers would therefore have had to be in the loop if the ISI had been helping him. The ISI would have had to ensure that neither the police nor the Army interfered with him or his hosts. They would have had to try to make sure that no one found him by mistake.[15]

For these and a variety of additional reasons it seems highly unlikely that the ISI and the Pakistan authorities were deliberately sheltering Osama bin Laden. Incidentally, the Western press is quite incorrect in thinking that bin Laden's house was virtually next door to the Military Academy; there is at least half a mile as the crow flies between them.

Schofield concludes her analysis of Pakistan's military and its appendages with the assertion that the future of Pakistan lies, 'to a considerable extent, in the hands of the Army'.[16] Such a claim may produce groans of despair from Western liberals who are passionately committed to democracy. But in a country in which large swathes of the population are without even rudimentary education, it is not clear that their votes will necessarily be directed towards their own betterment.

That the army remains a powerful force in Pakistan's affairs is evidenced by the fact that when the Afghan president, Ashraf Ghani, paid his first visit to Pakistan he called on the army chief before meeting Prime Minister Nawaz Sharif. And when Imran Khan staged a stand-off with the Sharif government in the summer of 2014, there were rumours that the army might attempt a coup. It is to their credit that they did not.

A critic of Pakistan's military, Aqil Shah, based in the USA, argues that the army bases much of its perceived role on the country's geopolitical insecurity – essentially the threat from India and a lack of internal cohesion.[17] In response to these dangers, the military has assumed for itself what Shah describes as 'traditions of tutelage' and a misplaced notion of its 'guardianship' of national interests and security. Extreme advocates of such a role for the military claim that it alone stands between anarchy and order, and therefore that any weakening of it might lead to administrative collapse. Many people appear to have believed this around the time of General Zia's presidency, but the more recent strengthening of other centres of power, such as the judiciary and the press, has rendered such a view much less tenable.

* * * * *

The activities of the Taliban and the Pakistan military in the borderlands adjacent to Edwardes College were further intensified by the presence of US drones in the region.

In 2004, US President George W. Bush authorised the covert use of drones inside Pakistan for the first time. In US military terms a drone is defined as a 'land, sea or air vehicle that is remotely or automatically controlled'. Predator surveillance drones had been used during the NATO intervention in Kosovo in 1999 and were first equipped and tested with Hellfire missiles in 2001, turning, as Grégoire Chamayou put it, 'an eye into a weapon'.[18] Hellfire missiles have a 'kill zone' of about 15 metres and there are plans for more precise targeting.

Forty-five drone strikes took place in the FATA areas during George W. Bush's tenure as US President, which ended in 2009. Nine occurred between 2004 and 2007, but additionally there was at least the one in Bajaur, which killed 85 *madrasa* boys and caused such anger in the province that the visit of the Prince of Wales to Edwardes College had to be cancelled, as mentioned. How many more such unacknowledged drone attacks were there during this period and subsequently?

US President Barack Obama considerably increased the use of drones inside Pakistan's borders, as the figures from the New America Foundation in Table 2 show.

Estimating the number of casualties from drone strikes is both difficult and controversial. A *Guardian* report describes the work of a local investigator in Waziristan, who has recorded the impact of drone strikes in the area where he lives:

> For every ten to 15 people killed, maybe they get one militant. I don't go to count how many Taliban are killed. I go to count how many children, women, innocent people are killed.[19]

Not only are many innocent people killed, but the entire population is radicalised by the attacks:

> There are just pieces of flesh lying around after a strike. You can't find bodies. So the locals pick up the flesh and curse America. They say that America is killing us inside our own country, inside our own houses, and only because we are Muslims.[20]

Even when the drones hit the intended target the blast also demolishes neighbours' houses, killing those inside:

> The youth in the area surrounding a strike get crazed. Hatred builds up inside those who have seen a drone attack. The Americans think it is working, but the damage they're doing is far greater.[21]

Table 2 Drone use inside Pakistan's borders 2004–11

	Number of strikes	Estimated casualties
2004–07	9	112
2008	33	314
2009	53	725
2010	118	993
2011 (to July only)	45	346

Another report, this time in the *Independent*, summarises the findings of a group of legal experts in Stanford and New York universities about drone attacks. It draws attention to what it calls 'double tap' drone attacks whereby a second Hellfire missile hits the same target a few minutes after the first on the assumption that this will kill those who go to the assistance of the victims of the first.[22]

This press account and the Stanford/New York report it is based on omit all reference to the October 2006 Bajaur drone. I therefore wrote to the *Independent*, which published my letter on 8 October 2012, following which I received confirmation of the strike as recorded by the Bureau of Investigative Journalism, describing it as 'one of the most shocking incidents in the entire series'.[23]

The identification of drone targets is based on information supplied by local informers and aerial photography. The CIA's spy network on the ground may include people with a grudge against individuals or groups, whom they name to their paymasters as militants. The manner in which such informers are recruited may be illustrated by the experiences of a former Edwardes student, originally from Waziristan, who emailed me to ask for advice about whether or not to accept from two Americans a large sum of money to act as a model. I advised him not to do so, but when they met him the second time it became clear that they really wanted him to spy for them in his home area. On 1 December 2012 he emailed as follows:

> They were not from a modelling agency. They wanted to hire me for information services (spy) and many more in Waziristan. I told them 'I am not a milk-feeding baby and I understand what is good and what is bad, and the world's biggest terrorist is America.' I don't hate the American people, only their policies.

The rest of the email is confused, but it seems to suggest that when the former student refused to cooperate he was threatened by the two.

Since 2009, security officials in Washington have met regularly to draw up for presidential approval a 'kill list' of candidates for assassination by drones. The precise criteria for being on these lists are not known, but are probably based on the concept of 'signature strikes' first approved the previous year by CIA director Michael Hayden. These allow drone controllers to fire a missile at any male of military age whose behaviour corresponds to a 'signature', which suggests suspicious activity.

The US authorities have tried to alleviate public unease about their use of drones inside the FATA areas by claiming that the Pakistan government is complicit. This has never been proved, and whatever one or two Pakistani government officials may be reported to have said, Imran Khan's electoral victories in Khyber-Pakhtunkhwa, based first and foremost on his opposition to drones, makes clear where public opinion lies on this issue. The pro-USA Western media have tried so hard to convince the public that 'drones kill militants' that they have converted the phrase virtually into a repetitive mantra. How else can anyone explain the media's threefold reports on separate occasions of the killing of Hakimullah Mehsud by drones?

US Ambassador Anne Patterson twice told her government that drones are counterproductive, but this only became widely known through the WikiLeaks disclosures. A former head of Britain's MI6 has expressed reservations about the use of drones, but his remarks are subject to Chatham House rules and cannot be attributed.

The robotisation of warfare represents a dangerous and slippery slope; it is an issue that needs to be put at the top of every electoral agenda.

5

In the Eye of the Storm

The first indications of violence following my arrival in Peshawar in 2006 came from the tribal areas close to the city. It took the form of rockets a few feet in length fired from distances of 15 to 20 kilometres. Initially most of these fell on the city suburbs, and it wasn't until October the following year that any landed near the college.

It was never particularly clear who was firing these rockets, and the semi-autonomous nature of the tribal belts made it difficult for the police to enter them. It appears that the Taliban progressively moved into these areas, but there was also a warlord called Mangal Bagh, whose militia attacked residential districts along the Jamrud Road leading to Landi Kotal. He was not associated with any Taliban group.

In addition to the tribal Khyber Agency, there was an unsafe area along Bara Road that I once visited to offer condolences to a teaching staff member whose father had died. It was customary on these occasions to sit in a group inside a courtyard or outside the house. There was a pleasant garden area outside the house gates but, instead of sitting there, we sat in a circle on rough ground further down the road.

'Why here and not there?' I asked Vice-Principal Naveed, who had accompanied me.

'Stray bullets,' he explained, simply.

I attended a wedding of two college students along the old Kohat Road, another tribal area. The father was especially happy because both his sons were marrying two sisters on the same day, and everyone would have saved a lot of money by combining the weddings. There were no bullets, but an armed guard loomed over most of the proceedings. Both the old and new Kohat roads were frequented by the Taliban, who would occupy the Kohat tunnel and demand ransoms from travellers. Other dangerous routes were Harichand Road, the road to Charsadda and beyond, and Warsak Road.

Warsak Road is a long road leading to a reservoir surrounded by hills. When I first visited the reservoir, which is a pleasant picnic area, I was advised not to go into the hills because they were full of Taliban. Subsequently, the Taliban moved progressively along the road towards the city until resistance from the army moved them away.

For the first few months I was able to travel by car through these tribal belts. I visited the Khyber Pass accompanied by two security vehicles in front and behind. We passed the huge house of the notorious Afridi family. I waved to boy soldiers, neatly attired in dapper uniforms and carrying AK47s, and they waved back. They may have worked for the Afridis, or possibly Mangal Bagh.

I went to Bannu, to attend the wedding of the brother of Zahoor Khan, lecturer in international relations, and called at the house of Khan Niaz, lecturer in biology, on the way back. On another occasion, we visited the Diocese of Peshawar's hospital in Bannu, their excellent Pennell Memorial High School, and a new church modelled architecturally on a mosque. On this journey the heat was too much for me, and I collapsed on arrival at the hospital, fortunately at the feet of the director, Dr Reginald Zahiruddin. I travelled almost as far as Bannu to meet the family of Waliullah, soon after he enrolled as a student.

There were no disturbances on any of these visits to Bannu, though Dr Zahiruddin, a member of the Church of Pakistan, was kidnapped at Christmas 2008 and held for three weeks. The Bannu Taliban disclaimed responsibility, but Bishop Rumalshah told me that he suspected the ISI on the grounds that the hospital had been treating wounded Taliban fighters. It was the hospital's policy to treat any sick or wounded person without asking questions.

We took two college students, Abid Ali and his brother Farooq Shah, up the Swat valley to Kalam, stopping to collect another student, Daoud, whose father owned several orchards. It was a beautiful journey, and there were no signs of the chaos that was to engulf the valley following the army's overthrow of the Taliban some months later. But at Kalam we were made aware of a social work camp organised there by Edwardes College, which had upset local people. Apparently, the college group had handed out medicines inappropriately to the villagers, and at one point had invited some *hijras* (transsexuals) to join them. This might have been acceptable at a wedding in Bannu, but not in the more orthodox Swat valley.

Chitral, like Swat, was originally a princely state, and neither is part of the FATA tribal group. The ruler of Swat lives in Islamabad, and can be seen at social functions organised by the British High Commission. The Chitral king is also there, and his former palace now serves as a hotel. Chitral introduced polo to the world, and is the home of the Kalash people, who trace their ancestry to early Indo-European encounters. They prepare an indifferent red wine,

Figure 14 Visiting the home of a student, Waliullah, near Bannu

and both they and their religious practices, which some claim to be of Greek origin, are protected by the Pakistan Constitution from interference by missionaries from other religions. I stayed with Asif Zaman, a college student, and his family.

These were my main excursions from Peshawar into or close to the tribal belt. With the exception of Chitral, they were possible for only a few months after I arrived.

* * * * *

Table 3 Security incidents relating to Peshawar: 2006–10

1 September:	arrival of principal at Edwardes College
19 September:	bomb in parking lot near the West Cantonment police station – no fatalities
? September:	bomb near Lady Reading Hospital; three passers-by injured
? October:	bomb near Daewoo Bus Stand on Grand Trunk Road; one passer-by injured
21 October:	bomb outside Jinnah Park on Grand Trunk Road kills eight and seriously injures 35
31 October:	proposed visit of Prince Charles to Edwardes College (cancelled following US drone attack in Bajaur killing 85)
1 December:	bomb attached to motorbike in the Defence Officers Colony kills one
27 December:	blast in parking lot at Peshawar International Airport kills two
2007	
11 January:	*The News* reports that nine bombs have killed a dozen Peshawarites since September; there have also been two rocket attacks and several dozen kidnappings
27 January:	suicide bomber in Dalgaran Bazaar kills 16, including capital city police officer

9/10 February:	bomb damages vehicles of International Committee of the Red Cross (ICRC)
18 March:	CD shops on Kohat Road damaged; two injured
27 March:	ICRC bombed for second time; no casualties
5 April:	bomb in Hashtnagri; two injured
16 April:	bomb in Badhbare; three killed, four injured
26 April:	motorcycle bomb outside Greens Hotel injures four
28 April:	bomb explodes inside airport
28 April:	suicide bomber in Charsadda kills 32 and injures 45 at political rally
15 May:	bomb at Marhaba Hotel kills 25 and injures 28
17 May:	*The News* reports 16 Peshawar bombs in eight months
29 May:	bomb at High Court; one killed, eight injured. (An earlier one had exploded during college admissions.)
30 June:	bomb at Hazar Khwani; two killed
21 October:	three rockets are fired at the US Consulate; one falls short near Edwardes College
8 November:	leaflets are distributed around College threatening to kill the principal
9 November:	bomb in residential area of Hayatabad; three killed, two injured
4 December:	Peshawar's first woman suicide bomber in Cantonment area – a nineteen-year-old woman
5 December:	Benazir Bhutto killed in Rawalpindi

2008

17 January:	bomb in Mohalla Jangi; 12 killed, 25 injured
30 January:	bomb in Badshah Dak; three killed
24 May:	bomb in Nasir Bagh; two killed, two injured

12 August:	bomb on Peshawar–Kohat road; 13 killed, 14 injured
26 August:	car of US Consul in Peshawar, Lynne Tracy, sprayed with bullets
6 September:	bomb on outskirts of city; 30 killed, 70 injured
20 September:	Marriott Hotel blown up in Islamabad
11 November:	bomb inside Qayyum Stadium; four killed, 13 injured
20 November:	six rockets fired at Pennell Memorial High School (Bannu) following US drone attacks in the vicinity
5 December:	bomb in Qissa Khwani Bazaar; 34 killed, 150 injured
13 December:	leaflets distributed at Elizabeth College (women) threatening Christian institutions

2009

12 January:	deacon at St John's Cathedral kidnapped and seriously injured
17 February:	bomb in Bazid Khel; five killed, 17 injured
7 March:	bomb in Mashogagar; eight killed
8 March:	bomb at Rahman Baba's tomb on southern Ring Road
? May:	Intelligence Bureau warns principal of 11-year-old boy who is targeting Edwardes College with a bomb
16 May:	bomb in Kashkal; 11 killed, 31 injured
22 May:	bomb in Kabuli Chowk; ten killed, 65 injured
28 May:	second bomb in Qissa Khwani Bazaar; eight killed, 68 injured
9 June:	Pearl Continental Hotel blown up; 17 killed, 60 injured
2 July:	bomb in Chistiabad area; two killed, two injured
23 August:	bomb in Momin Town; three killed, 15 injured

26 September:	bomb in Peshawar Cantonment; ten killed, 94 injured
9 October:	bomb in Khyber Bazaar; 49 killed, 94 injured
16 October:	bomb at CIA's Special Investigation Unit, Peshawar; 15 killed, 19 injured
28 October:	car bomb in Chowk Yadgar, Meena Bazaar; 117 killed, 200+ injured (mostly women and children)
13 November:	Inter-Services Intelligence building blown up; 13 killed, 60 injured
19 November:	bomb on Khyber Road; 20 killed, 50 injured
22 December:	bomb at Peshawar Press Club; three killed, 24 injured
24 December:	two suicide bombers kill and injure several on Mall Road near the Roman Catholic Cathedral
2010	
12 March:	bomb in Bara Qadeem; four killed, 25 injured
5 April:	several huge bombs explode near US Consulate; ten killed, 18 injured
19 April:	third bomb in Qissa Khwani Bazaar; 24 killed, 41 injured
28 April:	bomb in Pir Bala; five killed, 15 injured
20 May:	departure of principal from Edwardes College

Table 3 lists the major security incidents that occurred during the period 2006–10. Almost all were in Peshawar; if in the form of explosions, then most could be heard from the college. Some were so big that students rushed out of the lecture rooms in fear and windows throughout the college were broken. The worst attacks on soft targets seem to correlate with military operations against the Taliban in the Swat valley and Waziristan, or following the July 2007 storming by government troops of the Lal Masjid (the Red Mosque) in Islamabad on President Musharraf's orders.

Figure 15 The result of a bomb blast close to the college

Most of the incidents listed were not reported in the international press (with the notable exception of the Marriott Hotel explosion in September 2008), and it was not until the explosions that killed more than 100 worshippers at All Saints', Peshawar, in 2013 and the attack on the Army Public School the following year, that there was major global concern. But by this time large numbers of innocent civilians had lost their lives in a prolonged and furious series of attacks by Taliban extremists.

Pakistan's national newspapers are in both English and Urdu. On the whole, the Urdu ones are more outspoken; their journalists are young and tend to be anti-Western. English-medium newspapers such as *The News*, *Dawn* and *Tribune* largely downplay incidents of violence and terrorism unless they are so major that nothing can be suppressed. Whenever we heard a loud explosion at Edwardes College our immediate sources of information were our *chowkidars* at the college gates, who seemed to know at once what had happened, and local television, which always got a crew to any major incident in record time.

On 11 January 2007, four months after my arrival in Peshawar, *The News* carried a story headed 'Insecurity haunts Peshawar':

The situation is totally changed now. Along with a number of kidnapping and robbery incidents that took place during the recent past, terrorist gangs are also operating in the town for the past few months [...] a deputy inspector general (DIG), Abid Ali, was killed and after almost a month his murderers are still at large.

At least a dozen Peshawarites have been killed in nine bomb blasts that ripped through different parts of the provincial metropolis since mid-September. This was coupled with two rocket attacks that didn't result in any fatality but triggered panic among the citizens [...]

The public will relax only when they will feel secure while travelling though the Ring Road, Kohat Road, Bara Road at least within the jurisdiction of the city. So far, insecurity prevails across the city and [the] [...] public generally avoids coming out of their homes after the sunset.

None of these reported bombs or rockets had been near the Cantonment area where the college is situated. We knew that the DIG of police had been killed, but none of the other incidents had received more than a line in any newspaper. It was reported only later that there had been a bomb quite close to us in a parking lot near the West Cantonment police station on 19 September – there were no fatalities, and the police initially claimed that a faulty petrol tank was to blame. They said much the same about the next two bombs between late September and mid-October near the Lady Reading Hospital (three passers-by injured) and close to the Daewoo Bus Station on Grand Trunk Road (one passer-by injured). The police stated that the first of these was caused by a fault in an electrical transformer.

It was not possible to lightly dismiss the bomb on 21 October outside Jinnah Park on the Grand Trunk Road, which killed eight and seriously injured 35. On 1 December, a bomb attached to a motorcycle left in the Defence Officers Colony killed one person, and on 27 December a blast in the parking lot at Peshawar International Airport killed two.

All the bombs that exploded prior to the end of December 2006 had been planted in strategic locations. Then on 27 January 2007 a suicide bomber in Dalgaran Bazaar killed 16 people, including the capital city police officer (CCPO), a deputy superintendent of police, two union council *nazim*s (local government officials), a *naib nazim*, and six police. Two weeks later tragedy was narrowly averted when a bomb damaged vehicles belonging to the International Committee of the Red Cross (ICRC) in University Town; nobody was killed or injured.

On 18 March CD shops on Kohat Road were attacked with explosives and two people were injured. The ICRC was once more bombed on 27 March – again no casualties. On 26 April a motorcycle bomb exploded outside Greens Hotel on Saddar Road, injuring four, including a former Awami National Party (ANP) senator. Another bomb went off inside the airport on 28 April, and the same day a suicide bomber targeted a rally in support of the provincial Interior Minister in Charsadda killing 32 and wounding 45. On 15 May an explosion in the Marhaba Hotel on Naz Cinema Road killed 25 and injured 28.

All these incidents took place within eight months of my arrival. The targets ranged from the police and security personnel, busy transport centres and the airport, an international relief agency, CD shops widely believed by extremists to sell pornographic material, bazaars and predominantly Shi'i districts, to politicians. There was a steady increase in the number of individual bombs detonated by mobile phones and more suicide bombings. No group took any responsibility for these incidents.

On 17 May 2007 *The News* carried the headline '16 blasts rocked Peshawar in less than eight months', with the subhead 'Law enforcers still clueless about perpetrators of terrorist acts which claimed 52 lives and severely injured 108 others'. In actual fact there were probably more deaths and many more injured during this period. According to the report:

> The Peshawarites are more scared after the senior government functionaries as well as police authorities have surrendered by saying they cannot stop suicide blasts.

Senator Gul Naseeb, the top leader of the Muttahida Majlis-
e-Amal that is ruling over the province, was quoted as saying
in the press to replace the chief secretary and the inspector
general of police (IGP) for their failure in improving the law
and order situation in NWFP [...]

People have even stopped going to public places in the wake
of the worsening situation. But the law enforcers [...] have
failed to come up to the expectations.

Across the summer of 2007 there was something of a lull in violent
incidents in Peshawar. But elsewhere several regional and national
issues were very much on the boil. By the time I arrived in Peshawar
the Baloch rebel leader, Nawab Akbar Bugti, had been killed under
mysterious circumstances, and an insurgency was intensifying in
the neighbouring province of Balochistan.

In May 2007 several dozen people were killed in Karachi when
members of a party associated with General Musharraf blocked a
visit by the Chief Justice, Iftikhar Muhammad Chaudhry, to the
city. This was the result of a row that had been simmering between
them since March about several issues including Chaudhry's claim
that Musharraf had illegally transferred Islamist militants to US
custody. Musharraf invoked clauses in the Constitution to declare
Chaudhry a 'non-functional Chief Justice' – essentially a sacking.
Lawyers and many others campaigned across the country in
Chaudhry's favour and he increasingly won mass support.

Between January and July 2007 Islamic militants took over the
Lal Masjid in Islamabad and used it as a base for enforcing sharia
law on parts of the city. After a siege lasting for a week, government
forces stormed the mosque on 10 July, killing an officially estimated
154 protesters. This provoked militants all over Pakistan – but
especially in the FATA areas – to revoke a peace agreement with
the government. In September the TTP alliance of mainly Pashto
militant groups was formed, and in the Swat valley militants
threatened the provincial government.

Across the summer and into the early autumn of 2007 local violence
was exacerbated by tensions at the centre of government. Although
President Musharraf won most votes in the presidential election at the

beginning of October, the Supreme Court ruled that no winner could be announced until it had decided whether or not he was eligible to stand while still army chief. A newly sworn-in set of compliant judges eventually backed him; he resigned as army chief, and was sworn in for a second term as president at the end of November.

By the autumn of 2007 the stage was set for an increasingly violent confrontation between the militant groups united by a range of grievances and both the central and provincial governments. In the months ahead the law and order situation progressively deteriorated, and Peshawar and Edwardes College were in the eye of the storm.

* * * * *

On 8 November 2007, leaflets were distributed around college threatening to kill me, as principal. Several dozen double-page photocopies appeared on the ledges near the morning papers outside the library, and in a few other public places where incoming day scholars would see them.

I was sitting in the staff room when Vice-Principal Naveed rushed in and planted several copies of the leaflet in front of me. They were in Urdu except for a few scribbled words in English at the top: 'Think so much David Gosling'.

'Who are they from?' I asked Naveed.

'They say: "To the Principal, Edwardes College, Peshawar, from Commander Halifah",' he translated.

Other teaching staff sitting around me were curious.

'Who is Commander Halifah?' asked Yar Muhammad. Silence.

'Go on,' I encouraged the increasingly reluctant Naveed.

He continued: '"Islam is totally against female education, because it is against the sharia. But in today's sinful world more and more emphasis is put on so-called female education. People are unaware of the commandments of God. They are living a terrible life."'

By now all the teaching staff were listening.

'But that is not what Islam teaches,' stated Sardar Sabir Hussain from the Urdu department, who was responsible for the college mosque, and the practicalities of Ramazan and the annual Na'at event.

'But we were the first college in the province to introduce co-education,' protested Nasim Haider.

'But what really bothers them?' interrupted Donald Joseph. 'Is it women's education or co-education?'

I came to appreciate that this distinction is very important. When we eventually had to negotiate with Taliban extremists, they withdrew their objection when we offered to put all our women students – still calling them Edwardians – into Elizabeth College for women, and bus our teaching staff backwards and forwards for lectures. It didn't seem to matter, either, whether the teaching staff involved were men or women.

'What else does it say?' asked Mrs Nasira Manzoor.

'There are two notes,' explained Naveed. 'This is the first: "The principal of Edwardes College is a non-Muslim. God says in Surah Al-Ahzab that you don't make friends with non-Muslims; they are not your friends. They are enemies of your holy religion and prophet. Today our Pathans who are considered to be the bravest people have become slaves to them. Oh Muslims, wake up! Take your religion to the heights of the sky. Shake the foundations of non-believers and uplift the name of Islam."'

'Is this some sort of joke?' asked Francis Karamat.

'I don't think so,' said Sardar Hussain. 'If anyone makes a joke they will not try to quote from holy scripture, even if they quote it badly. This Halifah seems like a fanatic.'

'A bit more,' added Naveed. 'There's a second note. "We know what time Edwardes College closes. We have heard that students are not allowed to offer prayers in time. This is totally prohibited in our religion so act strictly upon what is in this letter."'

There was also an unpleasant threat relating to the time students went home after lectures, as though someone might be lying in wait for them.

'Is that all?' asked someone. Naveed said nothing.

I was indignant. Both I and my predecessors had done everything we could to accommodate the Friday prayers. But Naveed hadn't translated quite everything in this unwelcome message, and when

I showed the Urdu original later to Syed Kazmi, he translated the final line, which ran: 'If not [i.e. if I did not act in accordance with the letter] there is every chance of a suicide bomber attack. Be alert before this situation happens.'

I showed my death threat to the Governor's military secretary, who passed it to the Governor. The police and my minders from the Intelligence Bureau and the ISI came and read it through. The general consensus was that the threat was not from any Taliban organisation, but had been sent by an extremist group located near the main university campus. I never discovered the identity of Captain Halifah.

It was agreed that the military police at the road checkposts close to our gates would keep a careful eye on the college, and we were advised to employ security guards from a private company, which we did. These guards monitored all entrants through the main gates with metal detectors; one was a woman who checked incoming women. Most of the men were retired police and not particularly athletic. They had guns without bullets, and they dressed in smart uniforms, which weren't quite either police or military. My ISI minder, Inspector Qasim, repeated his earlier

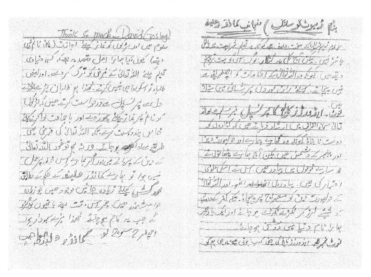

Figure 16 An Urdu death threat to the principal

opinion that if the Taliban extremists were to come, then these guards would probably climb up trees. But at least, in the eyes of officialdom and college members, we had taken sensible precautions.

I was more annoyed than frightened by the death threat with its sweeping assertion that we made it difficult for our Muslim students to practise their religion. However, the situation was somewhat put into perspective some months later at a convocation of the Khyber Medical University where I found myself sitting next to the principal of Islamia College. On learning of my death threat, he smiled reassuringly and told me that he had had three, but he didn't know who was making them. So at least we were not being targeted because we were seen as non-Islamic.

*****

On Tuesday 4 December 2007, Peshawar experienced its first suicide bombing by a woman – also the first of its kind in Pakistan. We heard the explosion, which occurred shortly after lunch, and I sent Shahzad to ask our *chowkidar* where it was. On learning that it was near a particular junction close to Khyber Road I decided to take a look to see if it was anywhere near St Mary's School, and whether or not this well-known Roman Catholic institution might have been the target.

I jumped into the car and was quickly at the site of the explosion. The body parts had almost been removed, and I approached a young military policeman (MP) to ask what had happened. He had seen two figures both clad in Afghan-style *burqas* moving near to the gates of residential quarters, probably belonging to the military or the ISI, close to where we were standing. When they were approximately 20 metres from his checkpost he pointed his gun at them and demanded identification. One unveiled her face, smiled at him and blew herself up. The other presumably ran off, but the MP was too shocked by the explosion to see where she (or he) went (male bombers sometimes conceal themselves in *burqas*).

The following day, *The News* carried more information. It stated that the woman was in her thirties, though the MP and subsequent

The News International, Wednesday, December 5, 2007

First lady suicide bomber misses target in Peshawar

Javed Aziz Khan

PESHAWAR: In the first suicide attack by a woman in Pakistan, a bomber blew herself up near the offices of the Inter-Services Intelligence (ISI) located in the maximum-security Peshawar Cantonment area Tuesday afternoon.

Except the suicide bomber, who was said to be in her mid-30s, no other casualty was reported in the blast. The bomber, according to sources, was clad in an all-enveloping, blue burqa normally used by Afghan women. She was reportedly carrying something in her hand.

The incident occurred at around 1:50 pm some 15 meters away from a checkpost of Military Police (MP) on Babar Road, which links Khyber Road with The Mall.

Head of the female suicide bomber at the site of the blast in Peshawar, Tuesday. — AFP

The site of the occurrence is located opposite the Saint Mary's School and on the back of the ISI regional headquarters.

"A soldier from the Military Police challenged a burqa-clad woman when she was 20 meters

from his post. The cop pointed the gun towards her when she didn't identify herself despite reminders," a senior investigator, requesting anonymity, told The News. He disclosed that the woman then unveiled her face and after giving a smile to the cop blew herself up some 15 meters from the MP Post.

The post is located at the start of Babar Road, which ends at the heavily guarded Corps Headquarters and is close to several army installations on all sides.

"We have recovered the legs and the upper body of the suicide bomber and it is confirmed that she was a female," Capital City Police Officer (CCPO) Tanvirul Haq Sipra told The News

Figure 17 Peshawar's first woman suicide bomber

information put her age as nineteen. A photograph of her severed head was published, and the Capital City Police Office coldly announced: 'We have recovered the legs and the upper body of the suicide bomber and it is confirmed that she was a female.' No other casualty was reported, and there was no reference to the bomber's companion.

* * * * *

Shortly before my death threat, on 18 October 2007, Benazir Bhutto returned from self-exile in London to lead the Pakistan People's Party (PPP) into an anticipated election. Her second government (1993–6) had been short-lived, and had been dismissed by President Farooq Leghari on charges of corruption. The consequent elections had led to a sweeping victory for the Muslim League of Nawaz Sharif. Three years later, both Benazir and her husband Asif Ali Zardari (later to become president) were formally convicted of corruption; Zardari went to prison, but she was already in London and decided to remain there.

In his autobiography Sir Nicholas Barrington describes her, when he first met her, as 'young, vigorous and glamorous [...] on prime form, looking elegant and beautiful, stylishly dressed as always, in simple colours. I knew that she had been the toast of Oxford with a yellow convertible [...] '[1] Her charisma in Pakistan was more in terms of mass appeal; according to Anatol Lieven, 'ordinary Pakistanis felt that they were looking at a great princess who had descended from a great height to lead them.'[2]

In May 2007, prior to her return to Pakistan, Benazir approached two contracting agencies, Blackwater and a British firm, to ask for additional security. On the day of her arrival in Karachi there were two explosions, which killed many of her guards and passers-by. Requests were made for her security to be enhanced. But on 27 December she was in Rawalpindi campaigning for elections scheduled for the following month. She had ended a speech and entered her campaign vehicle, but decided to stand up one final time to acknowledge the crowd. Shots were fired, and a suicide bomb exploded; she was declared dead at the Rawalpindi General Hospital shortly afterwards. A United Nations investigation into the incident later concluded that her death could have been prevented if adequate security measures had been taken.

Benazir's death seemed to unleash an unprecedented level of violence. In Peshawar, the police used tear gas and batons to break up angry crowds. Fortunately, Edwardes College was closed for the Christmas/New Year break and all but a few students were with their families.

The general elections scheduled for January 2008 were delayed until 18 February. The Pakistan Muslim League (PML-N) of Nawaz Sharif and the PPP secured most votes. They formed an initial coalition, and in March 2008 Yousaf Raza Gillani (PPP) became prime minister. The PML-N left the coalition, and the PPP formed an alliance with smaller parties, including the ANP. At this time General Musharraf was still the president, but in August the PPP and the PML-N began impeachment proceedings against him. In November he went into exile in London. By this time Asif Ali Zardari, Benazir Bhutto's widower, had been elected president.

In the North-West Frontier Province, the PPP and the ANP both emerged in the central and provincial elections as the dominant parties. This represented a decisive swing against the Muttahida Majlis-e-Amal (MMA) – a fairly religiously conservative party under the leadership of Akram Durrani since 2002. The ensuing coalition was led by Ameer Haider Khan Hoti, an Edwardes College graduate, who became Chief Minister.

It was inevitable that the Taliban would be held responsible for the killing of Benazir Bhutto, but it was not clear which particular grouping. Various al-Qaeda tributaries were said to have done it and the government and the ISI were also blamed. Benazir Bhutto had earlier emailed the British foreign secretary, David Miliband, to say that she believed that senior government aides were out to kill her. The Pakistani Interior Ministry may have been nearer the truth in blaming Lashkar-e-Jhangvi – a militant group linked to al-Qaeda and based in the Punjab. But Baitullah Mehsud's alliance of Pashtun militants, the TTP, could just as well have been responsible.

In Pakistan's most populous province, the Punjab, the PML-N of Nawaz Sharif had won an election and formed a government. Considering that Sharif had already been prime minister prior to being ousted by Musharraf, it seems surprising that at this point, with a sizeable national electoral vote, he was not more senior. But the unwarranted death of Benazir Bhutto had generated a considerable sympathy vote for the PPP, Zardari was ambitious to become president, and Musharraf had not yet been toppled from office. Meanwhile the army remained dominant, especially with regard to policy in issues relating to Afghanistan and India.

* * * * *

For several months following the February elections there were few bombings or kidnappings in and around Peshawar. Then in the summer of 2008 they began to intensify. On 26 August the car of the US Consul in Peshawar, Lynne Tracy, was sprayed with bullets as she set off for work:

Tracy, who is America's 'principal officer' in Peshawar, was attacked just after she was driven out of her home in the university area, the prime residential area in the city. Two gunmen, armed with AK-47 automatic weapons, reportedly leapt from a Toyota Land Cruiser, which blocked her vehicle's path, and sprayed hundreds of bullets. However, the bullets either did not hit or bounced off the armour. Tracy's chauffeur quickly reversed the vehicle back into her home, knocking over a rickshaw whose driver had to be treated in hospital.[3]

No group claimed responsibility for the attack. In Islamabad, politicians fawned over any US diplomats they could find saying how much they deplored this terrible incident. According to some strands of local gossip in Peshawar the militants were really targeting Tracy's neighbour, a prominent politician; I doubted it, and so did she.

My first encounter with Lynne Tracy came when I tried soon after my arrival to get to the bottom of the Edwardes College ACCESS project, whereby several of our English department teaching staff taught English to boys from local schools on Sunday mornings. The scheme was supported by funds administered via the US Consulate, and it worried me because none of the funding benefited the college itself, and some of the boys were known to be from a local *masjid*. Our English staff seemed reluctant to provide information, so I went to see Lynne, who immediately produced the colleague who had set up the programme. My fears proved to be well grounded, so I notified the Board and closed the programme. This upset some of the English staff.

Whenever a bomb went off close to the college, Lynne would phone to see if we were all right. One bomb in particular was very disturbing; it exploded on 22 December 2009 at the Press Club, which lies between the train station and the college. So huge was the blast that a woman being driven in a motorised rickshaw near the building had a heart attack and died. Students rushed out of their lecture rooms and many headed for the main gates – the worst thing to do in such circumstances.

I arrived at the gates just as a group of people carried someone in from the road. Word began to spread that the bomb had killed or injured a college member. But it was an epileptic student who had had a seizure. At this point the head of the chemistry department, Javed Hyatt, produced the loud hailer used during admissions and directed everyone to go to the main sports field and remain there. Students moved onto it where we told them to go home quietly in small groups. They did so and I closed the college for two days.

'Sir, you should not be here,' remarked a newly appointed lecturer as I walked back to my bungalow.

After such unpleasant occasions I usually received reassuring phone calls from Lynne and from the Governor's military secretary, and my ISI minder, Inspector Qasim, would come round the next day. But I rarely heard from the diocese though they also had their own problems with militant activity.

I recall a relaxed evening with Lynne watching *West Side Story*, and when the US Ambassador, Ryan C. Crocker, finally left office in 2007 she invited me to his farewell dinner. Diplomatic relations between Pakistan and the USA had deteriorated in the region on account of the drone strikes, and many invitees stayed away. I talked to a particular guest who was discreetly being served with an alcoholic drink in the hope that I might also be favoured. After some time I looked at my watch and speculated as to how long it would be before the ambassador arrived.

'I am the ambassador,' said His Excellency with a smile.

* * * * *

According to Ahmed Rashid:

> The Taliban made dramatic advances in the summer campaign of 2008, entering the settled areas of the NWFP for the first time, attacking police and army posts in Kohat, Hangu and the Swat valley. The military came under intense US pressure to move more decisively against them. On 6 August, after several government officials were killed, the army finally launched an attack in Bajaur, promising to clear the tribal agency of militants within six weeks. Over 250,000 people fled

Bajaur to escape the army's bombing. In retaliation the extremists launched suicide attacks around the country, and there were alerts for FATA-trained terrorists in Britain, Germany, Spain, Denmark and Holland.[4]

The army had gone into the Swat valley in 2007, but had been unable to defeat Fazlullah's well-armed militias. In 2008, the army tried again with 12,000 troops but was defeated by an estimated 3,000 Taliban fighters. Many inhabitants left the valley, and the Taliban imposed their brutal interpretation of sharia. Having failed to defeat the Taliban by force, in February 2009 the central and NWFP governments reached a deal whereby the Taliban could extend sharia law provided they abandoned their campaign of violence. This optimism was to prove short-lived.

On 20 September 2008, the first major terrorist attack in the capital took place. A British business friend was driving into Islamabad when suddenly the sky lit up and there was a sustained blast a few moments later. All traffic stopped, and drivers emerged from their vehicles clutching their mobile phones. At first they seemed nervous, but as it became clear that the target was the five-star Marriott Hotel they relaxed and some even began to applaud.

A vehicle had driven up to the Marriott Hotel carrying an estimated 600 kilograms of explosives, which had blasted a six-metre hole in the ground. Sections of the hotel had collapsed, and smoke was drifting across the site.

The media rushed in with their version of events. There had been a major political event in parliament and the chief guests, including the president and prime minister, were due to dine at the hotel but were delayed. So, clearly, the Taliban terrorists were out to get those democratically elected stalwarts who stand for law and order and stability. But a few hours later the hotel manager issued a statement that no such dinner had been planned; to the best of my knowledge his announcement was picked up by a single newspaper in Glasgow – everybody else ignored it.

Not only did the extremists bomb high-profile targets inside Pakistan, but shortly after the Marriott Hotel incident Lashkar-e-Taiba, a Punjab-based militant group active in Kashmir, carried out terrorist attacks in Mumbai, leaving 185 dead. This further damaged the already fragile relationship between Pakistan and India – even more when Pakistan refused to extradite the suspects to India.

The expansion of Taliban activity from the FATA areas into the so-called 'settled' ones (i.e. part of the NWFP, but non-tribal and away from the mountainous belt) was matched by US drone attacks deeper into the Frontier region. On 20 November 2008, a drone attack in the vicinity of Bannu was followed by the firing of six rockets into Pennell Memorial High School in Bannu city – an early indication of hostility towards Christians, who were probably seen as sympathetic to the USA.

On 13 December, just under a month later, Urdu leaflets distributed at Elizabeth College in Peshawar left no doubt that Christians were being targeted:

> We have seen the invitation letters of Christian programmes in the hands of many people […] Such programmes are organised in your college through which Muslims are invited to convert to Christianity. You were not our target, but such tactics on your part have compelled us to think about Christians […] America becomes happy over the blood of Muslims. Recently in India some Christians and Jews have been killed and that has alarmed America […] The purpose of our organisation is to wage holy war against infidels […] You have called Muslims on your Christmas Eid through a programme and remember we will blow up your college […] We will not hurt girls […] but we will teach a lesson to you before your Eid. We do nothing unless we inform […] We will do blastings and will take breath only after giving shock to America, Britain and Christian countries. We will do the same with other institutions along with yours. We have been sacrificing our lives for the sake of Islam. Those who spoil Islam will be eliminated. The flag of Islam is high. We will make it even higher through sacrifice.
>
> By the order of Allah to us we will end the conspiracies of Christians […] Allah has ordered us to warn first. Through

this letter you have been informed. Let us see what is the wish of Allah. We have done our duty in front of Allah.

Elizabeth College is a women's university college combined with a high school and founded as a Christian institution. It is located near Dabgari Gardens on the other side of the railway station from Edwardes College, and its principals have recently included Dr Asha Shafiq, the daughter of an Edwardes College vice-principal.

The threat to Elizabeth College mentions other institutions, which presumably could include Edwardes College. The principal is not named, as I was, and the author of the document is anonymous, though the plural 'we' is very Islamic. The reference to India clearly relates to the Mumbai attack the previous month. There is no mention of drones, but the USA, Britain and Christians are bracketed together.

Neither Elizabeth College nor Edwardes College has ever countenanced converting Muslims to Christianity, and since 9/11 all the organisations based in Peshawar, which might have encouraged this – mostly from the USA – have left. The accusation was therefore grossly unfair. The reference to Christmas as the Christian Eid is curious. Eid-ul-Adha, which relates to Abraham's near-sacrifice of his son, is often celebrated by Muslims close to Christmas and includes the distribution of gifts, but there the similarity ends. It is also incorrect to describe Christians as *kafirs* (infidels) – the same term was used to describe me in my death threat. Christians, Jews and Muslims all trace their ancestry to Abraham, and most Muslim scholars recognise this and avoid the term *kafir*. It is also worth noting that the Urdu handwriting on my own death threat differed significantly from that on the Elizabeth College document.

There were more unpleasant incidents, some involving Christians. On 12 January 2009 a young deacon at St John's Cathedral in Peshawar, who also assisted at a church in Charsadda, was kidnapped for three days, badly beaten up and thrown into the cathedral grounds. Bishop Rumalshah visited him in hospital, but I was surprised that the diocese gave no publicity to this event, though I notified the *Church Times* in the UK.

About this time (though I kept no record) a USAID worker was shot dead coming out of the American Club. His driver was also killed. But I saw no mention of it in any newspaper. So, like the presidential dinner in the Marriott Hotel in Islamabad, it can't really have happened!

*　*　*　*　*

The most important events in the early months of 2009 were regional. The peace deal between the NWFP provincial government, the army and the Taliban in Swat was signed into law by President Zardari on 14 April without even a debate in parliament. The Swat Taliban took control of the police, the local administration and education throughout the valley, and began expanding into Dir and into Buner, which lies geographically between Swat and Islamabad. Horrified Westerners interpreted the move into Buner as a preliminary to an invasion of Islamabad – which it may well have been, though it is also important to note that historically Buner had been part of the Swat kingdom so that a takeover there could be seen from the ground level more in terms of a natural expansion.

This particular period coincided with Easter, and the small church congregations in the Swat valley decided to ask the Taliban leaders whether or not to celebrate the festival. The response was very positive. Of course they must, they were told, 'and if any of your members don't attend, give us a list of their names'.[5]

A team of scientists visiting the area reported that the closing of hotels along the valley and a shortage of fertiliser for certain crops had considerably improved water quality in the rivers. There were also reports that anyone caught cutting down a tree without good reason would be publicly flogged.

Meanwhile, in the Punjab, by March 2009 relationships between the dominant PPP party of Zardari and Nawaz Sharif's Muslim League (PML-N) were deteriorating. Following a decision by the Supreme Court to declare illegal the elections of Nawaz Sharif and his brother Shahbaz, the Zardari administration was able to oust the Sharif provincial government. The PML-N responded with a mass march on Islamabad, and Zardari was forced to back down. Iftikhar Chaudhry was reinstated as Chief Justice and the PML-N resumed government in the province.

Peshawar continued to experience unprecedented levels of violence. In May 2009, an Intelligence Bureau official came to warn me that an 11-year-old boy was targeting the college. The boy could be identified by a number, which I was told, and would probably be carrying explosives in his underpants because they would be less visible than around the chest or waist.

I didn't know what to do. An 11-year-old could climb a tree overhanging a college fence and drop into the grounds – or go underneath the fence. The sons of all kinds of college staff were moving around all the time. If I made an announcement people might panic and start rounding up every boy in sight. In the end I told my secretary, Shahzad, and Changez Khan; they told some reliable proctors who patrolled the grounds. The boy never appeared.

By June Taliban rule in Swat, and especially its expansion in the direction of Islamabad into Buner, had unnerved the federal government so much that they sent a large military force into the valley. The Taliban were overcome, but their commanders, including Fazlullah, escaped.

During this period more than two million refugees fled Swat, Buner and Dir. Many of them moved into makeshift camps near Mardan, where two of our teaching staff, Nasir Iqbal and Ejaz Ahmed, set up a link with the college. A group of students went regularly to distribute floor mats, clothing and bottles of filtered water. I went on an early visit and met some of the refugees. One told me that they had problems both with the Taliban and with the army. Local people had never experienced a military curfew before, and there had been tragic incidents of soldiers shooting children who roamed at night. I was told off by an Intelligence Bureau official for going into the camps on the grounds that some refugees were probably Taliban militants. The Diocese of Peshawar also undertook relief work at the Christian Vocational Centre in Mardan.[6]

I wrote to Chief Minister Haider Hoti to request funds to help students whose families had become refugees from their homes in

Swat and Buner, and he responded with a generous grant. This was used to reduce or cancel the fees of these students, and when the time for admissions came in July we did the same for the incoming batch (we tried to avoid giving cash). They were known in official jargon as Internally Displaced People or IDPs.

* * * * *

On Tuesday 9 June 2009, 11 people were killed and 70 wounded (including a Briton and a German) when a suicide bomb went off at Peshawar's five-star luxury hotel, the Pearl Continental. Three men approached the hotel's main gate in a truck, firing at security guards, and blew the vehicle up close to the main building. In the words of one of the injured, 'The floor under my feet shook. I thought the roof was falling on me. I ran out. I saw everybody running in panic. There was blood and pieces of glass everywhere.' According to the *Guardian*:

> No one immediately claimed responsibility for the attack, but it comes after Taliban threats to stage a campaign of assaults in retaliation for a military campaign against militants in the Swat valley [...] The hotel is a favourite place for foreigners and elite Pakistanis, making it a high-profile target for militants [...] Last week it emerged that the US government was negotiating the purchase of the hotel in order to turn it into a new US consulate.[7]

Shortly after I had arrived in Peshawar I had paid a subscription to the hotel to use their heated outdoor pool and gym, but after a year the cost seemed prohibitive, so I stopped going.

The biggest bomb to be let off anywhere in Pakistan during my time there was probably the one that destroyed the ISI regional headquarters little more than a stone's throw from the college on 13 November 2009. An estimate by a senior member of the Pakistan High Commission in London put it at 1,000 kilograms. Windows broke all over college, and the doors and windows of the house of our law lecturer, Shujaat Ali Khan, were lifted from their frames. It appeared that the vehicle carrying the bomb had traversed Warsak Road from the hills, but, instead of continuing to the intersection with Khyber Road, close to the ISI building, had turned left into a new housing area and circled onto the main road at another point. As they deviated from this road into the ISI complex, a lone security guard challenged them, whereupon the bomb exploded. Huge slabs of concrete were thrown across the site like children's toys.

I tried to contact Inspector Qasim Zafar a few days later to see if he was all right. He had been away when the bomb exploded and they had relocated to a new headquarters, the whereabouts of which was secret.

Both these high-profile bombings were probably carried out by the TTP, based in Waziristan. In August 2009 the TTP leader, Baitullah Mehsud, was killed, probably in a US air strike, and was succeeded by Hakimullah Mehsud. The following weeks saw a build-up of the army preparatory to a major offensive against the TTP; this appeared to trigger a ferocious blitz on both military and civilian targets throughout Pakistan. On 10 October, Taliban militants attacked the headquarters of the Pakistani army in Rawalpindi, killing ten. The psychological effect of such an audacious act was considerable. In one explosion in a *masjid* in Rawalpindi the only son of our Corps Commander, Lt General Masood Aslam, was killed.

Not all bomb blasts were so large, but some of those which occurred in the bazaars close to our college during this period killed dozens of people, many of them Shi'i Muslims. On Saturday 26 September, there was a suicide bomb attack near the Askari Bank on the side of the Combined Military Hospital opposite to our campus. Deaths were between 13 and 20, with many more injured. The bank was used primarily by the hospital staff, but we also had an account there. It was tragic next day to see the manager in a smart white shirt standing outside the ruins of his bank explaining to customers that, although the bank had gone, their money was safe and could be accessed at another branch.

Fifty were killed by another bomb, and I visited the site of yet another explosion near Lady Reading Hospital. Worst of all was a huge bomb on 28 October, which killed more than 120 in Chowk Yadgar. I spoke with a local tradesman whose shop had become a pile of rubble.

A bomb went off during a meeting of our Board of Governors held at the Governor's spacious residence. Everybody paused for a few moments. The Governor beckoned to an aide, who went out of the room; on returning he whispered into the Governor's ear – presumably giving him details about the explosion. We concluded that something serious had happened and I dutifully thanked His Excellency for sparing his precious time to attend to the affairs of our humble college (he was an Edwardes graduate). We stood in silence as he left, and made our way to our means of transport and various residences – or whatever in some cases might have remained of them!

Figure 18 The Chowk Yadgar bomb on 28 October 2009, which killed 120 people

Figure 19 Clearing up the bomb debris in Chowk Yadgar

* * * * *

The security of the college, in these circumstances, was initially monitored by the Governor's staff and the findings were communicated to the police. On one occasion the secretary to the Governor had written to the provincial Inspector of Police as follows:

> *Enclosed please find copy of letter dated 27.12.2007 received from Principal, Edwardes College, addressed to the Governor along with a threatening note for your perusal/ necessary action. The Governor has desired that effective measures be taken by the concerned authorities for the safety of the College and its staff, on urgent basis.*

We employed security staff from a local firm, but there was little else that we could do. Various college members told me that I should own a gun, but I declined. For a brief period I had a small pistol in the house, which I had confiscated from a student called Jallal – but I eventually handed it over to his brother.

Various official communications about security reached me during the latter part of 2009. The Higher Education Regulatory Authority wrote on 27 October with some fairly basic recommendations, including the need for security guards 'inside the academic institutions especially at their roof tops'. On 17 November, the Intelligence Bureau faxed a report from their zonal headquarters advising us about the standard procedure adopted by suicide bombers prior to an attack:

Intelligence Bureau: Zonal Headquarters, Mardan   SECRET

Communication No. MR/MLtncy/2-85   Dated: 17.11.2009

Source Report

When terrorists decide to destroy a place with suicide bomb blast materials in a vehicle, they undergo a standard procedure at least 14/15 days before the blast.

1) *They first involve a local resident or worker sympathetic to their cause who knows the area well. With the assistance of this person they and their companions take the suicide bomber to examine the targeted place.*

2) *The suicide bomber visits the targeted place 3/4 times wearing different clothes.*

3) *The suicide bomber visits the targeted place 3/4 times in different vehicles by different routes.*

4) *After the blast a few associates of the bomber move among the gathered public to deceive them and the security guards by cursing the terrorists. From the exact place of the incident they then remove the head of the bomber and any other clue by which the bomber can be recognised pretending that they are shocked by the incident. They then disappear into the crowd.*

Therefore, all law-enforcing institutions must maintain careful vigilance for the signs of the abovementioned crimes.

Shaftifullah, ASI

Intelligence Bureau, WHRps, Mardan

[translated from Urdu]

Between 5 and 14 December, there was a burst of Intelligence information that reached my office mostly as faxes. The Corps Commander's office sent a blurred fax on 5 December warning of a 22-year-old Lashkar-e-Taiba courier 'having weak structure, small beard, black eyes, bended finger of right hand, wearing Afghan clothes, and speaks Dari and Pashto'. This courier was believed to be carrying a book filled with poisonous chemicals. This was to be given to the Afghan ambassador in Islamabad. (The Afghan consul in Peshawar, whom I had met in connection with our prison work, had been kidnapped some months earlier and his driver shot dead.) The same poison had also been placed in perfume bottles for distribution elsewhere. According to the memo, Afghan troops had alerted their Pakistani counterparts about this bizarre threat.

On 7 December, the National Crisis Management cell of the Ministry of the Interior faxed our provincial Home Secretary about a specific threat alert:

Terrorists are planning to target political personalities and high-ranking civil officials in Peshawar on regular/daily basis in forthcoming days. This merits extreme vigilance and heightened security measures at all times.

Later that day, I received a fax from the same source saying that 'miscreants have despatched five suicide bombers toward major towns (exact destination not known)'. On 10 December, they predicted suicide attacks in 'Bara, Khyber Agency, Peshawar and surrounding areas in the near future. LEA installations, universities, colleges and schools could be the targets.' The following day we were warned about 'an explosive laden truck registered number C-7075 for some terrorist activity in Hangu, Peshawar, Thall and Kohat'.

On 24 December, two suicide bombers on a motorcycle killed several people on Mall Road near St Michael's Roman Catholic Cathedral. It was not clear whether they were targeting the Pakistan International Airways offices or a Shi'i area nearby. The head of one of the bombers was found in the grounds of the primary school attached to the cathedral – fortunately the school was closed for Christmas.

At the time this bomb went off the priest-in-charge of the Church of Pakistan cathedral, the Revd Joseph John, was giving sick communion to a nearby parishioner. That same day, Christmas Eve, some church members received mysterious texts on their mobile phones, which said, 'We'll give you a nice Christmas gift – and it won't be the baby Jesus.' In spite of all this, attendance at the midnight Mass was as big as ever. Additional police were on duty at the gates, and the chief of city police sat next to me in my car all the way back to college.

* * * * *

Towards the end of 2009, US President Barack Obama intensified the war against the Taliban in Afghanistan and announced a surge in US troops. In Pakistan, the Supreme Court challenged legislation introduced by Musharraf giving President Zardari and others immunity from prosecution for corruption. Zardari was to come under further pressure three months later when he was forced to delegate many of his powers to the prime minister – a reversal of General Zia's dictatorial policies, which Musharraf did not repeal, though he seldom used them. Zardari was also forced to agree to rename the NWFP as Khyber-Pakhtunkhwa (KP), a move that provoked riots in the non-Pashto-speaking parts of the province.

At this time Imran Khan's party, Tehreek-e-Insaf (PTI), was little talked about, and there were no indications that by 2013 it would sweep the KP elections. Imran Khan entered politics in the late 1990s following a successful career in cricket. He came to Peshawar once during my time there, but nowhere near Edwardes College. However, the issue which eventually became central to his political programme, namely the collateral damage caused by US drones, was steadily gaining in importance, and college students were telling me of casualties among their family members.

Up to the end of 2009 few of our college members and their families had suffered violence at the hands of extremists. But on New Year's Day a suicide bomb killed ninety people in the Lakki Marwat district, including a police officer, who was the father of one of our students, Ghani Khan. Although the funeral of this man was several hours' drive away in the Swat valley, the same bombers managed to blow up several family members there, including our student's brother. One of the mourners who narrowly escaped death – a former pupil of Edwardes College School, Mustafa Kamal – later became a postgraduate student at Fitzwilliam College, Cambridge, where he gave me more details about this ghastly incident.

Students asked me to meet Ghani, who had returned to college to collect his belongings. We stood or sat in silence as he tearfully packed his bag, then I embraced him and he left. He returned in time to sit and pass his exams, and went into the army.

On 5 April 2010, five huge bombs exploded near the US Consulate in Peshawar. The interval between each was sufficient for my secretary, Shahzad, to photograph the last two – plumes of smoke billowing from the treeline upwards, distinguishable from clouds only by their yellow-brown edges. For a few moments we stood on the lawn and then went inside to watch the grim events on television: ambulances, the police, fire engines, and local politicians and officials incessantly describing what was happening.

In this particular event two or three carloads of militants had stormed the US Consulate with automatic weapons, but hardly any of its staff were in residence. By this time Lynne Tracy had left, to be replaced by E. Candace Putnam, who was more often in Islamabad than Peshawar. Little was said about this incident in the press, but it clearly demonstrated how confident the Taliban had become.

I left Pakistan a few weeks after these explosions, but not before I had to deal with a complex sequence of events involving the discovery of a huge embezzlement in college funds. In some respects these problems were more difficult to cope with than those caused by Taliban extremists!

6

Islam in Context

To: The Principal   Dated: 30/10/2006

Edwardes College, Peshawar

Subject: Application for Hajj leave

Sir,

With great respect and very humble submission I would like
to state that as discussed with you in our meeting of October
20, 2006 in your office that I have the intention of going on
Hajj (pilgrimage) this year. My scheduled journey to Hajj is
to be of 40 days, i.e. from November 25, 2006 to January
10, 2007, and fortunately for these days there are holidays
for Christmas as well as Eid ul Azha, which is going to
reduce the number of my absentee [days] from the
college [...]

The letter continued to calculate carefully how many lectures
would be missed during the period of absence and offered extra
classes on return. It was signed by Sardar Sabir Hussain, assistant
professor in the department of Islamiat.

There was, of course, no problem with sanctioning the leave,
and I was touched by the thoroughness with which this college
lecturer made provision for his teaching during his absence. The
same thoroughness was present in his arrangements for Ramazan

(which included the hiring of a *shamianah*), the Na'at celebrations and the upkeep of the college mosque.

Sardar Sabir Hussain's role was accepted and affirmed throughout the college. Although 'Sardar' can serve as a general title – the word is of Indo-Iranian origin and signifies authority such as that of the head of a tribe and is used by the Sikhs – in his case it was used as the first part of his name. It would not be correct to characterise him as a Muslim 'chaplain' and he would probably have shrunk from any association with the notion of a *maulana* with its overtones of authority. He was – in his own eyes and most of his colleagues' – simply a lecturer in Islamic education or Islamiat. He was also very good at organising college activities associated with Islam.

Sabir went to Mecca and on his return kindly presented me with a prayer mat. But much as I valued this gift I soon realised that I would eventually have to donate it to Waliullah, a first-year student who had seen him give it to me. Wali wanted it for his mother, whom I had visited at the family home near Bannu and who was disabled, and in the end I gave in to his entreaties.

As far as I knew, only two other college members undertook the Hajj. They were Muhammad Mushtaq, the head of the economics department, who also served as a capable vice-principal, and Attaullah Jan, a senior physics professor who followed Kalimullah as chief proctor. Mushtaq was worried about his physical ability to perform the Hajj, but both completed it satisfactorily.

The Hajj pilgrimage is one of the five pillars of Islam and a religious duty that must be carried out by every able-bodied Muslim at least once in his or her lifetime. Elements of the Hajj can be traced back to the time of Abraham, and at one time Christian Arabs were as likely to have made the pilgrimage as members of other belief systems. But in 630 CE the Prophet Muhammad (peace be upon him) performed the first all-Muslim Hajj by leading his followers from Medina to Mecca, where he destroyed various idols and dedicated the Ka'aba – the huge black stone circumnavigated by pilgrims – to Allah. There is also a lesser pilgrimage, or Umrah, which can be performed at any time of the year; it is recommended but not compulsory, and is not a substitute for the Hajj.

* * * * *

Islam in Pakistan is many faceted. There are historic sectarian divides within Islam, regional variations across the country, constitutional accommodations, and recent political events with far-reaching implications for the relationships between Islam and society. We shall begin with some of the less controversial areas.

Islam is the state religion of the Islamic Republic of Pakistan. Of a population in excess of 190 million, 95–97 per cent are Muslim, mostly Sunni, and 3–5 per cent are Christian, Hindu, Sikh, Kalash and others. The Shi'is are variously estimated at between 10 and 15 per cent of the Muslim population, and Ahmadiyya adherents – who are not permitted to call themselves Muslims in Pakistan, but whose numbers have included the Nobel Prize-winning physicist Abdus Salam – are about 2.2 per cent.

The arrival of Islam in central and southern Asia was a consequence of the eastern expansion of the Umayyad Caliphate, the dynasty that ruled the Islamic world from the death of the fourth Sunni caliph, Ali – who was also the first Shi'i imam – in 661 CE until 750 CE. In 711 CE, the Umayyads, based in Damascus, sent an army led by Muhammad bin Qasim against Raja Dahir, the ruler of Sindh. But although this army was composed of Arab Muslims, its objectives were not religious. According to John Esposito:

> The Umayyads' great expansion was primarily military and political, not religious; conversion to Islam was discouraged for some time since it would reduce the treasury's intake of taxes on non-Muslims.[1]

In 750 CE, the Umayyads were overthrown by the Abbasids, who established their capital in Baghdad, which became a major cultural, religious and scientific centre until sacked by the Mongols in 1261, whereupon they re-established themselves in Cairo. Although this dynasty subsequently lacked political power, it continued to exercise a strong religious and cultural influence on the entire Muslim world.

Contrary to the view that Muslim armies swept the various regions that became part of their empire, the course of events east of Baghdad was highly complex and too detailed to be covered adequately here. Olaf Caroe's study, *The Pathans*, though published some years ago, offers a thorough account of these events. Summarising the main features of Arab expansion to the east during its first 200 years, he observes:

> I have given this somewhat bald recital from original Muslim sources to establish how completely untrue it is to suppose that the people of Gandhara and the surrounding mountain regions were swept into the Muslim fold at an early period in the Islamic era. The general picture on the contrary is that during the first two Islamic centuries Arab control, except in Sind, was never effectively extended over any part of what had had been the eastern provinces of the Sassanian Empire.[2]

Much of the area extending from what is now the Khyber-Pakhtunkhwa Province to Kabul continued to be controlled by Buddhist and Hindu rulers. The strength of Buddhism at one time is evidenced by the huge Bamiyan statues, which were destroyed in 2001 by the Taliban. But, according to Caroe:

> it is probable that, much as in modern Nepal, [Buddhism] was fighting a losing battle against the Brahmins, finding its adherents pushed further and further back into the mountains [...] Long before the time of the Ghaznavids (from 960 on) the ruling creed, at any rate around Peshawar, had become a strict Brahminical Hinduism.[3]

Hindus today constitute the second largest religious grouping in Pakistan amounting to just under 2 per cent of the population. They are mostly in Sindh (93 per cent) with 5 per cent in the Punjab and 2 per cent in Balochistan. Buddhists may currently number no more than 1,500; it is claimed that they spread their beliefs via the Silk Road of northern Pakistan into central Asia, China and beyond.

Christians rank third, with numbers estimated at just under three million (1.6 per cent of Pakistan's population). They have inherited many of the fine institutions set up during the colonial era, and this has given them a level of importance out of all proportion to their size. Most are descendants of Hindus and Muslims from the Punjab region who were converted during the British colonial period. Outside the Punjab most Christians are located in urban areas, with a large Roman Catholic community of Tamil and Goan migrants in Karachi.

The Sikh reformist movement began on Pakistan's side of the Punjab, though the focus of Sikh worship, the Golden Temple, is in Amritsar across the border. There may be as many as 20,000 Sikhs living in Pakistan; in recent years a number have migrated from Afghanistan.

There are rather more Bahais than Sikhs in Pakistan, and as many as 4,000 Pakistanis who practise Zoroastrianism – most in Karachi, though a lot of their fine temples still exist in Balochistan. The wife of *Quaid-e-Azam* Muhammad Ali Jinnah came from a family of Zoroastrians (usually known as Parsis).

The Kalash number about 3,000, there may be a few Jains in Sindh, and there is a Jewish synagogue in Peshawar, though it does not appear to be used for any religious purpose.

When Pakistan gained independence in 1947 it was a secular state, and the original Constitution did not discriminate between Muslims and non-Muslims. But amendments made during the presidency of Zia-ul-Haq, however, based on literal interpretations of the early scriptures, led to the controversial Hudood Ordinance and Shariat Court. There have been subsequent moves to liberalise them by, for example, President Musharraf.

* * * * *

The different groupings within Islam are to some extent geographically represented in Pakistan. Shi'is are predominantly in the south and in enclaves such as Parachinar in the FATA hills close to Afghanistan – some of the best students at Edwardes College came from this region. Other Islamic groupings – we shall avoid the use of the term 'sect' – are based more on schools of thought (e.g. Deobandi) and law schools (e.g. Hanafi). Urban, educated Muslims may be influenced by nineteenth- and twentieth-century reformers such as Syed Ahmad Khan (1817-98) and Muhammad Iqbāl (1877-1938).

At least 85 per cent of the world's 1.2 billion Muslims are Sunnis. They derive their name from the Sunnah, the exemplary behaviour of the Prophet Muhammad. All Muslims are guided by the Sunnah, but the Sunnis place more emphasis on this and also on the importance of consensus. Each of the four schools of Sunni legal thought – Hanafi, Maliki, Shafi and Hanbali – stresses the importance of revelation and of the Prophet's example.

Shi'i Muslims constitute approximately 10 per cent of world Islam. Their origins go back to the earliest days of Islam, their name indicating that they are *Shī'at 'Alī*, 'of the party of Ali'. Shi'is believe that Ali was the legitimate successor to Muhammad; he ruled briefly as caliph from 656 CE until 661 CE, when he was killed and replaced by a member of the Umayyad dynasty. Ali's two sons negotiated with the new regime until 680 CE when the younger one, Hussein, was killed at the Battle of Karbala. This event, which marked an irrevocable split between Sunnis and Shi'is, continues to be commemorated by the latter on the Day of Ashura during Muharram.

A Shi'i religious leader is known as an *imām*, one who stands in front: a role model for the community in all its spiritual and secular undertakings. The largest subdivision within Shi'i Islam recognises twelve historic imams, and its members are therefore known as Twelvers (also as Ithna Asharis). Only seven imams are recognised by the Seveners, who are better known as Ismailis (including the Nizari Agha Khanis). Other significant Shi'i minorities are the Mustaali Dawoodi Bohras and the Sulaimani Bohras. Although the term imam is used primarily by Shi'is to designate a divinely appointed successor to Muhammad, Sunnis also use the title for prominent representatives of their legal schools.

Shi'i teaching, like that of the Sunnis, is based on the Qur'ān and *hadīth*, but incorporates additional *hadīth* and teachings of the imams, including the *Path of Eloquence*, attributed to Ali. Shi'is undertake pilgrimages to shrines of the imams, to Karbala and to Najaf.

The Shiʻi teaching staff and students in Edwardes College were identifiable as Shiʻi but were not in any sense clannish. They went home to their villages to participate in Muharram and observed Ramazan, but in the college took part only in *khatam-ul-Qurʼān*, the final night of the recitation of the Qurʼān. Many used the honorific title Syed (also Syad or Sayyīd), denoting males who are descendants of the sons of the Prophet Muhammad's daughter Fatima and son-in-law Ali.

The most prominent Shiʻi teaching staff were Syed Nasim Haider Kazmi, botanist and an outstanding vice-principal, and Asaf Naveed Ali, our technically skilled head of computer science with publications at an international level. Sadly, his brother was killed by extremists during my time as principal.

On the basis of the perceived academic ability of Shiʻi staff and students, it is tempting to argue that Shiʻis are more capable than their peers. But there are other factors. Many Shiʻis in Parachinar, and more generally in the wider Kurram Agency of FATA in which it is situated, belong to tribal groups such as the Turis. These place a high premium on education, and push their youngsters to work hard. By contrast, the Bangash tribe, whose members may be either Shiʻi or Sunni, is better known for physical prowess and its Sunni members have been involved in Taliban extremism in the region.

The Parachinar students in the hostel were frequent visitors to my house in the evenings. Often they came as a group, but individually they had close personal friends among other students, including women students from outside the hostel (hostel accommodation for women would have proved too tempting a target for extremists). Rafiq Hussain, studying for the Pre-Medical intermediate exams, would often come with his classmate, Muhammad Yaseen, nicknamed 'Einstein' on account of the picture in his room. Rafiq distinguished himself (and the college) by coming first in the entire FATA area in his exams, and gaining a place to study medicine at the prestigious King Edward's College in Lahore. He became a doctor in 2014. Yaseen, who had studied in a *madrasa* prior to coming to Edwardes, did not do so well, but went on to do research in geology in Peshawar University.

Syed Shahid Kazmi, like Rafiq, came from Parachinar. He spent a lot of time with Zaidi – whose full name I never discovered – possibly a cousin. Periodically they would quarrel, in which case I saw more of Shahid; on other occasions they would infuriate the second-year hostel warden, Naveed Ali, by missing dinner in order to eat out in Peshawar. Shahid was well connected with government officials and the military and was able to cadge lifts home in their helicopters. On one occasion I asked him to give me an outline of significant events in the Pak/Afghan region leading up to the then current spate of bombings. He promptly set out two pages of precisely dated events on both sides of the border – I was amazed by his ability to do this without a note, and I told him that he should get a job with one of the Intelligence agencies!

* * * * *

Five hundred years of Abbasid influence came to an end in 1258 CE with the sacking of Baghdad by the Mongols, originally led by Genghis Khan (1162–1227). Genghis' strategy had been to unite the Turkish and Mongol tribes of the Siberian steppe to create an empire stretching from the Mediterranean to the Pacific. Although his military campaigns were brutal, he was generally tolerant towards religions, including Buddhist and Christian minorities, and the Russian and Iranian parts of his empire eventually flourished as strong Muslim areas.

Timur, or Tamburlaine (1336–1405), succeeded Genghis Khan and was notorious for the ruthlessness of his campaigns (his armies are credited with the deaths of 17 million people, or about 5 per cent of the world population at that time). Visitors to the Khyber Pass can see on the Afghan side of the border one of Timur's castle-like prisons; on completion of their sentences prisoners were taken onto the roof and flung into vertical turrets lined with razor-sharp knives, which would cut them into shreds for the waiting dogs below. Hardly surprisingly, Tamburlaine becomes the representative of unconstrained power in the play of that name by Shakespeare's English contemporary, Christopher Marlowe.

We shall leave this unedifying phase of the history of the Pakistan/Afghan region until we come to consider the progressive educational reforms of the nineteenth century, but before doing this it is important to acknowledge an important development within Islam, namely the appearance of the Sufis.

Sufism (*taṣawwut*) is Islam's mysticism – an aspect or dimension of Islam. Sufi orders (*tarīqa*s) can be found in Sunni, Shi'i and other Islamic groups, and can be traced back to the years following the Prophet's death. Sufi teachers (*imām*s) base their authority on Qur'ānic verses such as the following:

Ask those who know if you know not (16, 43)
And follow the path of him who turns unto Me (31, 15)

Early Sufi teachers included women, of whom Rābi'a al-ʿAdawiyya of Baghdad is probably the best known. Their asceticism, characterised by rough clothes made of *ṣūf*, or wool, was a preparation for the search for *maʾrifa*, knowledge or wisdom, rather than familiarity with religious texts, though mystical union with God remained central.

The Sufis emphasised Qur'ānic verses such as 50, 15: 'We are nearer to him than his jugular vein', but held back from pantheism; at the moment of supreme illumination there remains a distinction between the mystic and God. In spite of their belief in monotheistic mysticism, their way of life fitted in with the sub-continent's tradition of Hindu holy men, and practices such as the veneration of shrines and tombs were readily accepted. By the late twelfth century, the Chishtī Sufi order had been founded in Kashmir, where it became popular on account of its emphasis on learning, contemplation, music and songs of devotion as ways of approaching God. It also appealed to Hindus who felt oppressed by the caste system.

Two popular Sufi shrines in Pakistan are Ali Hajveri in Lahore and Shahbaz Sehwan in Sehwan, Sindh – both established in the eleventh and twelfth centuries. Devotees gather for annual festivals, and especially on Thursday nights, to enjoy Sufi music and dance. But more orthodox Muslims are opposed to these populist activities, and in 2010 there were several extremist attacks directed against Sufi shrines and festivals, which killed more than 60 people.

Some stricter traditions such as the Barelvi, founded at Bareilly in Uttar Pradesh by Ahmad Raza Khan (1856–1921), rejected many features of Sufism, but supported devotion to holy men (*pīrs*) and their shrines. But the Deobandi tradition – a revivalist movement within Hanafi Sunni Islam – was strongly opposed even to these concessions to populism; Deobandis also carried considerably more weight in the *madrasas*.

* * * * *

The Sufi love of poetry, music, dancing, and other devotional activities – some ecstatic, such as the whirling *darwish*es – is strongly present in the Pashtun areas, but it is tempered by the older, more severe code of Pashtunwali, the basic tribal common law. This includes elements such as hospitality, honour and respect for women, tribal assemblies known as *jirgas* and other features, some of which are not readily compatible with Qur'ānic teaching. Also present in the border areas are Deobandi *madrasas*, some influenced by Wahabi teaching from Saudi Arabia, which was responsible for supplying funds for their expansion during the presidency of Zia-ul-Haq.

Pashto, used by most Pashtuns, is believed to belong to the Indo-Iranian family of languages. It is written in the Pashto-Arabic script, and is divided into two main dialects. The hard, north-eastern version, called Pakhto, is spoken in Bajaur, Swat and Buner, and by the Yusufzai, Bangash, Orakzai, Afridi and Mohmand tribes. The softer south-western Pashto is spoken by the Khattaks, Wazirs, Murwats and other tribes in the south. The earliest literary and poetic works were composed in the Yusufzai district of Pashto, which is reckoned to be the purest form of the language. Malala Yousafzai, the teenager who was almost killed by the Taliban, derives her name from this area – the name of which has been linked with 'Joseph' in the Hebrew scriptures.

Figure 20. The Pashto poet Abasin Yousafzai recites poems at the annual college mushaira

The first major Pashto poet was Khushal Khan Khattak (1613-89), who is reported to have authored more than 300 works of poetry and prose on a vast range of topics, including religion, medicine, sport and falconry. He was also a tribal leader; as such he fell out of favour with the Mughal emperor, Aurangzeb, and was imprisoned in the Gwalior Fort where he composed his finest poems, some of which have been compared with those of the English Romantic poets.

Abdur Rahman (1650-1711), popularly known as Rahman Baba, is famous for his poems, but is also venerated as a Sufi, though there is no evidence that he was ever ordained in any *silsilah* (order). He was a simple but learned man; in his own words: 'Though the wealthy drink water from a golden cup, I prefer this clay bowl of mine.'

Rahman Baba's tomb is set in a domed shrine (*mazar*) on the southern Peshawar Ring Road, and has become a popular place for local poets and mystics to meet. On 8 March 2009, the tomb was bombed and the grave almost destroyed. Apparently the bombers had tied explosives around the pillars of the mausoleum.

The following translated stanza illustrates the striking combination of mysticism and humanism in Rahman Baba's poems:

Humanity is all one body,
To torture another is simply to wound yourself.
When you don't look for faults in others,
They will conceal your weakness in return.
Make your path straight now, by the bright light of day;
For pitch darkness will come without warning [...]
The heart that is safe in the storm
Is the one which carries others' burdens like a boat.

If Rahman Baba was a poet of humanity, then Khan Abdul Ghani Khan (1914-96) was distinguished for his psychological, romantic and religious works, Ajmal Khattak (1925-2010) for his Marxist-Leninist views, and Rahmat Shah Sail (b. 1943) for his passionate socialism. These names have been chosen to illustrate the variety among Pashto poets – many others of comparable distinction could be added.

Khan Abdul Ghaffar Khan (1890-1988), better known as Bacha Khan or the Frontier Gandhi, was not a poet, though his son Abdul Ghani Khan was both a poet and an artist. Bacha Khan attended Edwardes High School, where the principal encouraged him to follow his brother, an alumnus of Aligarh Muslim College, to London. He refused, however, and by the age of 20 had opened his own school in Utmanzai.

Ghaffar Khan saw himself as a secular Muslim, and did not believe in religious divisions. He worked tirelessly to serve and support his fellow Pashtuns through education. During the 1920s he formed the *Khudai Khidmatgar* ('Servants of God'), more commonly known as the *Surkh Posh* ('Red Shirts'), founded on Gandhi's notion of *satyāgraha* (active non-violence). Gandhi and Ghaffar Khan were close friends, and on one occasion visited Edwardes College together. But when the Congress party finally refused a last-ditch compromise to stop the 1947 partition between India and Pakistan, Ghaffar Khan rebuked Gandhi with what

Figure 21 Bacha Khan and M. K. Gandhi visiting the college in 1933

turned out to be his last words to his lifelong friend: 'You have thrown us to the wolves.'

This accusation was tragically prophetic. After protracted and stormy relationships with Muhammad Ali Jinnah and Z. A. Bhutto, whose government he described as 'the worst kind of dictatorship', Bacha Khan died under house arrest in Peshawar in 1988. Two hundred thousand mourners attended the funeral, including President Najibullah of Afghanistan (an Edwardian), and the Indian government declared a five-day period of mourning in his honour.

* * * * *

During Gandhi's second visit to Edwardes College on 4 November 1938 he met with Kenneth Jardine, then a lecturer, who became principal in 1953 for a year. (The principal at the time of the visit was the Revd A. M. Dalaya.) Jardine recorded the following conversation with Gandhi:

Kenneth Jardine: I would be grateful if you would give me your opinion of the value […] of a college with a religious purpose such as that of Edwardes College.

Gandhi: If you mean by religious purpose missionary purpose, in my opinion it has no place. But if by the expression you mean a moral purpose that seeks to turn the students towards God and a godly life, such colleges have a definite place not only in India but everywhere.

Kenneth Jardine: You once advised all Indian students to study the life and teaching of Jesus while they are in college. Would you still give this advice?

Gandhi: Most emphatically, yes; only my advice was of a general character, *viz.* that the students should study the lives of all the great teachers of humanity. What you are referring to was a course of lectures I delivered on the Gospels. It was the beginning of a series that was to cover the teachings of all the other great faiths in the world.

Kenneth Jardine: But when I tell others of the life and teaching of Christ I cannot help telling them also what an enormous difference he has made to my own life – the joy and knowledge of God I receive from him. If they ask me how they may know God, how can I help telling them of my own experience? If they then wish to try the same path and ask me to help them to find God through Jesus, can I possibly refuse to allow them to come with me and become Christians?

Gandhi: I have written a great deal on this matter. In saying what you have said just now so frankly, you have not succeeded in saying the whole truth. What I mean is this. At the back of your mind must be the idea that the other faiths are either false or not as true as Christianity. If my interpretation of your view is correct, I regard it as a profound error. No one has the right to judge for others. There is no reason why Buddha or Krishna or Muhammad should not mean precisely the same thing to a Buddhist, Vaishnava or a Muslim that Jesus means to you. What I should do in your place is to invite Buddhists, Vaishnavas and Muslims to contact you so that you become better as a Christian.

* * * * *

During an expanded daily college officers' meeting I mentioned incidentally that a family member in Yorkshire had died. There was an immediate silence and everybody sat motionless for a few minutes, then Dr Yar Muhammad spoke some words in Urdu and there was a murmur of assent. We could continue the meeting.

Religious faith was deeply felt by all sections of the college in such situations. On this particular occasion three members of the group were Christian; their reaction was exactly the same as that of their Muslim colleagues.

I shall never forget the shock waves that spread through the college at the news that the parents of Muhammad Jamal, head of the Urdu Department, had both been killed in a car crash. We all converged on his house and sat together under a rapidly improvised *shamianah*. He was absent for a few days, but back remarkably quickly in the lecture room with his students.

A close friend of Khayam Hassan, the student I had intended would accompany the royal couple on their visit, was killed in a car crash late one night on the Peshawar roads. The family was involved in car manufacture, and the student had constructed his own vehicle. Tragically, while racing the car through the empty streets at night, he hit a tree and died.

I went to the house the next day and sat with the mourners. As I left, the father of the student told me how grateful he was that I had attended; I was touched by the intensity of his gratitude. But of Khayam, one of the deceased's best friends, there was no sign, though a week later he sent another student to my house to tell me how tragic the incident had been.

Two students attempted suicide during my time as principal, and a third succeeded after I had left. The two had overdosed on painkillers and were rushed to the Combined Military Hospital; their parents were notified. I was informed that one of these students kept a pistol and bullets in his room. I confiscated them, but when I tried to give them to the student's father he declined on the grounds that he could be in trouble with the military or police if stopped on the way home. I kept the gun in my house for a few weeks and eventually gave it to the elder brother, who was studying medicine at the Khyber Medical College. This was the only time I had a gun in my possession, though, as mentioned, several people urged me to have one.

'Sir,' protested Wazir, a postgraduate from South Waziristan, 'you are the least protected foreigner anywhere in Pakistan.'

This same student also invited me to visit his village:

'Only six hours by road,' he explained.

'But Wazir,' I countered, 'isn't your region the most dangerous centre of Taliban activity anywhere in Pakistan?'

'No problem, Sir,' said Wazir. 'My uncle is a good friend of Mullah Omar in Afghanistan. We will look after you.'

Nobody I met in college was in favour of suicide under any circumstances. Possibly the strongest arguments against it are to be found by comparing passages in the Islamic scriptures with corresponding Hebrew ones shared by Jews and Christians. Thus, for example, in the narrative about King Saul, his son Jonathan and David, the psalmist who became king, it is stated that Saul, following defeat in battle, 'took his own sword and fell upon it'.[4]

The Qur'ān nowhere mentions Saul's suicide, and elsewhere Islamic literature simply records that he died in battle. The Islamic Jonah does not ask to be thrown overboard, and Job does not pray for death. The suicidal aspects of Samson's death are absent from the Islamic scriptures, and in other places similar insinuations in the Hebrew scriptures are airbrushed out of the Islamic sources.[5] For Islam, suicide is always forbidden.

* * * * *

Students came regularly to my house in the evenings before and after dinner, which took place in three sittings because the dining hall was not big enough to accommodate all in residence. On certain occasions I had dinner with them; more frequently I sat inside the door and drank tea prepared by Bashir, who ran the tuck shop.

All the students I encountered in this way were resident in the hostel and therefore from outside Peshawar, which meant that I met a wide range from various parts of the frontier. The first of these was Irfan from Buner. I had been given several cakes on arrival, so I took the largest and gave it to the first student I saw. Within 15 minutes the cake had vanished and Irfan and friends came to my door to thank me. I served all visitors with 'Dew', a Pakistani soft drink, and never Pepsi, which I discouraged the college from supplying.

Students with something in common usually came round in small groups – they might be from Chitral or Swat, or have acted together in the college play, for example. Day scholars were more likely to come alone; on Saturdays after the prison visits Romail and Shahan usually stayed for some time. I made a special effort to get to know the student proctors by inviting them to the house, but abolished the position residential 'prefect', which seemed unnecessary and a bit reminiscent of English public schools.

Conversations covered just about everything. Politically, student loyalties were divided between the Pakistan People's Party (Benazir Bhutto) and the Pakistan Muslim League (Nawaz Sharif). Regionally, the Awami National Party was well liked, but not the Muttahida Majlis-e-Amal (MMA), which was the dominant provincial party when I arrived (it collapsed in the 2008 elections). General Musharraf was regarded favourably, but there was a general mistrust of his successor as president, Asif Ali Zardari. However, a group of young teaching staff in the college was totally opposed to Musharraf, labelling him a military dictator. There was a general liking for Imran Khan – Waliullah, from Bannu, became a great admirer and arranged for me to meet him during a visit to London. Muhammad Jallal, a friend of Irfan, surprised me by stating his historic admiration for Adolf Hitler!

Islam was always seen as a given feature of society and of college life. It was recognised that there are variants within Islam, but I never detected any disapproval by one variant of another. Questions I might raise about Islam were answered positively and descriptively.

During our evening discussions students sometimes asked about Christianity. Their questions were usually requests for clarification – what is the difference between a priest and a bishop, for example. Only one student ever indicated a desire to convert to Christianity, and he was a member of the Kalash from Chitral. I encouraged him to attend the chapel services on Friday lunchtimes.

A few of the hostel students had girlfriends who were discussed enthusiastically. Some women students were stigmatised as predatory, but most appeared uninterested in contact with the young men outside lecture periods. The women's centre, which I established next to the principal's house, was a great success as a private space for its occupants. I got to know a few of the women student proctors, such as Bushra, who upset the chief proctor Kalimullah by coming to college several times with her arms bared. After graduation she taught international relations for a few weeks after Zahoor Khan, the regular lecturer, was injured in a motorcycle accident. Bushra moved on to manage the Oxford University Press bookshop in Peshawar. I admired her for her independent spirit.

Although I never met Jallal's girlfriend, their bumpy relationship – to which his parents were totally opposed – was the topic of numerous discussions in my house. Usually, Irfan and Zeeshan Khan were also present. Zeeshan was known in college for being very outspoken, and he also had a girlfriend. On these occasions

– during which Jallal would periodically rush outside the door clutching his mobile phone – I was tempted to suggest that the relationship was going nowhere and needed to be terminated. But I said nothing.

One student in particular became something of an icon among several of the hostel students – we shall call him 'Prince' for reasons to do with his email address. In his first year he came to my house with his friends, always sat on the edge of the settee, and said nothing. At the end of the year he became more confident and began to blossom physically. Another student – let us call him 'Gul' – came to my office one day to ask if he could share a room with Prince during the second year. I passed the request on to the second-year hostel warden, Naveed Ali, who asked Prince, who agreed.

A month later Gul came to my house and begged me for a room transfer.

'But you were so anxious to share a room with Prince,' I observed. 'Why have you changed your mind?'

After a long pause the truth eventually came out.

'Sir, I wanted to share with him because he is so good-looking. But every night his friends come round and sit on his bed admiring him. I can't stand it any more!'

Naveed Ali was as amused as I was by this frank admission, though it wasn't easy to arrange the transfer.

Mohammed Hanif's *A Case of Exploding Mangoes* captures very effectively the manner in which male-to-male bonding over a period of time can lead to more explicit activity.[6] The transition from the seventeen preceding chapters to this brief episode in his book makes the development appear very natural.

In the context of the educational and social life of Peshawar and its surroundings, Islam is much more tolerant and accepting of diversity than it is elsewhere.

7

Educational Renaissance

One of the most severe critics of Pakistan's higher education system is Pervez Hoodbhoy, Professor of Physics at Forman Christian College University, Lahore. In a trenchant article published in 2009 he writes:

> Every country wants universities, and the more the better. There is a clear utilitarian goal behind this: universities have become the engines of progress for knowledge-driven economies in the age of rapid globalisation. They are the fountainheads of modern science, and of technologies that have changed the world more in the past fifty years than the previous 10,000 years.
>
> But higher education requires much more than just building structures and calling them universities or colleges. There is little to be gained from a department of English where the department's head cannot speak or write a grammatically correct non-trivial sentence of English; [...] a mathematics department where graduate students have problems with elementary surds and roots; or a biology department where evolution is thought to be new-fangled and quite unnecessary to teach as part of modern biology. Nor does putting a big signboard advertising a 'centre of excellence' make it one.

There are countless places in Pakistan where the above is not far from the truth. On the other hand, there are also some examples of high quality such as a world-class medical university and business schools, some good quality engineering and fine-arts colleges.[1]

Hoodbhoy traces the poor quality of many higher education institutions back to the period of British rule over the subcontinent:

In the early twentieth century, Muslims of the Indian subcontinent were, in general, poorly educated relative to Hindus. This was both because of British prejudice against Muslims, as well as resistance by orthodox Muslims to modern scientific ideas and to the English language.[2]

Historians may debate Hoodbhoy's assertions about relationships between Muslims and the British – certainly they soured after the 1857 Sepoy uprising – but what concerns us here is how some Muslims adapted to science and Western education in general that was made possible by the decision in 1835 to make the English language the medium of instruction in higher education.

* * * * *

In the days of the undivided subcontinent in 1835, James Prinsep – head of the Calcutta mint and an able scholar – was so impressed by the standard of a class of chemistry students examined by him at the Calcutta Medical College that he wrote:

I do not think that in Europe any class of chemical pupils would be found capable of passing a better examination for the time they have attended lectures, nor indeed that an equal number [...] would be found so nearly on a par with their acquirements.[3]

The same year Thomas Babington Macaulay (1800-59), president of the Committee on Public Instruction, issued a Minute on behalf of the British legislature announcing that in future all higher education institutions in the subcontinent were to disseminate their knowledge through the medium of the English language. Many complex motives underlay this decision, but it enabled countless talented young people to prove themselves at least as capable as their peers in Europe.

Unlike Prinsep, Lord Macaulay had no appreciation of the abilities of the 'native' population, as he contemptuously called it, but was guided by the philosophy of utilitarianism as set out by John Stuart Mill and Jeremy Bentham. Realism dictated that the limited resources of the British legislature could not educate the subcontinent's millions, and therefore a strategy had to be found for doing this via intermediaries:

> It is impossible for us, with our limited means, to attempt to educate the body of the people. We must at present do our best to form a class who may be interpreters between us and the millions whom we govern - a class of persons Indian in blood and colour, but English in tastes, in opinions, in morals and in intellect. To that class we may leave it to define the vernacular dialects of the country, to enrich those dialects with terms of science borrowed from the Western nomenclature, and to render them by degrees fit vehicles for conveying knowledge to the great mass of the population.[4]

Macaulay's sweeping educational vision was influential, though deeply flawed in many of its details, of which possibly the most significant was his inability to acknowledge the latent intellect among students, which James Prinsep had carefully noted. But the utilitarian concept of higher education institutions in places where 'interpreters' are fashioned did affect the ethos and role of a considerable number of colleges throughout the subcontinent – including St Stephen's College in Delhi and Edwardes College in Peshawar.

The nineteenth- and early twentieth-century renaissance in the northern subcontinent was dominated by charismatic Hindu reformers such as Ram Mohan Roy (1772-1833), Swami

Vivekananda (1863-1902), and, later, Rabindranath Tagore (1869-1941). There was also Mohandas K. Gandhi (1869-1948), though his distinctive fusion of politics and religion marks him out as atypical.

There is no doubt that these Hindu reform leaders were inspirational. Roy, for example, like many of his contemporaries, had his early schooling in a *madrasa*, where he learned Arabic and Persian (he already knew Bengali, his mother tongue). By the age of 15 he had learned Sanskrit in order to study the Hindu scriptures; later he mastered Greek in order to understand Christianity, and he published a book based on the teachings of Jesus.

Roy is often described as the 'maker of modern India'. On his first visit to London he astounded audiences with his wealth of learning – how different he was from anything the missionaries had led them to expect! Unfortunately, the English weather eventually proved too much for him and he died and was buried in Bristol.

Swami Vivekananda was as much a sensation in the USA as was Roy in London. His address to the World Parliament of Religions in Chicago in 1893 was masterly in both content and presentation. Roy was the inspiration behind the Brahmo Samaj – a small and rather eclectic organisation founded shortly after his death; Vivekananda was leader of the Ramakrishna Mission named after his guru, Sri Ramakrishna. The ebullient Dayanand Saraswati (1824-83) led the much less intellectually based Arya Samaj, and there were many additional luminaries, such as Sri Aurobindo, who collectively adorned this period with their reforming zeal.

These Hindu leaders welcomed the new knowledge from the West – especially science – for a variety of reasons. For some – Roy most of all – Western ways of thinking had made Britain a powerful nation and if similar ways of thinking were assimilated they might do the same for India. One of Roy's successors as leader of the Brahmo Samaj, Keshub Chunder Sen (1838-84), went further than any of his contemporaries in his adulation of science:

Science will be your religion [...] above the Vedas, above the Bible. Astronomy, geology, botany and chemistry, anatomy and physiology are the living scriptures of the God of Nature.[5]

Subaltern and Marxist historians criticise Western scholars who have relied exclusively on such English-language sources, which, they maintain, do not reflect the aspirations of the vast majority. While there may be some truth in this, it is surprisingly hard to find any sources among the vernacular languages relating to science, except for those written in Bengali and Urdu by the same reformers who express themselves so eloquently in English. However, the views that some of them voice in English to one audience are sometimes not the same as those they publish in their mother tongue. This was especially true of Ram Mohan Roy![6]

In addition to the charismatic leaders of the reform movements there were a number of capable scientists who identified with these increasingly nationalistic aspirations. They were mainly Hindu, such as C. V. Raman, who was awarded a Nobel Prize in physics in 1930; Abdus Salam wasn't too far behind with a Nobel Prize in 1979 for his outstanding work on electroweak unification – sadly, his membership of the Ahmadiyya Muslim community led to his exile from Pakistan.

The major Hindu reform movements were generally well disposed towards Muslim, Christian and other minorities. Ram Mohan Roy collaborated with the Scottish missionary Alexander Duff in setting up the Hindu College in what is now Kolkata in 1917. This has become Presidency University, arguably the best in India, with Nobel Prize-winner Amartya Sen (1933-) and many distinguished scientists such as Prafulla Chandra Ray (1861-1944), Jagadish Chandra Bose (1858-1937) and Satyendra Nath Bose (1894-1974) among its alumni.

The attitudes of Vivekananda and his followers towards religious minorities may be summarised as 'all religions are equal but Hindus, by virtue of acknowledging this, are slightly superior'. However, in his debates with missionaries, he was not beyond characterising the God of Christianity and Islam as 'hideous, cruel and ever-angry'.[7]

Dayanand Saraswati's Arya Samaj was largely populated by lower-middle-class Punjabis who were not well disposed to Muslims. His reassertive Hindu preaching had strong nationalistic overtones, preparing the way for the extremism of the so-called

Sangh Parivar, which included the Mahasabha, one of whose members killed Gandhi.

* * * * *

It is often claimed that Muslims in the north of the subcontinent made little progress in assimilating Western knowledge until the so-called Aligarh movement towards the end of the nineteenth century. However, the evidence rather supports the view that some Muslims took very rapidly to certain aspects of Western thought, but became more critical after the 1857 Sepoy revolt and its savage repression by the British.

Most Muslims had good reason initially to be more hostile than Hindus to the British. The rule of the Mughal emperors was progressively usurped and the foreign learning of the West was secular and needed the acquisition of a new language – something that Muslims, unlike Hindus, were unaccustomed to. There was a vast network of *madrasa*s that were patronised by some of the most brilliant pupils.

By the 1830s the Delhi College – now the Zakir Husain Delhi College, named after India's first Muslim president – was poised to play much the same sort of role among a small modernising group of Muslims as did many missionary institutions and the Hindu College among young Hindus. The Delhi College was founded as a *madrasa* in the 1690s by a general of the Emperor Aurangzeb; it closed for a short time towards the end of the eighteenth century but was reorganised as the Anglo Arabic College in 1828.

By 1831, in spite of opposition from Muslim leaders in the city, 300 students at the college were reading textbooks that were either in English or had been translated from English into Urdu by members of staff. Most of the science teachers at the college seem to have been religious men; for Muslims, the translation of science into Urdu would have helped to bridge the psychological gap between 'science' and 'religion'.[8] By the early 1850s much of the education in the north-west provinces was of a higher quality than that in Bengal, and the standard of science instruction and scientific literature available in Urdu at the Delhi College was exceptionally good.[9]

The importance of science as a strategic weapon in debates between Muslims and Christians at this time may be seen from the following incident recorded by Professor Yesudas Ramchandra of the Delhi College in his *Memoirs*:

> Once a learned Muhamedan came to me with a copy of the New Testament in Urdu [...] His object [...] was to get an English scholar and a teacher of English science to agree with him in saying how absurd Christianity and the Christians were [...] I briefly told him that, for my part, I considered not only Christianity, but also Muhamedanism, and all bookish religions as absurd and false. Upon this all Hindus and Muhamedans present paid me the compliment of a philosopher and departed with marks of approbation and goodwill.[10]

Ramchandra joined the Delhi College as a lecturer in science in 1844 and played an important role in the Delhi Renaissance, as it is sometimes called. He taught European science with a pioneering enthusiasm, which left a mark not only on his students but on the entire city. In his *Memoirs* he describes the impact of the new learning as follows:

> The doctrines of the ancient philosophy taught through the medium of Arabic were cast into the shade before the more reasonable and experimental theories of modern science. The old dogmas, such as 'that nature abhors a vacuum' and that the 'earth is the fixed centre of the universe', were generally laughed at by the higher students of the oriental as well as by those of the English Departments of the Delhi College. But the learned Maulvīs who lived in the city and had no connection with College did not like this innovation on their much-beloved theories of the ancient Greek philosophy, which for centuries past had been cultivated among them.[11]

But however much the city authorities may have resented the new learning, Ramchandra and his friends appear to have given them no opportunity to criticise their orthodoxy on social grounds. Together with a number of higher students of the college

Ramchandra published a bimonthly periodical *Fawā' id dani-i naz-rin* in which:

> Not only were the dogmas of the Muhamedan and Hindu philosophy exposed, but also many of the Hindu superstitions and idolatries were openly attacked. The result of this was that many of our countrymen, the Hindus, condemned us as infidels and irreligious; but as we did not advocate Christianity, but only recommended a kind of deism, and as we never lost our caste publicly, by eating and drinking, all our free discussions did not much alarm our Hindu friends.[12]

It is possible that Ramchandra was influenced in his decision to remain within the confines of orthodoxy by Ram Mohan Roy, who also preached a version of deism and maintained his caste. Ramchandra's ability as a mathematician helped the Delhi College to gain a wide reputation, and his proofs of Taylor's Theorem were an important landmark in pure mathematics.[13]

The Sepoy revolt cut short the achievements of the Delhi Renaissance, and Ramchandra, who had narrowly escaped death, moved to the Civil Engineering College at Roorkee in 1858.

It has been said that after the revolt Syed Ahmad Khan (1817–98) 'took the English section of the Delhi College to Aligarh'.[14] Syed Khan had been a private pupil of one of the Arabic teachers at the Delhi College, and there were certainly strong similarities between the lines along which the Aligarh College, which was raised from the status of a school in 1878, and the Delhi College were organised. Aligarh was also inspired to a large extent by the example of Cambridge University.

By the time of the third Decennial Missionary Conference in 1892, T. E. Slater had noted the emergence of a distinctive group among the Muslims:

> Among the Mohammadans of India there has arisen a small but cultured party, who deny the eternal nature of the Koran, take moderate views as to its inspiration [...] and advocate many social reforms.[15]

Slater was referring to Syed Khan and the Aligarh movement, which gathered momentum during the last quarter of the nineteenth century. He may be wrong in his statement that Syed and his friends denied the 'eternal nature' of the Qur'ān, but they certainly advocated a critical approach to it and, wherever an apparent conflict occurred with science, were willing to modify whatever views they had previously held:

> The Qur'ān does not prove that the earth is stationary, nor does it prove that the earth is in motion. Similarly it cannot be proved from the Qur'ān that the sun is in motion, nor can it be proved from it that the sun is stationary. The Holy Qur'ān was not concerned with these problems of astronomy; because the progress in human knowledge was to decide such matters itself [...] The real purpose of a religion is to improve morality; by raising such questions that purpose would have been jeopardised. In spite of all this I am fully convinced that the Work of God and the Word of God can never be antagonistic to each other; we may, through the fault of our knowledge, sometimes make mistakes in understanding the meaning of the Word.[16]

This particular extract from Syed's writings displays a number of typical facets of nineteenth-century thought, for instance the references to 'progress in human knowledge', 'the improvement of morality', and the acceptance of Western science at its face value.

Syed felt the need for a purer, more rational presentation of Islam, and he shared with many Hindu reformers a mistrust of miracles and the supernatural:

> It has become a habit with men that they ascribe miracles and supernatural attributes to an object or a person whom they consider to be holy or sacred. This is why men have interpolated supernatural factors into Islam, which are not worthy of belief, but such credulous persons believe in them.[17]

Syed saw the rise of science as part of the total growth of human knowledge, and he believed that once Islam had been purified it would take its rightful place alongside the best that the West had to offer.

* * * * *

If Syed Khan brought a rational, critical attitude and a desire for knowledge to the northern Muslims, Muhammad Iqbāl (1877-1938) gave them inspiration and an original philosophy. After teaching philosophy at the Lahore Government College, he went to Cambridge and Germany where he became acquainted with McTaggart, Bergson, Nietzsche and others whose influence is apparent in his poems.

Iqbāl's basic philosophy may be summarised as follows. Action is the key to existence, and human destiny is to remake the universe:

> You are creation's gardener, flowers live only in your seeing,
> By your light hangs my being or not-being;
> All beauty is in you: I am the tapestry of your soul;
> I am its key, but you are Love's own scroll.
> The load that would not leave me you have lifted from my shoulder,
> You are all my chaotic work's re-moulder.[18]

The human self is active, assertive, and imposes order upon nature. Iqbāl interpreted the human quest to subdue nature in terms of the accounts of creation in Genesis:

> The Quran teaches creative freedom of the human ego [...]
> The parable of Adam's fall from a state of primitive instinctive appetite to the conscious possession of a free self [...] signifies the emergence of a finite ego, free to choose [...] That God has taken this risk shows his immense faith in man. It is for man now to justify this faith.[19]

143

Thus God desires the development of the self to its fullest capacity, but this can come about only through identification with the community of Islam, and through 'love', which is the Sufi word for ecstatic devotion to God. Iqbāl differentiated between the quietist strand of the Sufi tradition, which he considered responsible for the decline of Islam, and the positive, optimistic side of Sufi thought.

But it is Iqbāl's understanding of space and time that is the most original part of his philosophy, and although the influence of Bergson and McTaggart is strong, his synthesis is striking:

> It seems as if the intellect of man is outgrowing its own most fundamental categories – time, space, and causality [...] The theory of Einstein has brought a new vision of the universe and suggests new ways of looking at the problems common to both religion and philosophy.[20]

Einstein's insight that space and time form an inseparable continuum is hinted at on several occasions in Iqbāl's poetry, as is McTaggart's view that temporal series are characteristics of appearances but not of reality, and Bergson's belief that everything is in a state of continual flux. In *The Secrets of the Self*, Iqbāl summarised his concept of time as follows:

> The cause of time is not the revolution of the sun:
> Time is everlasting, but the sun does not last forever.
> Time is joy and sorrow, festival and fast;
> Time is the secret of moonlight and sunlight.
> Thou hast extended time, like space,
> And distinguished yesterday from tomorrow.
> Thou hast fled, like a scent, from thine own garden;
> Thou hast made thy prison with thine own hand.
> Our time, which has neither beginning nor end,
> Blossoms from the flower bed of our mind.
> To know its root quickens the living with new life:
> Its being is more splendid than the dawn.
> Life is of time, and time is of life.[21]

Time is not the linear time, which we say we feel and express in terms of past, present and future, nor is it the time of science, because the scientist must assign limits to both space and time. Real time is everlasting and infinite, and can be thought of as an attribute of God. Only in such time can the Self find its fulfilment.

Iqbāl's concept of time is related to his activist attitude to life as a whole. If time is finite and limited, all that can be accomplished will ultimately disappear. Therefore life must look forward to a purposive irreversible goal – at this point he rejects both Nietzsche's 'eternal recurrence' and Bergson's concept of flux, which, though creative, is not purposive:

> Every moment in the life of Reality is original, producing what is absolutely novel and unforeseeable. To exist in real Time is not to be bound by the fetters of serial time but to create it from moment to moment. Life is free creative movement in time.[22]

History is important because it is the arena of human activity, and the religious community has a vital role to play in shaping the future:

> The modern world stands in need of biological renewal. And religion, which in its higher manifestations is neither dogma, nor priesthood, nor ritual, can alone ethically prepare the modern man for the burden of the great responsibility which the advancement of modern science necessarily involves, and restore to him that attitude of faith which makes him capable of winning a personality here and retaining it hereafter. It is only by rising to a fresh vision of his origin and future, his whence and whither, that man will eventually triumph over a society motivated by an inhuman competition, and a civilization which has lost its spiritual unity by its inner conflict of religious and political values.[23]

The Reconstruction of Religious Thought in Islam, from which this quotation has been taken, represents Iqbāl's later outlook, and contains elements of anti-Hindu sentiment. Objecting increasingly to the Sufi quietism, which seemed to have brought Islam into fatalistic depths in the eighteenth century, Iqbāl stressed the need for a type of biological renewal that would build a new elite into powerful units able to withstand the Hindus. However, this and other aspects of his thought are less significant than his attempts to interpret Islam in scientifically and philosophically credible terms.

* * * * *

The personalities with whom we have been so far mainly concerned, Syed Ahmad Khan and Muhammad Iqbāl, were anxious to adapt Islam to meet the challenge of Western science and the more general process of secularisation. There were also other Muslims who reacted much less sympathetically, perhaps the most influential being Mirza Ghulām Ahmad of Qādiyān (1838-1908) who came to prominence during the 1890s. The Mirza Saheb claimed to be both the Mahdī of Islam and the promised Messiah of Judaism, but from the point of view of the impact of Western science his ideas are relatively unimportant.

The idea of progress appears to have been readily accepted by all sections of society, and popular newspapers were echoing the need for it as early as the 1840s. In contrast to Europe and America, where Darwinism triggered off a series of dramatic reactions, society in the northern subcontinent was unmoved by it, and in spite of being preoccupied with the Sepoy revolt when *The Origin of Species* first appeared, subsequently assimilated the theory without undue comment. Most Hindu reformers incorporated the views of Herbert Spencer and Charles Darwin into their own religious and philosophical theories, and argued that they were comparable with traditional Hindu systems of thought.

It is difficult to say whether or not Muslims experienced initial misgivings about the implications of Darwinism. On the basis of Ramchandra's observations about the difference between the outlook of his students and that of the Delhi maulvīs, it would appear that Muslim orthodoxy was generally suspicious of all branches of Western science. But by the time the repercussions of the Sepoy revolt had died down, Syed Ahmad Khan and his associates had begun to advocate an interpretation of scripture which would have been much more amenable to Darwinism than earlier views.

Hindus, of course, would not in any case have run into difficulties with respect to their own scriptures and Darwinism since they were not in the habit of interpreting them in a literal, historical sense. But their estimation of Christianity was coloured by the scriptural dogmatism of the early missionaries, and by the time of later and more progressive thinkers – such as Slater and Farquhar – most Hindus were more interested in the possibility of reforming their own tradition than in listening to Christian apologetics. Unfortunately – from the point of view of the missionary enterprise as a whole – the higher criticism was ultimately used not in order to present the Christian faith in a less Western and conceptualised form, but as a weapon against the missionaries themselves. A few Hindus were impressed by the historical figure of Jesus Christ as revealed by European continental theologians such as Renan and Strauss.

The introduction of Western science into the nineteenth-century northern subcontinent was part of a process of secularisation whereby vast areas of life that had previously been determined by religious and social criteria came to be viewed according to secular standards – many of them directly associated with science. The Hindu reformers' beliefs were part of a much broader spectrum of political and philosophical ideas associated with secularisation. Within this process certain trends relating to higher education became more fully developed. Three types of response to secularisation – abandonment of traditional values, reaction against new ideologies, and the adaptation of the old with the help of the new – can be traced, and it can be seen that within these categories science had an important role to play. Among Muslims, comparable responses came later and were less clearly articulated.

The trends that we have described were only apparent among a small, modernising group of Muslims during the nineteenth and early twentieth centuries. They are important because they

147

occurred within the context of education, and because the institutions that they shaped can be regarded as role models for a progressive interpretation of Islam within modern society. Insofar as science became important for both India and Pakistan after Independence, the progressive and intellectually based views of Syed Khan and Muhammad Iqbāl were ahead of their time. Although temporarily eclipsed during the presidency of Zia-ul-Haq, they now deserve a prominent forum, and few better places exist for this to be achieved than higher education institutions such as Edwardes College.

8

The Dominant Minority

During the final part of General Musharraf's presidency it was reliably estimated that of the 18 or so senior military and government officials closest to him, a dozen had been educated in schools or colleges founded by Christians. And yet Pakistan's churches today, most of whose members are poor and subject to periodic ill treatment by the Muslim majority, represent a mere 1.6 per cent of the population. This ironic situation provides the context for understanding many of the most important aspects of the role of prestigious educational institutions such as Edwardes College.

My own dealings with a local church were at St John's Cathedral where I worshipped on Sundays. Usually I sat alone or with students that I knew, but at Christmas and Easter I helped the regular clergy with the administration of the sacraments. Although I continued to enjoy friendly relationships with all members of the congregation until I left, it was at Easter 2009 that there began to be a parting of the ways between myself and the Peshawar church leaders.

'Let's not spoil the principal's Easter,' said Donald Joseph to his associate vice-principal, Nasim Haider.

It was Thursday 9 April 2009. There had been very few bombs during the first quarter of the year, and after the Good Friday service at St John's Cathedral I was planning a long walk around an unfamiliar part of the city.

*Figure 22 Two outstanding vice-principals: Donald Joseph with
Nasim Haider*

Cathedral services tended to be long by European standards, but
on Good Friday I was not involved in any formal part of the
service, which was in Urdu. Following the service I enjoyed my
walk, which took me past the prison and the law courts, and on to
Chor (thieves') Bazaar, where a range of useful items was always to
be had, though I never tried to purchase anything there unless in
the company of a Pashto-speaking college member. I circled past
the five-star Pearl Continental hotel (which was blown up two
months later, with 17 killed), through the fairground, and back to
college, pausing briefly at the entrance of Aree Bazaar to talk to a
shop owner who had visited the UK.

On Saturday, I went to the prison with some of our regular
college visitors for an Easter service organised by the diocese. This
was for Christian prisoners, not more than two dozen, all male
adults and mostly serving sentences for petty crimes. Bishop Mano
Rumalshah usually presided on these occasions, which took place
each Christmas and Easter. The diocese also had a prison liaison
officer, the Revd Rashid Nazir, who became diocesan secretary
after the bishop retired in December 2009.

The Easter Sunday services began at sunrise with a communion service attended by more than 2,000 worshippers; a second service attended by as many or more took place mid-morning. These were normally led by the bishop and the cathedral priest (effectively a dean, though not in name) – the Revd Joseph John – a caring and committed priest, though rather timid, who was invited to the college at regular intervals to conduct communion services. There was always at least one other cathedral priest present, and we shared the distribution of bread and non-alcoholic wine between us – quite an exhausting task with such huge congregations.

On Christmas Day and Easter Sunday, I was expected to conduct a communion service in English. Congregations for these services seldom reached two dozen, but always included Professor Alwin Edwin and his family, whom I made use of for the readings and intercessions. Alwin has consistently reminded me of these seasonal events by email since I left. I couldn't help thinking how much more appropriate it might have been for either him or Donald Joseph to have done the job of principal instead of me. Both were academically excellent, good teachers, capable administrators and absolutely trustworthy – Donald's premature death soon after I left was a great loss to both college and diocese.

* * * * *

The first indications of a Christian presence in the subcontinent are associated with St Thomas, who is believed to have been brought before King Gundaphar (Gondophares – the name is spelled variously) at his capital, Taxila, a small city about 30 kilometres to the north-west of Islamabad. This might have occurred around the middle of the first century CE. St Thomas could have travelled to Taxila along one of the eastward trade routes collectively known as the Silk Road, continuing southwards to a Jewish synagogue in Kerala. This would have been consistent with the apostolic practice of preaching the Christian faith initially to the Jews.

Independently of the St Thomas tradition there is evidence of Christianity in Balochistan, Sindh and the Punjab by the end of the seventh century, which may have been the result of evangelism by Persian Christians.

By the sixteenth century European missionaries were in evidence, and in 1597 Jesuit missionaries based in Goa built the first Roman Catholic church in the Punjab, in Lahore. The period of British colonial expansion saw a considerable growth in missionary activity, initially limited to such as the East India Company chaplains, but eventually centred on schools, colleges and hospitals throughout the subcontinent.

British missionaries were of a high calibre and some, like William Carey and Henry Martyn, did impressive work translating the Bible into vernacular languages (Carey was also a capable botanist). Martyn, who translated the Bible into Urdu, made an entry in his diary relating to the Qur'ān stating that he 'felt much shame at being obliged to confess much ignorance of many things which I ought to know'. He urged his colleagues to recognise 'eastern ways of seeing, imagining and reasoning'.

The first Scottish missionary to what is now Pakistan, Thomas Hunter, came to Sialkot in January 1857. Both he and his family were killed during the Sepoy uprising later that year. The parish church in Sialkot, Hunter Memorial Church, is named after them. Relations between the British and their subjects hardened during the second half of the nineteenth century, though the first Anglican bishop of Lahore, Thomas Valpy French, was noted for his familiarity with vernacular languages. These British missionaries not only served in the areas of evangelism, health care and education, but they were also much concerned about civil rights, and even supported the move for independence from British rule. Sir Herbert Edwardes, in whose name Edwardes College was founded, was like-minded.

* * * * *

The Church of Pakistan belongs to the United and Uniting family of churches, and came into being in 1970 as the result of the union of four churches: Anglican, Methodist, Lutheran and Presbyterian (Scottish). The United Presbyterian Church did not join, though it was involved in the negotiations.

Initially, the united church was divided into four dioceses: Lahore, Karachi, Multan and Sialkot, but in 1980 four new dioceses were created: Hyderabad, Raiwind, Faisalabad and Peshawar. There are therefore eight active bishops in Pakistan, one of whom is elected moderator for a three-year term. The total membership of the church is approximately half a million and there are about 600 clergy or pastors. The United Church of Pakistan is the second largest church in Pakistan after the Roman Catholics.

Edwardes College was originally owned by the Church Missionary Society, but in 1956 it was handed over to the Lahore Diocesan Trust Association (LDTA) along with other properties. However, the Deeds of Transfer stipulate that former CMS properties should be used only for the purposes for which they were originally intended. Some church leaders have maintained that these stipulations are relics from the colonial past and that they are entitled to do what they like with these properties. But the courts have been more stringent about such conditions where consequent disputes have arisen. One such case involved the Mission Hospital in Peshawar. The diocesan leadership wanted to sell a central plot of land to a supermarket chain. The foundations were dug before legal objections from within the diocese and by the Cantonment Board were sustained. A huge gaping hole remains to this day.

In 1972/73 the federal government of Z. A. Bhutto attempted to nationalise all private educational institutions. But the NWFP government resisted, and clever manoeuvring by the then principal of Edwardes College, Phil Edmunds, secured a partial nationalisation whereby the Governing Board was reorganised with the Governor as chair and the bishop, who had previously been chair, as one of two vice-chairs. The bishop was the Bishop of Lahore. (The Diocese of Peshawar came into being only in 1980.)

The membership of the new Edwardes Board is specified on the Notification issued by the provincial government, but both the Ordinance which accompanied it and the Memorandum of Understanding between Dr Edmunds and the Governor have disappeared. When Governor Owais Ghani asked me to find a copy of the Ordinance, I searched the provincial archives for several hours with two colleagues to no avail. The Notification was there, but the Ordinance had gone.

The college constitution should have been revised when the Board was restructured, but it was not, with the result that it reads as a curiously hybrid document – still with the Bishop of Lahore as chair with consequent responsibilities, such as the appointment of principals, when in fact he had been supplanted by the Governor. Presumably this meant that the Governor was ultimately responsible for the terms and conditions of principals, but that was not how the bishops subsequently chose to understand it.

During the early part of the summer of 2009 the diocesan director of education, Humphrey S. Peters, had been ordained deacon. Normally this should have been done at a ceremony in Lahore cathedral with other candidates for the ordained ministry following two or three years of training at St Thomas' Theological Seminary in Karachi. But on the basis of the British colonial practice of Letters Dimissory from the Bishop of Peshawar to the Bishop of Oxford, it occurred in Oxford following an extremely brief period of training at Ripon College Cuddesdon theological college. The moderator of the Church of Pakistan, Samuel Azariah, later told me that it was done without his knowledge and that of the national synod, which might not have agreed. Neither would the Bishop of Oxford, had he known that within eight months of his ordination to the diaconate Peters would become Bishop of Peshawar following Bishop Rumalshah's retirement. (According to the by-laws of the Church of Pakistan, a deacon or priest can be considered as a bishop only after eight years of service.) When the Bishop of Oxford did find this out, he told a retired bishop in the UK that he was 'utterly devastated'.

* * * * *

On 31 August 2009 I wrote to Bishop Rumalshah informing him that my contract was due to end the following day. He did not reply, and so I sent a copy of his original appointment letter to the Governor's office with a covering note. A few days later the secretary for higher education, a Board member, phoned to say that my contract had been extended. The Governor had asked his staff to contact the Board members, and they were in favour.

'How long is this extension for?' I queried.

'Until the next principal comes,' was the reply.

I decided to press the matter further.

'And is the Governor himself happy with my performance?'

'Very much so,' was the reply.

Shortly before the middle of the month the bishop swept into my house clutching an official letter. He had had a 'robust' conversation with the Governor about my extension, and this letter was the outcome:

DIOCESE OF PESHAWAR

CHURCH OF PAKISTAN

      BISHOP MANO RUMALSHAH

14 September 2009

Dr David Gosling,
Principal,
Edwardes College,
Peshawar

      Extension of Service Tenure

Dear David,

Grace and Peace. I am sorry to be writing this rather late, but it is due to the fact that I was on sick-leave and have resumed my duties only couple of days ago. However, after due consideration and consultations I am offering to extend your tenure as the Principal of Edwardes College Peshawar, until 30 June 2010. This will be effective retrospectively as from 1 September 2009, rest of the terms and conditions of your appointment agreement will remain the same.

We thank you for your time at the College so far, but I am sure we are all aware that currently the College is going through its darkest period due its financial crises. We do hope that under your continuing leadership, it will recover from this fiasco and move forward with renewed purpose and hope. We further hope and pray that this College will

continue to serve the young people of this region with
selfless devotion and that its integrity will be restored for the
good of us all and in honour to our God Almighty.

So we on behalf of the whole Diocese of Peshawar offer you
our full support as you continue to respond to this challenge
under God.

With prayers and good wishes

[signature]

+Mano Rumalshah

Bishop of Peshawar

CC:

> *His Excellency the Governor of NWFP: Chair Edwardes*
> *College Peshawar*
>
> *The Secretary of Education: Diocese of Peshawar*

This was not what I had been told, but it was reasonably complimentary, so I decided not to argue. I assumed that the termination of my contract was timed just before the 2010 admissions so that Humphrey Peters could push poor quality candidates into the college without my resistance. However, the discrepancy between the Board's decision as communicated by the secretary for higher education and the bishop's letter became more mysterious when I met the vice-chancellor of Peshawar University some time later. Referring to my contract extension, he commented: 'We all signed it' – meaning presumably all Board members. If so, then what had happened to that document, which I never saw, and what did it specify, if anything, as the duration of my extension? I never found out.

Another problem concerned my work permit, which was given by the federal government and was due to expire in January 2010. I had originally entered Pakistan with a tourist visa and was told by the bishop that I should consult Humphrey Peters about a work permit. Peters told me that although my predecessors as principal had had three-year work permits, the government had changed the rules and foreigners now had to reapply each year. This was not true, but I didn't know that until my Intelligence Bureau minder pointed out that the original rules still applied. This was confirmed by Peter Armacost, the principal at Forman Christian College in Lahore, when I visited him; he also told me that although their college constitution stipulates that the principal must be a Christian, the appointment is done entirely by academics with no involvement on the part of any churches.

When I discussed these issues with Dr Nasser Ali Khan, the Old Edwardian Board member, he advised me to ask the Minister for Higher Education, also on the Board, to put in a request on my behalf to the federal authorities for an extension of my work permit. He agreed, and my work permit was extended to cover the whole of the following year (2010). This meant that my precise departure date could be negotiated with the Board without the additional complication of yet another extension – which involved lots of form filling and visits to Islamabad. But I was annoyed with Humphrey Peters for misleading me. At any rate, I had both my contract and my work permit extended until well into the following year.

* * * * *

While it seemed incongruous to have a contract in any higher education institution authorised by a church functionary, I had learned to live with such paradoxes over the years.

When I was a postgraduate physics student at Manchester University, churches had seemed far removed from our philistine world. At Cambridge I existed between Ridley Hall, an Anglican college to which I had been assigned to train for the ministry of the Church of England, and the newly established Fitzwilliam College of Cambridge University, through which I was to obtain a degree in theology (the Archbishop of York, Donald Coggan, a kindly if austere Evangelical, felt that I should do a theology degree to complement my physics qualifications).

This double existence between the two institutions suited a group of us well; if looked for in one, it was assumed that we were in the other, and vice versa. In reality much of our time was spent in the Granta pub! I also rowed for my college. But I made good friends with K. Azariah, a south Indian Christian with whom I was to spend several Christmases at his home near Dornakal in Andhra Pradesh. I also made the fleeting acquaintance of Rajiv Gandhi, who had joined Trinity College to read engineering and who was to become prime minister of India. He was affable, a bit shy for a 'Dosco' (i.e. a product of the ultra-British Doon School in Dehra Dun) and somewhat dominated by his Italian wife-to-be Sonia.

I was deeply impressed by some members of the divinity faculty, especially C. F. D. ('Charlie') Moule, who took me for long walks round the Botanic Garden, expatiating on its various fauna and flora, and Donald M. Mackinnon, who thundered about a range of existential conundrums to admiring audiences of self-confident undergraduates.

But it was Simon Barrington-Ward, dean of Magdalene College, who supervised early church history, who sensed my unease about the institutional church. He had himself taught at Ibadan University in Nigeria and was familiar with similar educational ventures such as St Stephen's College in Delhi. 'A Christian foundation which has become essentially secular – they will welcome you as a physicist,' was how he put it.

St Stephen's College had been founded by Cambridge missionary academics, and the Cambridge Mission to Delhi (CMD) had been set up to fund travel between the two centres. I met John Nurser, dean of Trinity Hall and secretary of the CMD committee, and then an elderly lady in an attic in Tufton Street, close to Westminster Abbey, who booked my air ticket. The Archbishop of York had no problem with my going to India 'for a year', he suggested.

Meanwhile war had broken out between India and Pakistan, and I had been booked on an Indian airline from Heathrow to Delhi. As we cruised across the Arabian Sea the pilot solemnly announced that as we were entering a war zone, we should kindly switch off our reading lights. I ordered another glass of wine, and acquiesced.

The years in India were – as Simon Barrington-Ward had indicated – free from overt involvement with the churches. In St Stephen's College, chapel was the responsibility of their splendid chaplain, Daniel O'Connor, capably supported by his wife Juliet. The Bishop of Delhi was Fred Willis, a dynamic Irishman who went everywhere on a sturdy bicycle, unleashing a stream of Punjabi expletives on any unsuspecting bus or taxi driver who challenged his right of way.

The college chapel was attractive and there was a branch of the Student Christian Movement, which invited several provocative speakers such as Nirad C. Chaudhuri. The nearest English-speaking church was St James, Kashmere Gate, which had been founded by Colonel James Skinner, a former mercenary recruited by the British military. There was also the Cambridge Brotherhood of the Ascension, an Anglican community run by a group of high-church priests who included Ian Weathrall, James Stewart and Amos Rajamoney, whose social activities included the organisation of a rickshaw drivers' trade union. There was a corresponding women's community nearby in Rajpur Road, which was associated with such medical luminaries as Dr Ruth Roseveare – in this respect the Indian churches were generally more progressive than their Pakistan counterparts, though Dr Ruth Coggan, the daughter of the Archbishop of York, worked as a surgeon at Pennell Memorial Hospital in Bannu for more than 20 years.

Outside Delhi I met and was impressed by Bede Griffiths, with whom I stayed at his Kerala ashram; M. M. Thomas, who helped me with a research programme during my second stay in India, in Bangalore, and Father Windey, a Belgian Jesuit who taught a group of us from St Stephen's how to blast wells in Bihar during the 1967 famine and drought (we nicknamed him Father Dynamite). During my second period in India I met Subhir Biswas, the dean of Calcutta cathedral, and travelled with him around his relief projects across the border following the establishment of Bangladesh in 1971. I also met Mother Teresa, who seemed to take an instant dislike to me and handed me over to one of her sisters to look around their work.

Figure 23 St John's Cathedral, Peshawar

I lived in India for three periods totalling nine years, the most recent being from 1995 to 1998, and therefore had more opportunities to observe the local churches there than while in Pakistan. But the quality of leadership and of church life generally appeared to be consistently better in the former than the latter. Admittedly, India is much larger than Pakistan, but I cannot think of more than a handful of Christian leaders in Pakistan as charismatic as their Indian counterparts – for example, Shahbaz Bhatti, the Roman Catholic federal Minister for Minorities, who was killed in 2011, Anwar Barkat and Priobala Mangat Rai, principals of Forman Christian and Kinnaird colleges respectively, and the former Bishop of Lahore, Alexander John Malik. Among foreigners might be numbered Ruth Coggan, G. D. Langlands and Ron Pont. Maybe others, such as former moderator Bishop Arne Rudwin, a Norwegian Lutheran, but not many more. But among the young Christians who passed through Edwardes College several possessed the kind of leadership qualities that the Pakistan churches badly need to enable them to display less of a siege mentality.

* * * * *

Every time I went into Edwardes College chapel (which was attached to the principal's house) I was aware of the foundation plaque dedicated to the Church Missionary Society in Britain. I was therefore surprised after some time not to have received any communications from the CMS – with which I had had friendly relationships for many years – and therefore I wrote to them.

The response from a senior executive of the Society, who has asked not to be named, was unexpected:

> You have my every sympathy! […] Robin [Brooke-Smith] was a friend as well as colleague and I knew some of his agonies as principal. These also continued under Huw [Thomas] from USPG (which the Bishop used to end the CMS era). We also withdrew from working directly with the diocese in general and Humphrey Peters in particular because of financial mishandling and lack of accountability (monies sent were not utilised for the given purpose). So we have kept a cautious distance […] I do believe if Humphrey Peters is made bishop it will be disastrous. (He has already functioned as a sort of 'lay bishop' running everything with almost unbridled power.)

By the time of this email (11 December 2009) Humphrey Peters was well on the way to becoming bishop.

My immediate predecessor, Huw Thomas, had been associated with the USPG, which may be designated as the 'high church' equivalent of the CMS, and they shared the same building in London until the CMS moved to Oxford.[1]

I had been a member of the USPG General Council for ten years, but did not want a formal link with them in Pakistan on account of their historic association with the missionary movement. This also suited them because their funds were at a low ebb and in any case Edwardes College was willing to pay my air fares plus a reasonable salary.

In Delhi, soon after I had arrived some years earlier, the Indian Government had announced that all foreigners working in church-related colleges would have to apply for missionary visas. I was summoned by a pro-vice chancellor of Delhi University (a Hindu) and asked why I should not be classified as a missionary. I showed him a monthly pay slip from St Stephen's College and explained that I taught physics. 'Then you are not a missionary,' he concluded.

I did not want to undergo a similar cross-examination in Pakistan, and I therefore avoided formal association with both the CMS and the USPG. To be fair to them, neither would have subscribed to the historic connotations of the term 'missionary', and both support high-quality educational and developmental activities in the subcontinent. My earlier Cambridge mentor Simon Barrington-Ward became General Secretary of the CMS, following the prophetic John V. Taylor, and the USPG was nurtured by the saintly Martin Heath. But where the Diocese of Peshawar was concerned, there were problems in relation to both these Anglican societies and the Church of Scotland. Granted that the CMS acted responsibly in severing its relationship with the diocese once financial irregularities had been detected, it remains a mystery why they did not tell the USPG and the Church of Scotland. And the latter pair can be criticised for ignoring later evidence about the systematic embezzlement of their funds.

Figure 24 Palm Sunday at St John's Cathedral

9

Trials and Tribulations

'Sir, money has been disappearing from the staff provident funds,' explained an agitated Nasim Haider on the Monday after Easter 2009.

'How much is missing?' I asked routinely.

'Sir, we are not sure because some of the Post Office passbooks have disappeared.'

I began to put together the various pieces in this financial jigsaw. I had never understood why the college staff deposited their monthly pay in Post Office accounts rather than in banks.

'Sir,' explained Nasim, 'on the first day of Ramazan each year the banks are legally required to deduct the *zakāt* tax from all accounts. This policy was introduced by President Zia in 1980 in accordance with one of the five pillars of Islam, which is to give alms. But this law does not apply to Post Office accounts.'

I did not consider it a significant part of my responsibilities to know what college employees did with their money once they had been paid. In fact Safaraz Khan, the chief accountant and deputy bursar, had once told me that my responsibilities were academic and his team would look after all aspects of college finances. My predecessor, Huw Thomas, had told me that there were some tensions between Safaraz and the bursar.

I needed to know the mechanism whereby college employees received their pay and deposited it in their Post Office accounts.

This was done by Haroon Shahid, the ebullient assistant accountant, who took the money to the Post Office where their staff entered appropriate sums in each passbook. Most of these passbooks were kept by Haroon in a locked cupboard in the finance office.

I was never happy with the fact that college staff borrowed from their provident and pension funds – sometimes quite large sums. After some time I was able to stop this practice and restrict borrowing to advances on monthly pay. I was also uncomfortable with the custom of giving allowances to people who undertook variants on their routine jobs during regular hours. Thus, for example, a *mali* (gardener) who mowed the tennis court three times a year would be given a monthly bonus for the whole year. On one occasion, I pointed out that lawn mowing with a mechanical mower was easier than most manual jobs and offered to do it myself to save the college money.

Safaraz and the bursar presided over the allowance scheme and operated a financial fiefdom, which struck me as being highly discriminatory. Certain low-paid staff – known as class four employees – were given a few thousand rupees in honour of some family occasion (e.g. marriage or the birth of a child), while others were ignored.

Things came to a head on this front when the bursar suddenly increased his own salary by fifty per cent, specifying it as an allowance on the monthly pay sheets. I decided not to be too confrontational, approved the payment, but set up a committee chaired by Nasim Haider to review all the allowances. But when this committee called the bursar to give evidence, he made excuses and refused to attend. This was the background against which I had to deal with a huge embezzlement in college funds.

A Board meeting on 30 July set up a committee chaired by Dr Nasser Ali Khan, director of the Institute of Management Sciences in Peshawar and Old Edwardian representative, to investigate the causes of the embezzlement and make remedial recommendations in time for the next meeting, to be held within three months. It also discussed the Governor's Inspection Team (GIT) report, which tended to blame the bursar, Kanwal P. Isaacs, for the embezzlement. The Governor, HE Owais Ahmed Ghani, an

Edwardian, made no secret of the fact that he was deeply distressed by what had happened. The original one had been written by the bishop in his capacity as a Board vice-chair, and on my arrival in Peshawar he had taken me to meet the chair, the Governor. But the respective roles of these two were never clear, and I knew that when the contract of an earlier – and most outstanding – principal, Dr Ron Pont, had been terminated by the bishop, the Board had overruled the decision.

One issue that this Board meeting should have discussed, but did not, was the extension of my contract as principal, which was due to expire after three years at the end of August (when I wrote to the bishop to remind him of this fact). The original one had been written by the bishop in his capacity as a Board vice-chair, and on my arrival in Peshawar he had taken me to meet the chair, the Governor. But the respective roles of these two were never clear, and I knew that when the contract of an earlier – and most outstanding – principal, Dr Ron Pont, had been terminated by the bishop, the Board had overruled the decision.

* * * * *

During the autumn of 2009 there was a dramatic increase in the size and frequency of bombings in Peshawar – probably a reaction by the Taliban to military operations in Waziristan. A bomb in the Khyber Bazaar on 9 October killed 49 and injured 94. A week later, 15 were killed and 11 injured at the CIA's Special Investigation Unit. The third and largest of these October bombs, in the Meena Bazaar, killed 117 and injured 200; the blast occurred towards the end of our Board meeting on 28 October.

At 11am on Wednesday 28 October 2009, we solemnly took our places for an Extraordinary Meeting of the Board of Governors at the Governor's spacious residence, our humble college a stone's throw away having been deemed too dangerous for His Excellency to conduct this meeting, the main purpose of which being to receive and discuss Dr Nasser Ali Khan's Finance Committee report on the embezzlement. I had been told in advance that only full Board members could attend, so it was no surprise when a pro-vice-chancellor representing the vice-chancellor was sent out of the room. When I subsequently noted in the first draft of the minutes (the Governor sent them back three times) that 'The Chair said that this was a special meeting,' the Governor added in the margin: '[…] convened to discuss the huge embezzlement in the College pension and other accounts which had placed the very survival of this prestigious College in jeopardy; therefore substitutes […] were not allowed.'

From the outset I knew that this would be a difficult meeting.

Dr Nasser Ali Khan gave an illustrated presentation of the findings of his finance committee, which included the controller of finance at the Institute of Management Sciences, whom I had met several times. Dr Nasser pinpointed the weaknesses in the existing system and made short-, medium- and long-term recommendations of what needed to be done.

Facts had been concealed from the Board over a period of several years. This was particularly true in relation to the auditors' annual reports (especially the qualifying statements and management letters), which had not been shown either to the principal or to the Board. However – Dr Nasser continued – the Board must take its share of the blame for not asking for information. Further, the Board of Trustees for the rent revenues fund had not met since 1995.

In the ensuing discussion, the bishop urged that those accused of mismanagement (e.g. the bursar) be given the chance to explain themselves. Dr Nasser replied that they had been given questionnaires and had offered explanations to his committee. The secretary for higher education recommended that there be a combination of departmental enquiries and criminal investigations. The Governor's secretary wanted the National Accountability Bureau (NAB) to be involved. Dr Nasser responded to this last point that a NAB enquiry would automatically follow the criminal investigations (but it never did). He wanted the Governor to see both the police and the FIA reports as soon as they were available.

I avoided participating in these heated discussions as much as possible. I told the Board that the college would implement all the finance committee's recommendations, and I made a special plea for the Board to approve two new finance appointments. This was agreed.

The Governor said that the situation was a matter of 'make' or 'break' for Edwardes College and that it must be 'make'. He summarised the priorities as follows:

1   New finance staff must be inducted.

2   The Board's finance committee must play an active role in college affairs.

3   Action must be taken against those responsible. The bursar's services must be suspended and his salary stopped until the investigations were complete. Others responsible for misconduct must be dealt with severely.

As if to underline the gravity of the Governor's summation, and of his mood throughout the meeting, a huge explosion was heard outside and the meeting was swiftly adjourned.

The bishop was due to retire at the end of the year, and there was little doubt that he wanted Humphrey Peters to succeed him. Peters was elevated from deacon to priest by the bishop, and a 'college' of about a dozen diocesan representatives – all chosen by the bishop – was appointed to commend a candidate to the diocesan synod. Initially, there were two candidates – Peters and the cathedral priest-in-charge, Joseph John, but the latter withdrew because, as he explained to me, Peters would have made his life a misery had he been elected. So only one name – that of Humphrey Peters – was submitted from the diocesan to the national synod.

At one point in this process the Church of Pakistan moderator, Samuel Azariah, came to Peshawar to meet members of the diocese. I was not invited, but was told that, with his arm around Bishop Mano Rumalshah's shoulder, he informed all present that during the interregnum during which the new bishop was approved by the national synod, Bishop Mano would be his commissary and would effectively continue as previously.

It therefore came as something of a surprise when, the day after Bishop Rumalshah retired on 15 December 2009, a notice signed by the moderator announced that Humphrey Peters would be his commissary until further notice. Bishop Azariah later informed me that a group of Peters' friends had driven through the night from Peshawar to Lahore and 'persuaded' him to change his mind. He told me that when he tried to discuss the matter with Rumalshah, he discovered that he had vanished – possibly to the UK – without explanation. When I met Rumalshah later at a farewell function for the British High Commissioner, Robert Brinkley, in Islamabad, he was clearly miffed by the incident. Being deprived of the continuing role of commissary meant that the bishop was not given – to the best of my knowledge – a single farewell after many years of diocesan service and as vice-chair of the college Governing Body.

* * * * *

During the first few months of 2010 – which proved to be my final ones in Peshawar – the pace of life quickened considerably. The bursar was arrested by the FIA mid-January, but allowed bail. I wasn't informed officially, but Professor Shakil Ahmad Nisar told me. Our college lawyer explained that bail-before-arrest can only be granted with the consent of the aggrieved party. I would not have opposed it but I wasn't asked.

On Monday 18 January I met the FIA regional director, Inam Ghani, in his office in Hayatabad. He was very sanguine about the whole affair:

> *Yes, it is a huge sum of money that has gone from your college. First we arrested Haroon, who admitted his guilt. He has started naming the 'big' people who helped him. We arrested Kanwal Isaacs and his signatures have been verified, but we believe that another senior church official is also involved.*
>
> *We are still investigating the chief accountant, Safaraz Khan, who is Haroon Shahid's line manager. He did not sign any authorisations for improper withdrawals of cash by Haroon, but it seems extraordinary that he never noticed any irregularities over so many years. We have also arrested two Post Office workers.*

We were urged to get our accounts audited and send a copy of the auditors' report to the FIA and notify the Governor. The next day I sent a summary of my conversation with the FIA director to the Governor, receiving a reply on 22 January urging the college to take a number of precautionary measures.

I was becoming increasingly dependent on the college lawyer, Qazi Jawad Ehsanullah, whose offices were conveniently located on Mall Road, a short distance from the college. Qazi Jawad was an Edwardian, youngish, and a graduate in law from Cambridge University (St Edmund's College); also, he had two sons in college. At one point in the following weeks he told me that the FIA investigator had approached him to say that he was being pressurised to reduce the charges against the bursar. I was also informed that the FIA prosecutor had a bad reputation and was frequently moved from court to court. The legal playing field was definitely not level.

Meanwhile, I was hard at work implementing all the proposals of the finance committee following the October Board meeting. The two main new finance positions attracted more than 200 qualified applicants, and a professional panel interviewed and appointed the best – Safaraz Khan was not even shortlisted. During this period we also revived several finance-related committees, such as the Trustees.

While all this was happening I was told that there were several legal Stay Orders against the appointment of Humphrey Peters as bishop, but in March 2010 there was a consecration ceremony in St John's Cathedral. I received an invitation to attend from Naveed Attaullah by phone on the morning itself, but since I was on the way to Swabi with Kalimullah to offer condolences to Dr Nasser Ali Khan on the death of his mother, it was impossible for me to be present. A Stay Order against the appointment drawn on the Sindh High Court was still in place when the consecration occurred; the deputy moderator (Bishop Sadiq Daniel of Karachi) did not attend, nor did he sign the moderator's later notification.

The criminal proceedings over the embezzlement against the four accused rumbled on until I received a summons to give evidence at the anti-corruption court on 5 May. It was necessary to assemble all relevant documents, which I did with the assistance of Qazi Jawad, who also briefed me on how to deal with the cross-examination from three lawyers representing the bursar, Haroon and the Post Office employees.

On arrival, I was told by the judge that I could take the oath on either the Holy Qur'ān or the Bible, but there was no Bible to hand

and I said that I would be equally happy with the Qur'ān. The first part of my evidence was concerned with the documents. The next part involved further clarification of them, then came the detailed and lengthy cross-examination. After three hours the judge permitted me to sit on a high wooden chair; after four and a half I was offered a glass of water.

I was struck by the fact that the lawyers were preoccupied with the college provident and pension accounts, which were administered by Haroon, but they were not interested in the general account, which he did not have access to. Haroon was in prison and therefore not in court; the bursar and Post Office employees were standing at the back. At the conclusion of my long ordeal, the court was adjourned. I thanked the judge and went over to the bursar to ask if he thought that my answers were accurate and fair; he replied affirmatively.

I had become rather disillusioned with the legal proceedings, which I discussed with the secretary of the Garrison Military Club, where I went several evenings a week for exercise. He suggested that I write to the Corps Commander, Lt General Masood Aslam, whom I had met socially at the Cantonment flower show and who had seemed to take a warm interest in the college. During our conversation I had offered my condolences over the death of his only son, who had been killed by a bomb inside a military *masjid* in Rawalpindi. I now wrote to him explaining my frustration with the legal processes. A colonel at the Corps Commander's office phoned to say that they had received my letter, but his boss was about to retire and he did not know what would happen.

My final Board meeting was held on Thursday 13 May at the Governor's residence. My contract was due to expire in five weeks and I had not requested an extension, but I expected the Board to at least set up a search committee for a successor before I left. I had told one of the Board members, Sarah Safdar – a professor of social work and a member of the Church of Pakistan, that she should apply for my job. But when I mentioned this to Dr Nasser Ali Khan he disagreed; she was too much 'in the pocket of the bishop' and also a cousin of the bursar.

Robin Brooke-Smith has given a dramatised account of my final Board meeting in *Storm Warning*.[1] The Governor made it clear at the outset that he had to leave by early afternoon and it should have been possible to complete the agenda by then, but the auditors' report dragged on interminably. The Governor's higher education section officer, Arif Arbab, had told me in advance that only full Board members could attend, which excluded our vice-principal Nasim Haider, and yet when I arrived at the meeting various substitutes who were never introduced were present. The Minister for Higher Education, a vice-chair, was mysteriously called away during the meeting.

I presented my annual report, which the Governor commented on very favourably (see Appendix 2). Then I gave an update on the embezzlement, which provoked some discussion and a further recommendation that the National Accountability Bureau be contacted.

'Did you realise,' asked one of the substitutes, staring at me across the table, 'that once the NAB gets involved none of us will be permitted to leave the country until they have finished?'

The Governor excused himself and left without handing over the chair to anyone. Bishop Peters cleared his throat and moved to the last item on the agenda, which was about my contract. I was asked to leave the room. By now only four full Board members were present: the bishop, Sarah Safdar (diocesan representative), Dr Nasser Ali Khan (Old Edwardians) and Kalimullah (teaching staff representative). The substitutes remained, plus the auditors' representative. After about an hour I was called back in, and the meeting closed.

Early the next day I received the following letter from Humphrey Peters:

DIOCESE OF PESHAWAR – CHURCH OF PAKISTAN
BISHOP'S OFFICE

14 May 2010
No.DoP/EC/BOG/589
The Rev. Dr David Gosling,
Edwardes College,
Peshawar

Dear David,

Your case of extension in service, including Bishop Mano Rumalshah's letter dated 14 September 2009 was discussed at the Board of Governors' meeting held on 13 May 2010. The Board of Governors, Edwardes College, Peshawar, has unanimously decided not to extend your service any more. I have been asked by the Board of Governors to inform you that you are relieved from the position of the Principal, Edwardes College with immediate effect, it means as from today (14 May 2010) you cease to be the Principal of the College.

May I request you, as per Board of Governors' decision, kindly hand over the charge of Principal to Syed Nasim Haider Kazmi, Vice Principal, Edwardes College, Peshawar. He will be the Acting Principal till further orders. You will also be required to vacate the Principal's residence.

Thank you for your time at the Edwardes College, Peshawar and may God bless you in your future endeavours.

Regards and prayers,

[signature]

+Humphrey Sarfaraz Peters,

Bishop of Peshawar,
Vice Chair, Board of Governors Edwardes College

cc.

1) *His Excellency the Governor, Khyber Pakhtunkhwa, Chair, Board of Governors, Edwardes College, Peshawar.*

2) *The Additional Secretary Education, Diocese of Peshawar, Church of Pakistan.*

3) *Syed Nasim Haider Kazmi, Vice Principal, Edwardes College, Peshawar.*

Such a decision by four Board members was inquorate. It was also illegal because under Pakistan law you must serve a 'show-cause' notice on any employee, giving them a specified period of time to respond, before terminating their contract. It was unconstitutional because the college constitution states that a principal must be given three months' notice before their contract can be ended by the Board. The claim that the decision was unanimous was a lie and it was later established in a conversation between the Governor and the British High Commissioner that the former knew nothing about the whole matter.

I went immediately to see Qazi Jawad, who told me that he could get a Court Order against the termination letter from the High Court the next day.

'It doesn't make sense, because your contract ends in five weeks anyway, and college is closed for the summer break,' he observed.

'But the bishop wants to save the bursar, who is also his diocesan treasurer,' I countered.

'And the other three Board members?' he wanted to know.

'Kalimullah may be one of the "big people" Haroon was going to name in court. Dr Nasser is his good friend and may want my job – he's an Edwardian and soon due for retirement. And Sarah Safdar is a cousin of the bursar and may also want my job,' I offered.

The next day I went to Jawad's office in order to go with him to the High Court. But his mood had changed.

'I'm sorry, but they have been to see me. I cannot go with you. The bishop's people have threatened violence if I do. Every time you have come here they have been watching.'

The threat of violence to the college lawyer, whose small office on the Mall Road could so easily be firebombed, was clearly a proxy threat of violence to me; it was at this point that I decided to leave. I therefore booked a return flight to the UK for the Thursday of the following week.

However, before I left I received an unexpected visit from Major Adnan of Military Intelligence, who explained that, following my letter to Lt General Masood Aslam, he had been asked to conduct an investigation into the embezzlement and would be giving his findings to the new Corps Commander within a couple of days. His conclusions were confidential, but he believed that I should know them.

At Major Adnan's request I called our newly appointed finance officer, who was sent back to his office to find several large payment authorisations from the main college fund. Major Adnan then invited us to compare the signatures on those authorisations – one in particular – with those on regular payments. Clearly, the first set were forgeries based on an account to which Haroon did not have access. Either the FIA had not detected these or else this information had been deliberately suppressed during the court hearing. But with the threat of violence hanging over me, I decided to leave and pursue matters through correspondence.

It remained to say good-bye to the staff at a farewell dinner. Kind words were spoken, and then it was my turn. I went through the circumstances of the previous days, noting in particular the hostile role of the diocesan leaders. In the middle of my denunciation I was interrupted by the *maghrib* prayer from a nearby minaret, so I stopped respectfully. But in that pause I understood the need to change direction, so I began to thank by name all those – church members included – who had been particularly supportive.

The next day the women's officer, Mrs Nasira Manzoor, came to my house to thank me for everything I had done for the women in college. The prison superintendent phoned, and many students came to see me. On Thursday 20 May Fayyaz, Shahzad and Changez Khan bade me a sorrowful farewell at Peshawar airport.

10

Finally – A New Beginning?

During the period following my departure from Pakistan in May 2010, the most significant events were the general elections of 11 May 2013, which brought Nawaz Sharif's Muslim League party (PML-N) to power in a coalition. The People's Party of Pakistan (PPP) were pushed into second place, and Imran Khan's Pakistan Tehreek-e-Insaf (Movement for Justice) party came third. But in the Khyber-Pakhtunkhwa provincial elections Imran Khan's PTI party swept the board largely on a programme of opposition to US drone attacks in the FATA areas and corruption in high places.

There were substantial complaints that the elections were rigged, and in August 2014 Imran Khan and his supporters marched into Islamabad and mounted a campaign for regime change. By September, he was collaborating with the radical cleric Muhammad Tahir-ul-Qadri in a major confrontation with Sharif's government, resulting in three deaths and several hundred injured. Khan believes in negotiations with the Taliban, and that the Pakistan army should withdraw completely from the FATA areas.

On 1 May 2010, a Pakistani-US American attempted to detonate a car bomb in Times Square, New York. The US Secretary of State, Hillary Clinton, subsequently warned Pakistan that had the bomb exploded there would have been 'very serious consequences'. At the end of the month, 29 May, 97 members of the Ahmadiyya community were killed at two mosques in Lahore. On 2 July, suicide bombers attacked the revered Data Ganj Bakhsh Sufi shrine in Lahore, killing 47 worshippers, and on 9 July two suicide bombers killed 102 people in the Mohmand tribal region. On 1 September, a triple suicide attack killed 65 Shi'i worshippers in Quetta, and on 5 November an attack on a Sunni mosque in Darra Adam Khel killed approximately 70 worshippers during the *jum'a* prayers.

Peshawar was relatively free from attacks during this period, but at the end of July the heaviest monsoon rains on record left 1,900 dead and more than 20 million displaced. Most of these were in the northern parts of Khyber-Pakhtunkhwa and the Swat valley. The PPP Zardari administration was strongly criticised for its failure to provide adequate relief. The Diocese of Peshawar set up centres to accommodate the refugees, though there was some uncertainty over the efficiency with which donated funds were managed. Edwardes College was not affected by the flooding.

In the early autumn of 2010, a US helicopter killed a number of Pakistani troops inside the Pakistan border; the government retaliated by closing the Khyber Pass to NATO transport into Afghanistan. Shortly afterwards WikiLeaks revealed information about the presence of US special forces inside Pakistan and the misuse of US military assistance. WikiLeaks also disclosed confidential reports by the US Ambassador to Pakistan, Anne W. Patterson, to Washington, advising against the continued use of drones in the FATA border areas on the grounds that they were counterproductive.

There were no major incidents involving Christian minorities until 4 January 2011, when Salmaan Taseer, the liberal-minded Governor of the Punjab, was shot dead for his criticisms of the blasphemy laws. His killer was one of his own bodyguards, a conservative Barelvi Muslim. On 2 March Shahbaz Bhatti, Minister for Minorities in the Federal Government, and a Roman Catholic, was shot dead by extremists. On 13 May, two suicide bombers killed 80 police recruits in Shabqadar, allegedly in retaliation for the killing of Osama bin Laden. On 20 September, militants killed 26 Shi'i passengers on a bus near Quetta.

The years 2012 and most of 2013 were relatively free from such terrible incidents in Peshawar. On 5 January 2012, militants killed 15 Pakistani frontier police after holding them hostage for several months. On 22 November, a suicide bomber killed 23 members of a Shi'i procession in Rawalpindi. On 10 January 2013, 81 people were killed by bombs in a Shi'i district of Quetta; and on 3 March, 45 people outside a mosque in Karachi were killed by one or more bombs.

On 22 September 2013, two suicide bombers killed more than 100 worshippers at All Saints' Church, Kohati Gate, in Peshawar. According to some estimates 127 were killed and 250 injured. Four of the church members killed were Edwardes College graduates, two known personally to me. An Islamist group calling itself Jundallah claimed responsibility for the attack, maintaining that Christians and non-Muslims would continue to be targeted because they were enemies of Islam. They also said that they would not stop until US drone attacks inside Pakistan ceased. The umbrella Taliban group Tehreek-e-Taliban (TTP) denied any part in the incident.

During the first quarter of 2014, there were three incidents in which a few died but which could have been more serious. Then on 8 June there were at least 24 Shi'i victims when militants attacked a bus carrying pilgrims from Iran to Quetta. On the same day at least 30 died in an attack on Jinnah International Airport in Karachi – the subsequent combat lasted for five hours during which all ten militants appear to have been killed.

There were several smaller incidents across the summer of 2014, but on 6 September there was an extraordinary attack by militants on a navy frigate, which was briefly captured before a rogue officer detonated a suicide bomb inside the ship. Apparently, the plan had been to use the frigate's missiles to attack the US Navy fleet in the Arabian Sea – an indication of how confident the militants had become! On 2 November, 60 people were killed in a suicide attack on the Wagah border close to Lahore and Amritsar.

Nawaz Sharif's government had been reluctant to crack down on militant Taliban groups in North Waziristan, close to the Afghan border. This was partly on account of predictions by Imran

Khan and others that this would lead to a backlash against 'soft' targets in the cities. But the USA and the Pakistani military favoured confrontation, and in June 2014 General Raheel Sharif ordered an operation which, by all accounts, led to the brutal repression of militants and civilians alike. Bodies were mutilated and thrown onto the roads for animals to consume.

Taliban extremist revenge was uncompromising. On the morning of 16 December 2014, nine members of the TTP entered the Army Public School in Peshawar through a back entrance, bypassing several army checkposts. They opened fire on school staff and children, killing 145 people, including 132 schoolchildren aged between eight and 18. As the killers left, one was heard to ask: 'What shall we do next?'

* * * * *

My own tribulations were of a lesser order, but I had left Edwardes College and Pakistan on account of a proxy threat of violence made to the college lawyer, Qazi Jawad Ehsanullah, on behalf of one of the vice-chairs of the college governing body, the bishop. I therefore approached Lambeth Palace, which expressed regret at the manner in which I had been treated and advised me to write to the Pakistan High Commissioner in London. This I did on 8 June 2010 by registered post, but received no acknowledgement or reply; nor was there any response to subsequent letters until early 2014, when the newly appointed head of chancery, Syed Mustafa Rabbani, an Edwardian, began to take an interest. He had been in college at the same time as Qazi Jawad, who had subsequently graduated in law from Cambridge University.

On 18 August 2010, I wrote to the new provincial Corps Commander, Lt General Asif Jaseem Malik, about the investigation into the college embezzlement conducted by Military Intelligence (MI), but did not receive a reply until after I wrote again on 29 September 2011. This reply, dated 13 October 2011, was the first written evidence that there had been an MI investigation. It informed me that the results had been communicated to the Governor the previous year, on 23 October 2010.

I had written to the Governor, HE Owais Ghani, in May 2010 about the illegal and unconstitutional termination of my contract and the threat of violence, but was not surprised not to receive an acknowledgement since I had reason to believe that his section officer for higher education was part of the conspiracy to get rid of me. On 13 September 2010 the former Bishop of Coventry, Simon Barrington-Ward, who had visited Edwardes College some years earlier, wrote to the Governor protesting at the way I had been treated. Still there was no acknowledgement or reply.

I had kept the British High Commissioner in Islamabad, HE Adam M. Thomson, informed about college matters and on 18 October 2010 I received an email from him to say that he had discussed my case with the Governor, who clearly knew nothing about the circumstances of my departure but said he would try to find out:

> *I'm grateful to you for helping to fill in my picture of what has happened [...] It is important that this story should not end on a defeatist note. Edwardes College is a jewel in Pakistan's crown. You added lustre to it. And it should not be tarnished.*
>
> *You might like to know that since I responded to Simon Barrington-Ward, I've had an opportunity to speak to Governor Owais Ghani about the situation. He assured me that he was looking into it and promised me that he would take action, reminding me that he himself had been a student of the College. I hope that this and your efforts to mobilise an independent investigation will bear fruit.*

* * * * *

During the year following my return to the UK I was invited to give talks about my time in Pakistan at several Cambridge University colleges and to the Intelligence Seminar (held under the aegis of the University's Faculty of History). A church with which I had been associated and two deanery groups were interested, and a senior representative of the Church Mission (formerly Missionary) Society who had worked in Pakistan invited me to meet him in Oxford, but I was unable to go.

However, from most of the London-based Church of England junta, there was silence. This was particularly strange with regard to the United Society for the Propagation of the Gospel. I had been a member of the USPG General Council, and during my time in Peshawar had become aware of major financial irregularities not only in the college but also in the diocesan pension funds. In spite of documentary evidence about the arrest of the college bursar/diocesan treasurer in connection with the embezzlement of college funds, the USPG were not interested. Neither was the Church of Scotland, which I knew had been giving regular financial support to Peshawar diocese.

Following my lecture to the Intelligence Seminar, one of the Seminar's sponsors, a former White House aide, asked me to contribute to a report he had been commissioned to compile for the US Defense Secretary, Robert M. Gates, who was under pressure from sections of the US Administration to be more hawkish in relation to Afghanistan. My task was to evaluate Pakistan's potential role in the Afghan endgame. The final report was completed in March 2011 and submitted before Gates left office in July. The CIA duly paid me £2,000 for my contribution.

My report is included here as Appendix 3. Some of the material contained in it is slightly dated and has been overtaken by events. However, several of the points and the recommendations remain valid. In particular, the report urges the need for education at all levels, with particular emphasis on science and vocational technological studies as a priority throughout the Pakistan/Afghan region.

* * * * *

My letters to the Pakistan High Commission in London drew a blank, and so on 30 June 2011 I wrote to the Prime Minister of Pakistan, Yousaf Raza Gillani, setting out my concerns about the college embezzlement and the failure of various authorities to take appropriate action. I enclosed relevant documents, including the British High Commissioner's email relating to his discussion with Governor Owais Ghani and a second letter from Bishop Simon

Barrington-Ward to the new Governor, Syed Masood Kausar, who had taken office in February 2011. I copied my letter to the British High Commissioner and the Archbishop of Canterbury.

On 6 August 2011, I received a letter from the Prime Minister's Secretariat as follows:

Prime Minister's Secretariat

Prime Minister's Overseas Grievances Wing

Islamabad

PMS/OGW/599/UK/11   *6th August 2011*

Subject: REQUEST FOR INVESTIGATION OF FINANCIAL IRREGULARITIES IN EDWARD'S [sic] COLLEGE PESHAWAR

Please find enclosed herewith petition received from Dr David L. Gosling, residing in United Kingdom on the abovementioned subject.

2)   You are requested to take an appropriate action on the petition in accordance with the relevant rules and policy. This Secretariat may kindly be informed of the outcome at the earliest.

[signed]

(Muhammad Sadiq Sanjrani)

Chief Coordinator

The Director General,
Federal Investigation Agency,
Islamabad.

Copy to: Dr David L. Gosling, University of Cambridge, Clare Hall Cambridge, CB3 9AL, United Kingdom.

So it was back to the Federal Investigation Agency (FIA), but at a higher level than the provincial FIA investigators who had initially handled the embezzlement case. I was undergoing surgery and was unable to write to the FIA until 20 October 2011. My letter gives a concise state-of-the-art account of the embezzlement situation just over a year after I had left the college:

CLARE HALL CAMBRIDGE CB3 9AL

University of Cambridge

Dr David L. Gosling

20 October 2011

Director General
Federal Investigation Agency
Islamabad

Dear Sir

I am in receipt of a copy of the communication to you from the Prime Minister's Secretariat dated 06.08.11, reference PMS/OGW/599/UK/11. The communication was signed by Muhammad Sadiq Sanjrani, Chief Coordinator.

I wish to draw to your attention the attached letter dated 13.10.11 sent on behalf of the Corps Commander 11 Corps, resident in Peshawar, concerning the embezzlement of 6 crores of rupees from the accounts of Edwardes College, where I was Principal from 2006 until 2010.

This letter confirms the fact that Military Intelligence (MI) conducted an investigation into the embezzlement. The results may be confidential, but the MI investigator came to tell me that his findings concerning forged signatures contradicted those of the anti-corruption court which acquitted three of four accused, including the former bursar of the college, who had earlier been arrested by your Peshawar FIA. I believe that those court proceedings, directed by your FIA prosecutor, Mr Ikramullah, were improper, and that in the light of the MI findings you should now order a retrial of all four accused.

In addition to the new evidence of MI not presented to the court, the following points are relevant:

1)   The main accused, Mr Haroon Shahid, the assistant accountant who handled the stolen cash for 7–10 years, was tortured by your officials into making a confession. I saw his injuries, as did my secretary,

*when I met him in the prison hospital. He had a right
to withdraw his confession, but was denied that right
by a judge who acquitted all three other accused
before the evidence was completed.*

2) *Your FIA investigator in Peshawar complained to our
college lawyer that he was being pressurised by your
FIA prosecutor, Mr Ikramullah, into reducing the
evidence against the former college bursar, Lt Colonel
(rtd) Kanwal P. Isaacs. Mr Ikramullah has a bad
reputation in Peshawar legal circles and keeps getting
transferred from court to court. He invited me out for
lunch, which may seem innocent enough, but here in
the UK we have a saying that there is no such thing as
a free lunch. Maybe you have it in Urdu.*

3) *Neither our college lawyer nor I was notified that
Colonel Kanwal P. Isaacs had been granted bail before
arrest. A small point, but indicative of a bias in his
favour at the outset.*

4) *You will note that the Corps Commander sent the MI
report to former Governor Owais Ghani on 23.10.10,
but the Governor took no action. I believe that there
was a conspiracy among a small group of members of
the Board of Governors of Edwardes College to cover
up the embezzlement. The former college bursar is
also the treasurer of the Diocese of Peshawar [...] I
believe they pushed me out of my job to halt the
criminal proceedings against the bursar, and so far
they have largely succeeded. But both the college and
the diocese will benefit if justice is done and the guilty
are punished. (Incidentally, when I went for advice
about my dismissal to the college lawyer – a
Cambridge graduate – he told me that he couldn't help
because he had been threatened by an interested party
in the embezzlement!)*

5) *At my last Board of Governors meeting in May 2010 it
was decided to approach the National Accountability
Bureau. But once I had gone the college has refused
to take this action, and there have been no further*

Board meetings. The former bursar continues to live illegally on the college premises and claims that the courts totally support him.

6) *I have written to the new governor, HE Barrister Masood Kausar, to request him to send to you the Military Intelligence report, the contents of which have been communicated verbally to me, and I hope that when you see this you will order a retrial of all four accused. May I respectfully suggest that both Military Intelligence and the Governor's Inspection Team (GIT) be involved in the retrial.*

Yours sincerely

[signed]

David L. Gosling (Dr)

cc Prime Minister's Secretariat

There was no immediate response to my letter; when the reply eventually arrived, it came as something of a surprise.

* * * * *

Following a lecture by General Pervez Musharraf in June 2011 at the Cambridge University Union Society I asked a question about science education, in the course of which I mentioned my role at Edwardes College. He asked me afterwards for further details about my time in Peshawar and at my suggestion agreed that I should visit him in London. The meeting took place on 4 November at his London residence.

General Musharraf explained that he had been a student at Forman Christian College in Lahore. He had visited Edwardes College twice in a private capacity, but not as president. We discussed distinctive features of the college such as its ability to attract the best students in the science areas, especially engineering and computer science. I pointed out that Edwardes had been the first college in the province to introduce a degree-level course in computer science, and that the first woman to be admitted to the college was a student in this subject.

Musharraf acknowledged the importance of women's education and the significance of the college with regard to its closeness to the FATA tribal areas. He asked if I knew Major Geoffrey D. Langlands, the British principal of the secondary school, recently renamed after him, in the mountainous region of Chitral. I said that I had visited the school and also admitted some outstanding pupils from there to Edwardes College – including Asif Zaman, with whose family I had stayed. We agreed that independent schools and colleges had played a vital role in Pakistan in maintaining high academic standards and must be encouraged to continue to do so. He explained that the government increasingly wanted universities to be federally funded and the colleges provincially funded.

During tea I showed Musharraf some photographs taken during my time in Peshawar, including the bombing of Chowk Yadgar close to the college, which killed 117 people.

'Was that the college?' he asked, referring to the carnage.

'It could have been,' I replied.

I also showed him my two-page Urdu death threat, which he read carefully.

'This is not from the main Taliban,' he observed. 'Probably a local branch of extremists inside Peshawar – but a serious threat.'

I asked if he remembered a missile in 2006 while he was still president, which killed 85 *madrasa* boys in Bajaur and led to the cancellation of a visit to the college by Prince Charles.

'It was a US drone,' he responded.

'But your government didn't say that at the time,' I replied.

'What was the *madrasa* being used for?' he queried.

I replied that according to college students from Bajaur there was no militant activity anywhere near that *madrasa*.

I had been asked by the US academic who had commissioned my report about my time in Pakistan, to question General Musharraf about his government's alleged support for the Haqqani network based in North Waziristan. But when I raised this issue with Musharraf, he shrugged his shoulders, so I decided to change the subject back to education. Would he clarify the policies that he had set out in 2002 when he replaced the University Grants Commission (UGC) with the Higher Education Commission (HEC)?

Musharraf explained that the UGC had been cumbersome and ineffective. He had therefore replaced it and had constituted a fund, backed by Saudi Arabia, designed to promote education and health care and to reduce poverty. He believed Information Technology (IT) must be made available everywhere in Pakistan and this meant that there should be a technical school in every *tehsil* in the country. While president, he had partially implemented a collaborative plan for several technological and vocational universities with foreign assistance.

I said that I had already heard about this from Professor Haroon Ahmed, former Master of Corpus Christi College in Cambridge University, who had been very disappointed when Musharraf left office and the new PPP government abandoned the plan.

'We had guaranteed financial assistance from France, Germany, Sweden, Austria, Japan, South Korea and possibly other countries – but not Britain or the USA,' he continued, adding that Dr Atta-ur-Rehman, Pakistan's most distinguished scientist and a Fellow of the Royal Society, had also been involved in the scheme. 'Preparations had reached the stage at which former airports had been cleared to create university campuses – all abandoned as soon as I stepped down as president.' He was clearly sad at what had happened.

Bearing in mind the article I had been commissioned to write about the future of Afghanistan I asked if he considered that a comparable programme might be appropriate there; he replied, 'Possibly, yes.' I pointed out that some of our brightest students at Edwardes College came from *madrasa*s – did he think that his technological plans should have included them? The answer was affirmative.

I presented the General with a copy of my book about Einstein and Tagore, apologising for the reference to India in the title when, in fact, I was writing about the entire subcontinent.[1] Thumbing through the pages he commented approvingly on the inclusion of sections about Syed Ahmad Khan and Muhammad Iqbāl.

Figure 25   Meeting General Pervez Musharraf in London in November 2011

As I was about to leave I mentioned the problems at Edwardes College concerning the embezzlement of funds, and showed him the letter I had received from the Corps Commander's office confirming that there had been a Military Intelligence investigation. He read it carefully and offered to facilitate meetings for me with the Director General of the FIA or the Minister for the Interior if either visited London. He concluded by telling me that he planned to return to Pakistan in March 2012. Upon his eventual return – which was delayed – he was debarred from taking part in elections, and in March 2014 was charged with high treason for implementing emergency rule in 2007 and suspending the constitution.

* * * * *

There were several significant developments relating to Edwardes College and the Church of Pakistan during the period 2011-14, culminating in the appointment by the Board of the college's first Pakistani principal, who took up office on 16 December 2014 – the same day as the terrorist attack on the Army Public School, which claimed the lives of many children. We shall consider some of these developments, not necessarily in chronological order.

During my final year at Edwardes College I had become increasingly aware of divisions within both the Diocese of Peshawar and the wider Church. On one occasion I was visited by Bishop Peter Majeed of the Northern Diocese of Mardan, an hour's drive to the north of Peshawar, who told me why he had separated from the main diocese. He had trained for the ministry at St Thomas' seminary (Church of Pakistan) in Karachi, pursuing further studies in Norway prior to taking up a position at St John's Cathedral in Peshawar and then another at the Sarhardi Lutheran Church in Mardan. Quarrels between church leaders in Peshawar and Mardan led to a territorial split between the former Anglicans and the Lutherans, and Peter Majeed was eventually consecrated bishop of Mardan by bishops in the Norwegian Lutheran Church. On 27 September 2012, there was an article in *Dawn* about disturbances between two rival church groups in Mardan relating to an embezzlement of donated funds.[2]

There were further problems between the church in Peshawar and the Diocese of Karachi. I met Sadiq Daniel, one of two Karachi bishops, at a Peshawar diocesan triennial at which he was the chief guest. Or so I assumed when Bishop Mano Rumalshah handed me a memorial plaque and pointed to him. I had become familiar with these occasions, and so I placed the plaque in the visiting bishop's hands, turned and smiled as everyone applauded.

To my surprise the bishop handed the plaque back to me, and smiled to the applauding audience. Clearly, he thought that I was the chief guest – I could see that Bishop Rumalshah was looking worried. Not to be outdone, I handed the plaque back, moved several feet away, gave a huge smile and began to clap furiously. Thankfully, the uncomprehending audience continued their applause without a break.

A Pakistani Anglican priest whom I met in 2014 while he was working in London explained the reason why there are two bishops of Karachi as follows: 'The difference is very simple. One was elected but not appointed; the other was appointed but not elected.' What this amounted to was that Ijaz Inayat (from the Lutheran tradition) had received more votes in the episcopal election than Sadiq Daniel (with an Anglican background). The Anglicans proceeded to claim that the election was rigged and appealed to the then Archbishop of Canterbury, George Carey, to adjudicate. Carey decided in favour of Sadiq Daniel, who was therefore consecrated bishop. But Ijaz Inayat had already moved into the bishop's house and remained there, supported by a large following.

At one point in these shenanigans, Sadiq Daniel was arrested on trumped-up charges of molesting a woman in a church hostel. The moderator, Bishop Samuel Azariah, told me that he rushed from Lahore to Karachi to get him released from prison.

I never met Ijaz Inayat, but saw him once on the British Channel 4 News, clearly identified as Anglican Bishop of Karachi. Bishop Ijaz was responsible for a Sindh High Court Stay Order against the consecration of Humphrey Peters as Bishop of Peshawar. Peters' consecration took place in March 2010 in St John's Cathedral, Peshawar, and although an announcement was made that all Stay Orders had been cleared, this was not true; this particular one (Suit 970/2003) was not due for review until the following month (4 April 2010). Furthermore Sadiq Daniel, who had become deputy moderator, was neither present at the ceremony nor did he sign the authorisation. For these reasons, the opponents to the national Anglican ruling group maintained that the consecration of Humphrey Peters as Bishop of Peshawar was invalid. On the basis of the maxim that my enemy's enemy is my friend, I marvelled at the fact that Humphrey Peters was able to alienate both rival bishops of Karachi. And yet, within a few months, he had replaced Sadiq Daniel as deputy moderator!

There was also strong opposition to Humphrey Peters from within his own diocese. On 17 October 2013, following the bombing of All Saints' Church, the Shoebat Foundation (run by Walid Shoebat, a Christian convert from Islam) reported local church members as saying that 'the bishop and their priests were busy only with the funerals of their loved ones whereas the rest of the funerals were conducted by Roman Catholic and Salvation Army pastors without considering that the dead belonged to the Church of Pakistan'.[3] The same report maintained that funds sent by foreign agencies to help the victims of the bombing never reached them. This was echoed by emails I received from former Edwardes College students who worshipped at All Saints' Church.

The main leader of the opposition to Bishop Peters in the Diocese of Peshawar was Tanvir Shirazi, chair of the United Christian Committee. At a press conference at the beginning of April 2014 he described the bishop as illegal and self-proclaimed, 'making propaganda to create tension between the Muslim and Christian communities and take over Edwardes College, Peshawar'. The report in *The News* on 3 April 2014 quotes Shirazi as alleging that 'Humphrey Sarfaraz Peters wanted to appoint a man of his choice as principal of the college to embezzle funds and other assets of the institution'.[4]

* * * * *

In May 2011 a new college principal, Canon Titus L. Presler, was 'appointed' by Bishop Humphrey Peters. His appointment was made independently of the Board of Governors and without reference to the teaching staff. He was scheduled to visit the UK en route for Pakistan to take up his appointment and I had agreed to meet him close to the airport. But his flight route was changed mysteriously at the Pakistan end at the last minute. We met subsequently in Cambridge, and he also visited four other British former Edwardes principals, Huw Thomas, Robin Brooke-Smith, Ron Pont and Timothy Woolmer. But in spite of these credible initiatives on his part, his tenure got off to a bad start on account of the manner of his appointment. Another issue was that his qualifications in missiological theology were not appropriate to the needs of a college with a strong science bias and he had no prior experience of administration in any secular educational institution. Not surprisingly there were problems from the outset, culminating in his dismissal by the Board in December 2013.

My acknowledgement from the Prime Minister's Secretariat relating to the referral of the college embezzlement to the FIA had come three months after Titus Presler's arrival in college. I had written to the FIA on 20 October 2011, but it was not until the middle of the next year that I received three emails in reply. One of these, from Jia Desusa, dated 17 June 2012, announced cryptically that: 'We know what happened in Edwardes College during the embezzlement case'; this wasn't very helpful.

The other two emails seemed much more interested in Canon Presler than in anything I had complained about to the Prime Minister. On 30 June 2012, Jia Desusa informed me that the matter was being referred to the ISI:

> One of the ISI majors is taking over this case. He is currently working as an assistant to the commander of ISI in Khyber-Pakhtunkhwa. Current principal may be informed about this via email or phone. He must be warned about it. He must not come back to Pakistan and if he comes he may be put into investigation. This is a very sensitive issue and we know the consequences.

I had played no part in the appointment of my successor and saw no reason to get involved in his activities, so I did nothing. Since leaving Pakistan I had kept in touch with my former ISI minder, Inspector Qasim Zafar, but I suspected that he was too junior to be involved in negotiations between the FIA and his own organisation.

Things were not going well in the college. It had always been the custom that on public occasions, such as the Golden Night dinner in March, the proceedings began with a reading from the Qur'ān followed by one from the Bible. Titus Presler insisted that the order be reversed, whereupon all the students walked out, only returning at the request of Changez Khan, the lecturer in computer science with whom I had collaborated closely. Far from being grateful to Changez, Presler suspended him for sending me a critical email, which somehow got intercepted. Relationships between the principal and the teaching staff began to deteriorate.

The Board of Governors officially had two vice-chairs, the Minister for Higher Education and the bishop, though it was customary for the bishop to chair the Executive. Important matters were increasingly decided between the principal and the Executive without reference to the Board. The ultimate plan underlying this strategy appeared to be to remove the Board altogether and replace it with another one chaired by the bishop. This could be done by applying to the Higher Education Commission for degree-awarding status, independent of the University of Peshawar. If granted, then the chair of the sponsoring authority (i.e. the bishop) would become the chancellor of the new institution with a completely new Board of his own choice.

Not surprisingly there was opposition to this plan from within the college, especially the Edwardes College Teachers Welfare Association (ECTWA), led by Gulzar Jalal. The Old Students' Association (ECOSA) was also against the plan. But a more significant issue concerned the ownership of the college itself. Was it owned by the Lahore Diocesan Trust Association (LDTA), to which the CMS in Britain had passed it on, subject to conditions? Or did it belong to the government, which had part-nationalised it in 1974 and never given it back (unlike the case of Forman Christian College in Lahore)? I was asked by ECTWA to submit to them what documentary evidence I possessed, and this was presented together with other contributions to a variety of committees and to the High Court in Peshawar.

At about this time (early 2013), I became aware of antagonism towards me within the UK originating from the Diocese of Peshawar. Two Church of Pakistan bishops (they did not leave their names) tried to meet the President of my Cambridge college, Sir Martin Harris, to give – as they described it to the secretary – an 'alternative view' of my time in Pakistan. He refused to meet them. On 15 March 2013, the *Church Times* published a letter from Bishop Humphrey Peters responding to one from me relating to a provincial government grant to Edwardes College. The editor, Paul Handley, later told me that the bishop had originally stated that I had personally embezzled half a million pounds from the college, but he had refused to publish that part of the letter. A General Secretary of the USPG, an English bishop, told a former church-related official in London that I had left every job I had ever done 'under a cloud'. I had rocked the ecclesiastical boat and there appeared to be a coordinated campaign against me.

According to a report dated 11 December 2013 in *The News*, Titus Presler had been deported from Pakistan in November 2011 but had managed to return. But early in December 2013 'spy agencies' (presumably the ISI) visited him at the college and ordered him to leave on the grounds that his visa was not in order. Disturbances arose within the college and in late December 2013 the Board formally dismissed him, the main reasons being that he was constantly absent in the USA and that the college's results were at an all-time low.

The Board appointed a search committee chaired by the vice-chancellor of the University of Peshawar to advertise for a new principal and interview shortlisted candidates. Following this procedure three names were submitted to the Governor, who recommended Dr Nayer Fardows to the Board, which gave its approval, though the bishop had wanted another shortlisted candidate who was a cousin of his diocesan treasurer (the former college bursar). Dr Fardows, a distinguished academic, a former brigadier, and a member of the Church of Pakistan, was an excellent choice.

The Board of Governors, representing the college, the University, the provincial government – and the Church of Pakistan (even though the bishop had disagreed with the decision) – had finally triumphed, and in the process the first Pakistani principal of Edwardes College had been appointed. But one of the shortlisted candidates withdrew his candidacy, alleging that a speech given by Imran Khan in Islamabad had influenced the selection committee's choice. His petition to the High Court in Peshawar on 13 January 2015 received a positive response on 6 March requesting all parties concerned to comment on the appointment proceedings.[5]

A huge embezzlement of college funds that had been going on for many years had been stopped, though none of the stolen funds had been recovered and a major culprit was still in post. The bishop's wings had been severely clipped, the Governing Body was firmly in charge of college affairs, and a well-qualified Pakistani principal had been installed.

11

Afterword

Edwardes College was founded during the heyday of British imperialism. It was located in the military Cantonment area of Peshawar close to the Governor's palatial residence, the administrative seat of local government, the law courts and the prison. The railway station, the airport and a few colleges are nearby, though the main university campus is some distance away.

As far as the pragmatic and geographically distant colonial rulers were concerned, the creation of Edwardes and many comparable colleges was part of a master plan to train a class of intermediaries between the Raj and 'those whom we govern', to quote the imperious Lord Macaulay, one of the utilitarian architects of this far-reaching enterprise.

And yet, even from its earliest days, Edwardes College sat loose to this great vision of empire. Contrary to Lord Macaulay's 1835 diktat that the medium of instruction in colleges of higher education should be English, both Edwardes College and its sister college in Delhi, St Stephen's, initially adopted local vernacular languages for teaching purposes. Both also obtained their degrees through the University of the Punjab, located in Lahore.

There was also the influence of Christianity. Sir Herbert Edwardes, in whose name the college was founded, was a staunch supporter of the Anglican Church Missionary Society. All the principals were ordained clergy until the mid-twentieth century, when Philip Edmunds, an Australian layman, began his lengthy tenure of 23 years. The ethos of the college during these early years has been well summed up in the frequently quoted words of the Revd R. H. Noble, who was principal twice, from 1924 to 1928 and from 1948 to 1951:

> We are people of different communities, faiths and races, living in harmony and friendship. We work together and try to learn the secret of fellowship and peace. We hope our lives may be more useful and this spirit of helpfulness will enrich the province in which we live to the greater glory of God.

The final sentence contains the college motto ('to the greater glory of God'), which would be acceptable to members of most religious traditions; the quote also implies service to the province ('enrich the province'). All the college principals, including more recent ones, would have endorsed the college's role in terms of offering academic excellence to the whole province rather than to any particular section of it (e.g. the church). The Christian dimension of the college's life was envisaged by successive principals in terms of inclusiveness and service instead of the more traditional missionary concepts. In planning to give his longest speech (to be on the subject of interfaith dialogue) at Edwardes College during his visit to Pakistan, Prince Charles and his associates had chosen an appropriate venue; unfortunately, his visit never took place (see Chapter 1).

Most of the principals prior to and including the author have been British, with the exceptions of Phil Edmunds and the Revd A. M. Dalaya, who hailed from the Indian part of the subcontinent. The latter's tenure was from 1937 until 1948 – which covered World War II and Independence. Little, if anything, appears to have been written about the college during these tumultuous years. When Dalaya left, Noble returned for three more years. The shortest tenure of any principal was that of J. D. Murray, who arrived in 1978 and left a year later as a result of a mental breakdown.

All the four British principals before me made enormous contributions to the well-being of the college and are remembered

Figure 26 FATA student recipients of UK scholarships meet with High Commission staff person, Amna Jatoi

with affection by the teaching and administrative staff. Among them, Ron Pont made major improvements to the buildings and Robin Brooke-Smith was responsible for the admission of women to the college (an achievement for which he does not give himself sufficient credit in *Storm Warning*, the account of his tenure from 1995 until 2000, the year of the college's centenary).[1] Huw Thomas, my immediate predecessor, set up the department of professional studies and introduced the Higher National Diploma, to which I was able to contribute some lectures.

Three of the most recent British principals experienced difficulties with the local church leadership, which wanted the college to give unfair priority to their own community. Bishop Mano Rumalshah tried to terminate Dr Ron Pont's contract, but was overruled by the Board. Robin Brooke-Smith clashed with the diocese over the organisation of the college's centenary, and Huw Thomas left abruptly following a stand-off with the bishop lasting several months. By the time I arrived, Humphrey S. Peters, bishop-in-waiting, was gearing up for a confrontation that he was determined not to lose.

* * * * *

The nostalgic colonial ethos of the first chapter – shattered by a US drone – gave way in the second and third chapters to a dynamic account of Edwardes College as it has now become. Chapter 2 included a brief account of the local educational catchment areas from which Edwardes College draws its students; it is impossible not to remember that this includes the Army Public School, which was subjected to an appalling terrorist attack in December 2014. The inordinate amount of time spent each year over student admissions and the court cases arising from them were described, including a meeting with the Chief Justice in which he blamed the British for the overall complexity of the legal system. There is an account of an ugly – though thankfully very rare – incident between two students in the resident hostels, the role of my ISI minder in personal and college affairs, and details of the annual trip to the Murree Hills.

Chapter 3 began with an example of the stark differences that can exist between the liberal ethos of Edwardes College and the repressive realities of some students' domestic circumstances. There is a brief account of the varying social situations of women in the province, and of some typical day-to-day events in college. The chapter closed with a description of the weekly prison-visiting programme in the course of which the author was able to meet the elder statesman of Pakistan's Taliban, Sufi Muhammad.

These two chapters, and parts of Chapter 6, offered a dynamic account of the college as it has become, and it would be difficult to find an appropriate metaphor to summarise its character. It has certainly moved a long way from the utilitarian objectives of the British architects of higher education – if it ever fulfilled them. It is certainly not a 'mission' college, as politically rightist Hindus in Delhi used to stigmatise St Stephen's. It is also not a Western liberal institution. But the college as we have described it is not far removed from the vision of its founders, expressed in terms of a quality of inclusiveness and service, which owes its original inspiration to Christianity, and it is also compatible with other religions, including Islam.

It is a great pity that the leadership of the local church did not appear to understand this.

* * * * *

In Chapter 4, we considered the inception and rise of the Taliban against the background of events in Afghanistan, especially those leading up to and including the Soviet 'intervention' ('invasion' is too strong a word) in 1979. Resistance to the Soviets came primarily from orthodox Sunni tribals in the Pashtun belt, giving rise to the *mujahideen*, who played a large though not exclusive part in the Soviet withdrawal ten years later.

The *mujahideen* were backed by General Zia-ul-Haq and the USA, which viewed the Soviet involvement in Afghanistan as an extension of the Cold War. Zia expanded the ISI, which became his executive arm in his relations with the *mujahideen* and promoted the growth of *madrasas*, especially along the Pakistan/Afghan border, where new recruits could be trained. Much of the funding for this came from Saudi Arabia, and the brand of Islam that was consequently promoted was the ultraconservative Wahabi tradition.

The Taliban emerged under strong leaders, such as Mullah Omar and Jalaluddin Haqqani, and gained control of Kandahar (1994) and Kabul (1996). From its inception it was more cruel and ruthless than its later equivalent in Pakistan. Osama bin Laden established his headquarters in Peshawar, then left the region, returning from the Sudan in 1996 to Kandahar, where he and Mullah Omar consolidated a combined network, which enabled al-Qaeda to carry out global activities such as the 1998 bombings of US embassies in Kenya and Tanzania, leading to the 11 September 2001 attack on the World Trade Center and the Pentagon.

Following the US-led invasion and the fall of Kabul, many Taliban leaders took refuge in Pakistan's porous border areas. The main groupings were the Quetta Shura and the Haqqani network, geared towards the ongoing Afghan struggle, and, eventually, the TTP, earlier tributaries of which had been led by Nek Muhammad and the Mehsuds, based in Waziristan. The Swat valley Taliban, led by Sufi Muhammad and his son-in-law Fazlullah, followed a different sequence of events until 2013, when Hakimullah Mehsud was killed by a US drone (three times?), and Fazlullah assumed leadership of the TTP.

It is widely believed that the TTP under Fazlullah's leadership was responsible for the attack on the Army Public School in Peshawar in December 2014, killing 145 people, mostly children. Such appalling events raise serious questions about the credibility of Imran Khan's call for 'dialogue' with the militants. But equally the US drone attacks in the Pakistan/Afghan border areas are no solution, and, as mentioned, there is strong evidence that they are counterproductive.

Chapter 5 gave a chronological account of the security incidents that occurred mostly in Peshawar during the author's time there between 2006 and 2010. Most were bomb explosions and were within earshot of Edwardes College. The floor would shake, windows smash, and people would shout and run. The most accurate information usually came from the gate *chowkidar*s, who picked up gossip from passing vehicles or people fleeing from the scene. Where was the bomb? How many estimated dead? The *chowkidar*s knew first. But the television cameras were quickly on the scene, showing graphic images that European and other Western audiences would never have been permitted to see.

The most intense periods of bomb attacks against soft targets can be approximately correlated with military operations in Swat and Waziristan and shortly after the storming of the Red Mosque in Islamabad in July 2007. The main targets were prominent buildings (e.g. hotels), crowded bazaars and minority neighbourhoods, especially those of the Shi'is but also and increasingly those of some Christians. The author received a death threat for promoting co-education, but the general consensus, including the opinion of General Musharraf (Chapter 9), was that this was the work of an extremist group in the city, and not a threat from any Taliban tributary.

In a review of *Dara*, the story of two warring brothers at the head of the seventeenth-century Mughal Empire, in the *Independent*, Holly Williams summarises the differing interpretations of Islam on the part of Aurangzeb, a brutal fundamentalist, and Dara, a Sufi poet. Of the latter she says:

In the central trial, where Dara is accused of apostasy, [he] gives a passionate, compassionate speech on why all religions are but paths to God. He preaches tolerance, love and understanding of our shared humanity – a wonderful message.[2]

This is the kind of Islam that was represented in Chapter 6, which dealt with the religious aspects of Edwardes College. These include the observance of the Hajj pilgrimage by members of the teaching staff, Ramazan, and the Na'at celebrations. It is the Sufi tradition, based for example on the poems of Rahman Baba, which is most popular and is reflected annually in the college Pashto *mushaira*. Another inspired local leader was Bacha Khan, nicknamed the Frontier Gandhi. The influence of such people will ultimately be stronger and more enduring than the Wahabi version of Islam imported into the Pashto regions by General Zia and his backers in Saudi Arabia.

In Chapter 7, we moved away from the Pashto areas to pre-Independence Delhi and considered a Muslim college that began as a *madrasa*. The Delhi College rivalled the standards of the mission and other institutions set up in the first half of the nineteenth century, and it was associated with Muslim reformers such as Syed Ahmad Khan. Although the major renewals in Indian Islam during this period were shaped by the Deobandi and Barelvi movements, Syed Ahmad pioneered a small modernising group based initially on the Delhi College, which encouraged a critical interpretation of Qur'ānic texts, especially with regard to science. This progressive approach was continued by Muhammad Iqbāl, who, for all his militant communal sentiments, was even more willing than Syed Ahmad to accommodate scientific advances, such as Einstein's theories, within his Islamic worldview.

If we now consider together the Sufi-inspired poetic and musical Pashto culture and the more intellectually and science-based Islam of Iqbāl and others, we have some enriching alternatives to the conservatism that has often been imposed from outside. What is far more important for Muslims than any discussion with other faith systems is internal dialogue between different schools of

Figure 27 Rafiq Hussain, who came first in the FATA areas of the province in the Pre-Medical exams and is now a doctor

thought within Islam – the kind of debate portrayed in *Dara* and *Khuda Kay Liye* (which we showed in college).

* * * * *

Chapter 8 dealt with the Christian minority in Pakistan and the complex relationships, in part historical, between Edwardes College and the local church. There is no doubt that Christians are often badly treated in Pakistan, but so also are other minorities. As the superintendent of the Central Prison, Peshawar, pointed out (Chapter 3), not only are the blasphemy laws used to discriminate against the Christian minority, but *all* laws can be used to discriminate against anyone who does not have sufficient funds to pay lawyers or is not supported by some powerful group. Christians may also be increasingly discriminated against on account of their perceived association with the USA-led war against the Taliban in Afghanistan.

Compared with their counterparts in India, the Pakistan churches have failed to make major contributions to nation-building, and continue to appeal to the West for moral and material support. By contrast, M. M. Thomas, the Mar Thoma theologian, was appointed Governor of Nagaland by the Hindu rightist BJP government and could have become India's first Christian president but for his untimely death. By and large the Indian churches have responded to Nehru's challenge in 1947 to 'vindicate yourselves'.[3] The churches in Pakistan have never been confronted in this manner and have produced few outstanding leaders, with notable exceptions such as Shahbaz Bhatti, the Roman Catholic Minister for Minorities who was shot dead by extremists in March 2011.

The interests of the Church of Pakistan have been poorly served by its foreign partners, especially in Britain. The intervention of Archbishop George Carey in the internal affairs of the Diocese of Karachi has produced a split between rival groups supporting two different bishops. It was irresponsible of Ripon College Cuddesdon and a former Bishop of Oxford to fast track the ordination to the diaconate of a man destined to become a bishop in eight months, and to do this behind the back of his national church. Robin Brooke-Smith has given an account of the implications of the appointment by the USPG of a serving Pakistani bishop as their General Secretary.[4] And the persistent refusal of almost all the Church of England hierarchs in London and their Church of Scotland counterparts in Edinburgh to face up to the rampant financial corruption in Edwardes College and elsewhere, represents a gross dereliction of responsibility and a betrayal of their donors. Bland phrases, such as 'partners in world mission', are no substitute for normative procedures of accountability.

However, it should also be pointed out that the financial problems encountered at Edwardes College and in the Diocese of

Peshawar are symptomatic of broader ones throughout the south Asian region and to some extent reflect unsatisfactory relationships between local churches and their foreign supporters. Within a period of several months in 2014 three south Asian bishops – two in India (Delhi and Chennai) and one in Sri Lanka (Kurunegala) – were sacked by their dioceses for embezzling money.

This is good news in that local churches are increasingly holding their own leaders to account, but what does it say about the quality of leadership and the apparent ease with which some bishops put money into their own pockets? Few people can hear of Kurunegala without recalling Bishop Lakshman Wickremasinghe (1927–83), who made his mark on the entire Anglican Communion but refused to attend a Lambeth Conference for bishops because he would not permit what he regarded as an inordinate sum of money to be spent on his air travel. Such an attitude contrasts sharply with that of many more recent episcopal appointees for whom air tickets and foreign hospitality (always in the West) are a major reason why they want to become bishops. The Western churches are largely to blame for letting such a situation arise.

Figure 28 Letting their hair down; Edwardians on a visit to Lahore University of Management Sciences

The Western churches and their agencies, such as the USPG, need to give much more thought to the nature of their relationships with their mission and developmental partners. Why are these so consistently shaped in economic and monetary terms, when in fact – as the Indian Nobel Prize-winner Amartya Sen has pointed out – human deprivations cover a much broader range of needs and affect certain groups, such as women, in different ways? Visitors to south Asia (and elsewhere) are sometimes surprised to experience sumptuous hospitality from people officially designated as the poorest of the poor – and yet those same people may face incredible hardship when suddenly faced by illness or extortion. And church members in, say, Peshawar, who are employed – if at all – as sweepers and rickshaw drivers will never be able to take time off to vote in diocesan elections – so much for ecclesiastical democracy!

Chapter 9 included a detailed account of the huge embezzlement that was discovered in the accounts of Edwardes College and the measures taken – largely unsuccessful – to remedy it. (Part of the investigation into the embezzlement is given as Appendix 1.) At least it was stopped, but the consequences rumbled on for several years, as described in Chapter 10, culminating in a stand-off between the college governing body and the local church. This was finally resolved at the end of 2014 with the appointment by the Board of the college's first Pakistani principal, also a church member, signalling a potential new dawn for this splendid but troubled institution.

Appendix 1

The investigation of the embezzlement

Following the discovery of large sums missing from the provident and pension funds, I told the two vice-principals to investigate the missing money and recover all the passbooks, and on 27 April 2009 wrote to them, associate professor Francis Karamat and the bursar, instructing them to investigate all funds associated with Haroon Shahid, the assistant accountant. Two days later, I wrote to Haroon stating that there were deficits in a number of accounts amounting to a large sum and that if he didn't deposit the money then disciplinary action would be taken against him. On 7 May Haroon replied as follows:

The Principal
Edwardes College, Peshawar

7 May 2009

Respected Sir,

Thank you very much for your letter dated 29 April 2009.

As you know, Sir, that we are still working on it and within two or three days we will be able to see the clear picture, that how much deficit is in the accounts, and I will deposit the entire remaining amount to the college authorities, whenever the clear picture of the problem comes [...] Sir, I have only one request that to please give me one month time for depositing the deficit. I shall be thankful to you for your kindness.

Thanking you,

Haroon Shahid (Assistant Accountant)

The following day, I wrote to Haroon to tell him that a month was too long and that he must respond within seven days. By this time it was clear that money was missing from the pension as well as the provident funds. On the same day, I also wrote to the Postmaster General of the Cantonment Post Office asking him to permit Donald Joseph and Francis Karamat to check the balances of all college accounts. The following day I wrote again, specifying two particular pension accounts and several passbook entries.

The Post Office replied the same day (9 May) to give details of the balances in the two specified accounts, adding that 'nothing has been deposited on behalf of the collage [*sic*] to these accounts. The passbooks produced by the college are neither signed/stamped nor issued by the Post Office.'

Saturday 9 May was also the day on which the two vice-principals and Francis Karamat – not including the bursar, who did not sign – completed their preliminary investigation report, noting huge sums missing, as follows:

Pension fund accounts (SB 353135 and SS 187)	Rs. 20,000,000/-
College saving account (SS 427)	Rs. 35,000,000/-
General provident fund account of college staff	Rs. 5,000,000/-
Total deficit	Rs. 60,000,000/-

The report also noted that signatures for the withdrawal of funds from these accounts were forged, and – most alarming of all – that the previous day Haroon had withdrawn 1.3 million rupees from account SS 427. We notified all banks in which the college had accounts and the Post Office.

At this point I contacted the vice-chair of the Governing Body, Bishop Mano Rumalshah, who came to the college. He recommended that a First Information Report (FIR) be lodged against Haroon Shahid, and I wrote to the Station House Officer at the East Cantonment Police Station to this effect.

The police issued the FIR on Tuesday 12 May, authorising Haroon's arrest, and also recommending that he be put on the Exit Control list to stop him leaving the country. I wrote to the Governor on 13 May to inform him of these events, and the following day the Governor's Office sent me a copy of a letter to the Ministry of the Interior recommending that Haroon be prevented from going abroad. He was arrested in Rawalpindi, where he had fled with his family. The case was handed over to the Federal Investigation Agency (FIA) because Post Office staff, who were federal employees, were involved in the embezzlement.

* * * * *

Following Haroon's arrest, the pace of events slowed down considerably. The staff needed reassurance that when they reached retirement age there would be sufficient funds to pay them their dues. On a staggered basis this would be possible. The Teaching Staff Welfare Association (later registered as the Edwardes College Teachers Welfare Association (ECTWA)) unhelpfully released a press statement accusing the bursar and chief accountant of being involved in the embezzlement; this was picked up by the *Dawn* newspaper. I told the staff that there was insufficient evidence for them to make such an accusation.

I would not normally have tried to meet Haroon Shahid, thinking that this might prejudice the legal procedures, but I met him unexpectedly during a Saturday morning visit to the prison. On arrival, I was told by the superintendent that Haroon had been taken ill with a heart condition and was in the hospital wing, so I decided I could meet him on compassionate grounds. He was lying on his bed looking reasonably comfortable and invited me and my secretary, Shahzad, to sit next to him. He beckoned one of the prison assistants and ordered us soft drinks.

During the ensuing conversation Haroon showed us the bruises he had received through being beaten up by the FIA following his arrest – a fairly standard procedure, which explains why people of sufficient social standing opt for bail-before-arrest. His main concern was to tell me that he was not alone in stealing money from the college, and would name the 'big people' – as he put it – when his case came to court. In the event it took almost a year for his case to materialise, but he never gave evidence, and was released soon after I had left the country.

The Governor and the Board members had been notified about the embezzlement, and there was no urgent reason to hold a meeting until the legal proceedings were further advanced and steps had been taken to prevent future financial losses. I had to negotiate two independent enquiries by the Governor's Investigation Team (GIT) and the FIA, both of which involved filling in lengthy questionnaires and being interviewed on the basis of my replies by the investigators. The following extract from my responses to the GIT illustrates the level of detail in this process:

> *[Prior to the embezzlement] at no time has the present principal received any queries or complaints concerning the provident or pension funds. It is understood that the previous principal called in auditors in 2002 to investigate certain problems, and this led to the introduction of the Double Entry Accounting System (DEAS), which was computerised in July 2004. Until then the college had maintained books of accounts under a single entry bookkeeping system and prepared a statement of affairs instead of a balance sheet. The DEAS categorises entries under the headings of income, expenses, assets and liabilities. The computer software programme for this is the responsibility of the chief accountant.*
>
> *The principal deals periodically with issues concerning students' fees, especially where these are in dispute. He does this in collaboration with the bursar and occasionally the other college officers (vice-principals). All fee concession requests are monitored jointly by the bursar and the principal, who may also meet with students and their parents. Where fees are not paid on time, the principal is notified by the chief accountant, who issues default or struck-off notices on the principal's authority.*

Student fees are the college's main source of income, and are paid into the college main account. A computerised system is run through special software by three assistant accountants under the supervision of the chief accountant. The student fee deposits are made directly by the parents through the college's authorised bank, which is the HBL branch on Police Road.

The college's accounting procedure was based on four separate accounts, as follows:

- college main account;
- provident fund account;
- pension fund account;
- hostel mess and canteen account.

There was also a 'mission account', for which I was joint signatory with the bursar, which related to the diocese. It received funds from rent paid by staff resident in the housing colony, and could be used for fee concessions. There was also an endowment fund.

These and other details were submitted to the GIT on 23 June, and their consequent report was discussed at a Board meeting on Thursday 30 July.

The FIA questionnaire covered some of the same ground as the GIT one, but was more focused on the roles of the finance staff, who were obliged to complete similar ones. By the time I submitted mine on 4 August, Safaraz Khan was still not ready with his, and both he and the bursar appeared to be dragging their feet. At the end of my interview the FIA investigator urged me not to take any actions to protect the bursar from criminal prosecution. I said that I would continue to play an impartial role with the best interests of the college in mind.

Appendix 2

Annual report to the Board of Governors, May 2010

Edwardes College, Peshawar
PRINCIPAL'S ANNUAL REPORT TO THE BOARD
OF GOVERNORS

1   General introduction
2   Admissions
3   Academic results
4   Lecturing staff
5   Sport
6   College activities
7   Relationships with external bodies
    i.   German language classes
    ii. The UK-FATA scholarships programme
    iii. UK universities
8   Finance
9   Security
10 Conclusion
    Annex A
    Annex B
    Annex C

David L. Gosling (Dr)
Principal, Edwardes College

1 General introduction

During the last 12 months the college continued to offer academic excellence to young people of the province as an expression of service, and has largely succeeded. There have been setbacks, of which the security situation and an internal financial crisis have been paramount, but these have been largely overcome. More will be said of these presently.

Academic standards continue to rise, especially on the part of women students, and there have been substantial achievements both in terms of high marks in examinations and of academically related activities such as the national Olympiad put on by the Lahore University of Management Sciences (LUMS) and the Pakistan Young Leaders Conference at which two third-year students were nominated Leaders of the Future. One first-year student won the LUMS e-computing competition.

Students and teaching staff participated in a social welfare programme in the camps for Internally Displaced People (IDPs) in the summer of 2009, and the degree students' social work camp in Thandiani went extremely well. German language teaching was introduced as part of a substantive collaborative programme with the Goethe Institut, and the British High Commission set up a scholarships programme for Intermediate students from Federally Administered Tribal Areas (FATA) under their *Strengthening Human Resources in the North-West Frontier Province* scheme.

The Edwardian came out after many years, and the alumni *Directory* was updated (and will shortly be republished), five lecturing staff on contract were offered regular service, and three new finance staff were inducted. The principal gave the Teape lectures on *Darwin, Science and India* in Calcutta University and St Stephen's College, Delhi University, and several teaching staff published substantive articles and books in English, Urdu and Pashto. The Pashto *mushaira* was held on 31 March 2009.

The Board of Governors met three times.

On account of the security situation it was not possible to hold public functions, such as the Science and Culture Fair, but hostel students came off well with their Bara Gali first-year camp, sports and hostel nights, culminating in the Golden Night dinner at which the Speaker of the Provincial Assembly was the chief guest. More will be said about other activities later.

A new hostel has been constructed between the basketball pitch and the principal's residence. It accommodates 21 students in seven rooms. Two classrooms have been added to the lower floor of the Science Block. There are plans to replace the garages in the Arts block with a lecture room (or rooms) and to relocate vehicles at the back of the new hostel building (where there is already a gate). The college has purchased a bus, which plies every day around parts of the city, collecting and depositing students at a modest cost. Another bus, or at least a minibus, is required.

There are currently 1,870 students studying in courses ranging from Intermediate level to Masters in Business Administration. Eleven per cent are women, compared to 10 per cent last year. The detailed breakdown is shown in Table A1, as follows:

Table A1 Student enrolment in all courses: Session 2009–10

Course	Part	Male	Female	Total
Intermediate	First year	404	53	457
	Second year	441	65	506
Degree (BA and BSc)	First year	225	28	253
	Second year	178	29	207
A-levels	First year	58	7	65
	Second year	47	10	57
Higher National Diploma (HND)	Business	113	5	118
	Computing	31	1	32
Bachelor in Computer Science (BCS)	Years 1–4	113	19	132
Masters in Business Administration (MBA)	First year	15	1	16
	Second year	23	4	27
Total		1648	222	1870

Admissions to these courses are staggered, beginning with Intermediate level (Faculty of Science (FSc) and Faculty of Arts (FA)) in mid-July, then A-levels (mid- to late August), and degree levels (late September). HND admissions occur twice a year and follow the term system, and MBAs are admitted in November. Bachelor of Computer Science admissions take place in August – this is a four-year course.

2 Admissions

This year (summer 2009) first-year admissions started three weeks earlier than previously, which meant the Intermediate classes could begin on 18 August 2009. This made it possible to complete all courses on schedule in March 2010 in spite of occasional closures for security reasons. It also gave the college a better chance of securing the best applicants.

The total number of eligible students who applied for first-year Intermediate admissions was 4,298, of whom 496 (11 per cent) were enrolled (slightly fewer than the previous years). Fifty-seven of them were women. Of those admitted, 457 continued on the rolls, the remainder (8 per cent) having left or been struck off for poor attendance, low marks or ill-discipline.

The breakdown of Intermediate first-years still in college is as follows:

Pre-Medical	178 (188)
Pre-Engineering	182 (205)
Computer Science	51 (50)
Arts	46 (90)
Current total	457 (533)

Numbers in brackets indicate last year's comparable figures. The lower numbers this year reflect the overcrowding experienced last year on account of shortage of space in lecture rooms. The situation will continue until Edwardes College School moves to its new location.

Most second-year Intermediate students continue from their first year, but it is worth noting, in passing, their current breakdown, as follows:

Pre-Medical	185 (197)
Pre-Engineering	199 (189)
Computer Science	46 (48)
Arts	76 (89)
Current total	506 (523)

Figures in brackets show last year's comparable figures. Sixty-five of this year's second-years (11 per cent) are women, as compared to 53 last year (10 per cent).

Admissions were strictly according to merit, both in the open categories and within quotas (e.g. minorities, physically challenged, etc.). This enabled the college to win all court cases brought by aggrieved parents. The breakdown of all first-years according to their geographical home locations is given in Annex A. In the Intermediate figures for the three two-year periods 2007–9, 2008–10 and 2009–11, the highest collective percentages for admissions tend to be from Swabi and Kurram Agency, with Dir and Swat not far behind. Swabi is an established and fertile area, which contains the Ghulam Ishaq Khan Institute of Engineering, Science and Technology (GIKI) and the Tarbela Dam, which employ highly qualified professionals. Kurram Agency includes Parachinar, which contains a high proportion of bright intellectual Shi'as and Turi tribals who push their youngsters to work hard.

Dir and Swat can be similarly characterised, though the latter has experienced major dislocations in its local schools and colleges, which have encouraged parents to send their children elsewhere. The high collective percentage for Kurram Agency for 2009–11 (4.9 per cent) may reflect the attractiveness of Edwardes College on account of the UK's *Strengthening Human Resources in the North-West Frontier Province* scholarship scheme. It is noticeable that many of the students benefiting from this scheme are from Parachinar.

The overall FATA student percentages for admissions are in the region of 10-12 per cent. Approximately half of these may be classified as 'genuine', which means that they were schooled and domiciled in a FATA area. Otherwise, the FATA category means that they still live in a FATA area with their parents, but may have gone to school in Peshawar or, in the case of some Parachinar students, to Al-Asar Public School Usterzai Payan in Kohat (but part of Kohat is FATA and part is not, so the distinction is a fine one). All in all the college is catering for an increasing proportion of FATA students.

In first-year A-levels 100 applications were received. Sixty-six students were admitted, of whom 65 remain (58 males, seven females). Of these, twice as many do science as arts subjects (this is also true in the second year). Although a high proportion of A-level students come with good grades, a number of poorer-quality candidates obtain admission with lower marks because they can't get into Intermediate courses and because A-level admissions remain open until a late date.

The first year of the degree courses (BSc and BA) received 542 applications, of which 262 were admitted. Two hundred and thirty-two are males and 30 females. All are still on the rolls. This year applicants with lower than C grades were not admitted. There is a precedent for this at a Board meeting some years ago when it was formally decided not to pursue such a policy. However, in recent years the practice has lapsed. Following its reintroduction several D-graders who were turned down took the college to court, claiming that as 'Edwardians' they had a 'right' to admission. They lost their cases.

The Bachelor of Computer Science (BCS) degree received 100 applications, of which 50 were admitted. Thirty-eight remain on the rolls (34 male and four female). Edwardes College was the first in the province to introduce this four-year course; within the college it was the first course to admit women.

The Higher National Diploma (HND), introduced in 2003, overlaps to some extent with Computer Science in that students can opt for either Computing or Business within it. One hundred and thirty applications were received for the business component and 52 were accepted, of whom 47 remain (45 male, two female). Thirty-five applied for HND Computing, 20 were accepted and 17 remain (16 male, one female). The Diploma is validated by Edexcel in London. For a time there was uncertainty as to whether or not it is an adequate qualification for the University of Peshawar MBA. As from late March this year and following recognition of equivalence by the Higher Education Commission, this obstacle has been removed. Even before this decision, the Institute of Management Sciences in Hayatabad had accepted a good Edwardes HND as sufficient for admission to its BA (subject to a satisfactory interview).

The Edwardes MBA has been running for two years. This year they received 40 applications and accepted 17 (16 male, one female). All are still enrolled. In the most recent MBA examinations in April, Miss Heena Stephen was in the top three in Peshawar University and first in the college.

The overall admissions figures are given in Table A2:

Table A2 Admissions for the session 2009–10

Serial number	Faculty (Year 1)	Total applications	Admissions	On roll	Males	Females
1	Intermediate	4298	496	457	404	53
2	Degree	542	262	262	232	30
3	A-levels	100	66	65	58	07
4	HND Business	130	52	47	45	02
5	HND Computing	35	20	17	16	01
6	BCS	100	50	38	34	04
7	MBA	40	19	17	16	01
Total		5245	965	903	805	98

3 Academic results

This summer's second-year Board of Intermediate and Secondary Examination (BISE) exam results were better than in previous years, and the FSc and FA pass rates were as follows:

Faculty of Science (FSc): Pre-Medical: 100%
Faculty of Science (FSc): Pre-Engineering: 99%
Faculty of Science (FSc): Computer Science: 79%
Faculty of Arts (FA): 89%

The Computer Science results were slightly disappointing, which is surprising considering that the department boasts the highly prestigious Bachelor of Computer Science degree, but the FA results show a marked improvement compared with last year.

The overall top three BISE position holders were as follows:

Name	Group	Part II marks	Position
Muhammad Numan Khan	M1	948 out of 1100	First
Imran Farooq	M2	939 out of 1100	Second
Obaid Ali Shah	E1	925 out of 1100	Third

The first-years also did well, but the most significant difference was that, although only one of the 12 second-year toppers in the four FSc and FA groups just mentioned was a woman, six of the first-year toppers were women.

The overall top three first-year students were as follows:

Name	Group	Marks	Position
Miss Nimra Zafar	M2	472 out of 550	First
Ahsan Javed	E2	469 out of 550	Second
M. Waqas Afridi	E1	468 out of 550	Third

The trend towards improvement in women's academic standards is mirrored by the annual awards (April 2009). Though representing only 10 per cent of the total student body, women students carried away 36 per cent of all the prizes and 54 per cent of gold medals.

A-level results were extremely good. Out of a total of 126 students, 80 per cent got marks in excess of 90 per cent.

It is not difficult to find reasons for this all-round improvement in academic standards. Admissions are now firmly based on merit, and even within the decreased number of quotas, such as minorities and *hafiz-e-Qur'ān*, students are admitted with only slightly fewer marks than the merit cut-off. Most of the FATA students admitted were above merit, but the small FATA quota of 2 per cent is already yielding good results (and drawing financial support from the British High Commission).

Teaching standards also continue to improve. Just to give one example – the Biology department (which spends more time than any others with the Pre-Medical students) has just appointed a new contract lecturer, for which post only first-class Masters degree-holders could apply. Forty-five did so, and the seven best were set a two-hour written test the day before the interviews. Of these, four were offered interviews – in the course of which they had to give a short presentation – and the best was selected. With teaching staff appointment procedures as rigorous as this, is it any wonder that students' academic standards are rising?

In the June 2009 exams the majority of A-level students scored A or B grades, and together with a number of Intermediate graduates went on to do courses at reputable universities such as the Ghulam Ishaq Khan Institute of Engineering, Science and Technology (GIKI), the University of Engineering and Technology (UET), the Lahore University of Management Sciences (LUMS) – where a group of 38 students recently took part in their Olympiad – and the National University of Sciences and Technology (NUST). The previous year one Pre-Medical Intermediate student came fourth of all candidates in Pakistan in the medical colleges entry test and first among all FATA applicants; he therefore secured a very prestigious place at King Edwards Medical College in Lahore.

Results for the BSc/BA annual examinations for 2009 were an improvement on previous years. The top position holders were as follows:

Table A3 Position holders in BSc/BA annual examination for 2009

Fourth year BSc	Name	Marks	Percentage
1st position	Miss Marjan Akhter	389/550	70.72%
2nd position	Ahmad Yar	382/550	69.34%
3rd position	Miss Kausar Tayyab	381/550	69.27%
Fourth year BA	Name	Marks	Percentage
1st position	Miss Fizza Irshad	398/550	72.36%
2nd position	Miss Faryal Khan	357/550	64.90%
3rd position	Miss Irum Afridi	354/550	64.36%
Third year BSc	Name	Marks	Percentage
1st position	Miss Shumaila Manzoor	224/285	78.59%
2nd position	Miss Ruhama Taj	221/285	77.54%
3rd position	Miss Farah Noreen	207/285	72.63%
Third year BA	Name	Marks	Percentage
1st position	Sohail Akhter	208/285	72.98%
2nd position	Mashood Hassan	187/285	65.61%
3rd position	Gulzar Ahmad	186/285	65.26%

The high proportion of women position holders is noteworthy. The exclusion of 'D' grade applications from the most recent BSc/BA admissions should raise standards even higher.

The Bachelor of Computer Science and HND and MBA results are given in Annex B. These are assessed in a different manner from Board and Degree results except for the MBA, in which Miss Heena Stephen came second in the University of Peshawar Examination. One BCS student got second position in the University Examination. The results as a whole are satisfactory, and it is gratifying to know that the University of Peshawar now recognises the Edwardes HND as an appropriate qualification for admission to their MBA.

4 Lecturing staff

There are currently 81 lecturing staff in the college. Fifty-four are regular, eight are re-employed, three are visiting, and 16 are on contract. Six contract staff were offered regular employment following re-advertising of their positions and interviewing. Details are given elsewhere.

Considering the difficulties experienced by the college during the last 12 months, it is a major achievement that all courses were completed on time. Teaching staff must be congratulated for this, though it is also true that it was possible because the academic year began earlier this year than previously.

Academic publications by teaching staff are listed in Annex C. Some of these have been published in international journals, and are extremely impressive (e.g. those of Muhammad Naveed Ali and Fazl-e-Mahood). Mrs Rubna Masoud's research on organo-phosphorus pesticides is not so recent, but is currently of great importance in international circles dealing with the environment. The principal teaches in the environmental management section of the HND. Dr Yar Muhammad Khattak Maghmoom's Pashto book on Sufi mysticism is also very topical as a timely antidote to those with a primarily political interpretation of Islam.

Lecturing staff who are capable of such high-quality publications deserve the opportunity of doing doctoral research, and for this reason it is vital for the college to secure recognition and financial support from the Higher Education Commission.

5 Sport

College sport takes place at several levels. Intercollegiate sport tournaments occur at Intermediate and Degree levels. Within the college there are competitions between different teams, which include both day and hostel scholars. Last, but not least – because they are often the most fiercely and raucously competitive – are the hostel tournaments.

This year intercollegiate sport was severely hampered by security considerations, and Edwardes College took part in only two

Degree tournaments: football and hockey. More intercollegiate Intermediate matches took place; these were in football, athletics, hockey, cricket, basketball and volleyball. None was won, but college acquitted itself well in all of them.

Within college, the Degree team won the football tournament, and the second-years won the basketball. In the hostel, basketball and cricket were won by the second-years, football was won by the seniors, and most students participated in indoor games (table tennis, carrom board and snooker).

6   College activities

The social work camp for degree students, held in Thandiani from 13 to 19 August, went extremely well under the leadership of Professor Noor Muhammad. Students cleaned the area, planted trees, distributed simple medicines and improved roads. Blood donation camps were organised by the H. M. Close Memorial Blood Donors Society, led by Professor Atteq ur Rehman. The principal and student volunteers went to the Central Prison on Saturdays to assist prisoners, with a break across the autumn on account of Taliban activity in the prison.

The college now has a regular doctor, Dr Haider Ali from the Kuwait Hospital, Peshawar, who is available for three hours every evening in the first-year hostel, and a nurse is available during the mornings.

Debating has been reduced on account of security concerns, and there has been no play this year. The women students have been on a much-enjoyed outing to Murree in the college bus (accompanied by our women's officer, Mrs Nasira Manzoor), as has the Student Christian Movement. Chapel services have been well attended, as was the *Tarawih* during Ramazan last September.

Hostel students have been particularly privileged, with activities stretching from the Bara Gali camp for first-years to the Golden Night Dinner in March. Hostel football, cricket, basketball and hockey are fiercely competitive, and Friday night films have been much appreciated, including *Ghajini, Kurbaan, Khuda Kay Liye* and *Avatar*. More hostellers than usual remained in residence to revise for their exams on account of power cuts caused by electrical load-shedding at home.

7 Relationships with external bodies

i. *German language classes*

Following preliminary discussions in the summer of 2009 with representatives of the Embassy of the Federal Republic of Germany (FRG) in Islamabad and the Goethe Institut in Karachi, the college started German language classes last autumn. These have been conducted primarily by Professor Shah Jehan Sayed, Dean of the Faculty of Management and Information Sciences in the University of Peshawar. Approximately a dozen college members have so far enrolled – the cost is according to status.

From 2 to 10 December, Professor Kalimullah attended the programme's 'Partners for the Future' visit to the FRG and the subsequent regional conference in Sri Lanka in January. The Goethe Institut will be responsible for refurbishing the room on the right of the stairs of the main administrative block as a seminar room. It is anticipated that Edwardes graduates who speak German will be able to pursue research and find jobs readily in Germany.

ii. *The UK–FATA Scholarships Programme*

For the past two years the UK High Commission in Islamabad has been providing scholarships for approximately 40 Intermediate students from FATA areas. These scholarships are to cover tuition and boarding fees (since most FATA students reside in the hostel), and are only for students schooled and domiciled in FATA areas (i.e. 'genuine' FATA students).

The programme is entitled *Strengthening Human Resources in the North-West Frontier Province*, and its aim is 'to equip many young adults and professionals' to contribute to long-term good governance in the province by 'building capacity of human resources to undertake a more robust analysis of the issues affecting the tribal areas ...' Students and their parents have very much appreciated this programme, which has been carefully monitored both by the college and from Islamabad. More is the pity, therefore, that it has now been terminated.

This decision to reduce educational and developmental support to Pakistan drew strong criticism in the UK press in January, and it is to be hoped that, following requests to the UK High Commission from the Minister for Higher Education of the Provincial Government and the College Board of Governors, support for the college's genuine FATA students will be continued.

iii. *UK universities*

Many Edwardes students continue to pursue their further studies in the UK, though some have experienced difficulties and delays in getting visas recently. This is on account of changes in visa rules, a general tightening up of procedures and the move of a section of the UK Consulate in Islamabad to Abu Dhabi.

The largest number of Edwardes graduates at UK universities continue to be at Liverpool Hope University predominantly doing Business Studies (BBA) and Computer Science (they have a large range of optional courses, and Edwardes students go directly into their Masters degree). An increasing number are going to the universities of Hertfordshire, Northumbria and Glamorgan on the advice of visa consultants in Peshawar who are paid commissions to recruit students, and some go to bogus institutions such as the West London College. The UK Consulate in Islamabad seems to be increasingly turning down requests for visas to study at such places.

8 Finance

Details of the college's finances are found in the Budget and the reports of the auditors and the Finance Committee set up by the

Board of Governors in response to the embezzlement of approximately 60 million rupees from college accounts. This has shaken the college to its core, but it has also provoked a thoroughgoing and comprehensive analysis of finance and administration that should guarantee that there is no recurrence of these tragic events.

The embezzlement took place over a period of seven to ten years and was mostly from the provident and pensions funds in GPO accounts. The main architect is in prison; the fact that he appears to have been assisted by one or more GPO employees means that the Federal Investigation Agency is conducting the enquiry. The former college head of finance is being co-charged. The court case is proceeding and the matter is therefore *sub judice.*

The Board's Finance Committee, chaired by Dr Nasser Ali Khan, Director of the Institute of Management Sciences, set out short-, medium- and long-term proposals to check abuse and streamline finance procedures. All have been implemented as reported elsewhere, and three new competent and experienced finance staff have been inducted. The college is already feeling the effects of this capable team and confidence is slowly returning.

Administration has been separated from finance, and a capable administrator has taken the place of the former bursar. Support staff are being relocated and in some cases replaced by recently graduated Edwardian interns (costing only Rs. 5000/- per month). *Chowkidars* having no previous security training (e.g. as police or military personnel) are being replaced.

Attempts to obtain financial support for the college have been put on hold pending implementation of improved financial mechanisms, but now they must be pursued with vigour. The Chief Minister is to be thanked for a donation of Rs. 5.105 million towards Internally Displaced Persons (IDPs), who were homeless following the military operation in Swat. The former Chief Secretary, Mr Sahibzada Riaz Noor, kindly donated Rs. 2 million to kick-start the Endowment Fund, and smaller donations have been received from various bodies such as the local ECOSA (Old Edwardians) group. But funds offered by the former Governor shortly prior to his resignation and by the FATA Secretariat have not materialised. These must be pursued. But the most important source of funding to enable lecturing staff to obtain PhDs is the Higher Education Commission, and contact must be made with this body as soon as feasible.

9 Security

During the summer and autumn of 2009 Peshawar was in the forefront of bombings, kidnappings and other acts of violence. The main five-star hotel was blown up, as was a bank frequented by college members – quite close. In September, the principal was informed that an 11-year-old boy was targeting the college. A huge bomb – larger than the one that blew up the Marriott Hotel in Islamabad – devastated the provincial headquarters of the Inter-Services Intelligence agency; a bomb close to the college at the Press Club sent students rushing out of their classrooms in a panic, and a suicide bomber on a motor bike blew himself up near the Roman Catholic church on Christmas Eve. Since then there has been less violence, though three bombs exploded near the US Consulate not far from the college early in April.

In these extreme situations the college's policy has been to follow the advice of the Department of Education and close – not to do so would have worried parents and might have exposed the college to being targeted. Otherwise, security has been increased at every possible level with the introduction of road blocks, armed guards and night patrols. No members of the college have been seriously injured, though some have lost close family members as a result of Taliban activity and US drone attacks near the Afghan borders. The cousin of one college lecturer was murdered by extremists on the main university campus in March.

10 Conclusion

The past year has been difficult, but the college has completed its main responsibilities on time, with some improvements already made. This has been possible largely on account of the dedication and hard work of various groups and individuals such as the college officers (meeting every morning), the new finance team, the wardens, the college lawyer, the women's officer, the proctors, our Board members (especially Dr Nasser Ali Khan), and many others. Collectively, the teaching staff are understanding better the problems of management – thus, for example, they allowed their demand for a 15 per cent pay rise to be overruled by the Board pending a proper investigation of the college's finances. Individually, some are publishing high-quality research in international journals, which should entitle them to doctoral opportunities and scholarships. In order to facilitate this, the college must explore avenues for cooperation with the Higher Education Commission. This may lead to a rethinking of relationships in other areas.

To highlight some of the points already made:

1   Strict emphasis on merit has made the whole admissions process more transparent and streamlined. It has also enabled the college to win every court case brought by aggrieved parents. The *Prospectus* needs to state the college's policy and procedures more clearly. Fee concessions must be reduced, and should be negotiated with parents during admissions.

2   Steadily improving academic results reflect admissions based on merit. Women students are consistently producing the best results. The policy of excluding 'D' grades from BSc and BA degrees should be continued (as agreed by the Board more than a decade ago) and admissions for A-levels need to be tightened up so as to exclude weaker applicants.

3   Student records must be centralised via a single database for the purposes of admissions, finance and ID cards.

4   Relationships with the Goethe Institut should be continued, and an attempt must be made to persuade the UK High Commission to continue its scholarship scheme for FATA students.

5   The recommendations of the Board's Finance Committee, which are summarised elsewhere and which have been carefully implemented, must remain in place indefinitely. Ways must be sought to increase funding for the college.

These must include approaches to the Higher Education Commission and potential provincial sources such as the Chief Secretary and the FATA Secretariat (which has already promised funds that never materialised). Alumni could do much more for the college, and need to be reached via the website.

6   As important as external funding – perhaps even more so – is generating additional finance by recruiting more fee-paying students. This can only be done when Edwardes College School moves to its new designated site. In the meantime, the school should return the upper section of the college second-year hostel, which it took over without any notification to the Board.

7   All *chowkidars* employed by the college must have security experience (e.g. as ex-military, police or in security firms).

8   The full Board should attempt to meet a minimum of twice a year. For whatever reason, the three meetings held in 2009 constitute a record in the college's history!

As the academic year draws to a close, we are thankful to the Board and all others who have encouraged us to continue in our God-given responsibility of offering academic excellence and our shared Edwardian values as a form of service to young people of the Province and beyond.

Annex A: Distribution of student homes according to course: degree and A levels

District/Province/Country	A levels 2007-9 Nos.	%age	A levels 2008-10 Nos.	%age	A levels 2009-11 Nos.	%age	Degree 2007-9 B.Sc Nos.	%age	B.A Nos.	%age	C %age	Degree 2008-10 B.Sc Nos.	%age	B.A Nos.	%age	C %age	Degree 2009-11 B.Sc Nos.	%age	B.A Nos.	%age	C %age
Abbottabad	0	0.0	0	0.0	0	0.0	0	0.0	1	0.7	0.6	1	1.3	1	0.6	0.8	4	5.9	0	0.0	1.8
Afghanistan	1	2.2	3	4.5	1	1.3	1	2.3	3	2.2	2.2	0	0.0	3	1.7	1.2	0	0.0	0	0.0	0.0
Attock	0	0.0	1	1.5.	0	0.0	0	-0.0	0	0.0	0.0	0	0.0	0	0.0	0.0	0	0.0	0	0.0	0.0
Azad Jamu Kashmir	1	2.2	0	0.0	0	0.0	0	0.0	0	0.0	0.0	0	0.0	0	0.0	0.0	0	0.0	0	0.0	0.0
FATA Bajaur	0	0.0	1	1.5	2	2.7	1	2.3	1	0.7	0.6	0	0.0	0	0.0	0.0	0	0.0	0	0.0	0.0
Balochistan	0	0.0	0	0.0	0	0.0	1	2.3	2	1.5	1.7.	0	0.0	0	0.0	0.0	0	0.0	0	0.0	0.0
Bannu	1	2.2	0	0.0	4	5.3	1	2.3	3	2.2	2.2	2	2.7	3	1.7	2.0	0	0.0	3	2.0	1.4
Battagram	0	0.0	4	6.0	0	0.0	0	0.0	0	0.0	0.0	0	0.0	0	0.0	0.0	0	0.0	0	0.0	0.0
Buner	0	0.0	0	0.0	0	0.0	0	0.0	1	0.7	0.6	0	0.0	3	1.7	1.2	0	0.0	0	0.0	0.0
Chilas	0	0.0	0	0.0	0	0.0	0	0.0	0	0.0	0.0	1	1.3	0	0.0	0.4	0	0.0	0	0.0	0.0
Chitral	0	0.0	0	0.0	0	0.0	2	4.5	1	0.7	1.7	1	1.3	3	1.7	1.6	5	7.4	5	3.4	4.6
Dera Ismail Khan	0	0.0	2	3.0	0	0.0	0	0.0	0	0.0	0.0	1	1.3	2	1.1	1.2	0	0.0	0	0.0	0.0
Dir	0	0.0	0	0.0	0	0.0	1	2.3	3	2.2	2.2	2	2.7	4	2.3	2.4	1	1.5	6	4.0	3.2
FATA (unspecified)	0	0.0	1	1.5	0	0.0	0	0.0	2	1.5	1.1	0	0.0	3	1.7	1.2	3	4.4	7	4.7	4.6
Gilgit	0	0.0	0	0.0	0	0.0	0	0.0	1	0.7	0.6	0	0.0	3	1.7	1.2	0	0.0	0	0.0	0.0
Hangu	0	0.0	0	0.0	0	0.0	0	0.0	1	0.7	0.6	1	1.3	1	0.6	0.8	0	0.0	1	0.7	0.5
Haripur	0	0.0	1	1.5	0	0.0	0	0.0	1	0.7	0.0	1	1.3	0	0.0	0.4	0	0.0	0	0.0	0.0
Karachi	0	0.0	2	3.0	0	0.0	0	0.0	0	0.0	0.0	0	0.0	0	0.0	0.0	0	0.0	0	0.0	0.0
Karak	1	2.2	0	0.0	1	1.3	0	0.0	0	0.0	0.0	3	4.0	3	1.7	2.4	1	1.5	1	0.7	0.9
Khushab	0	0.0	0	0.0	0	0.0	0	0.0	0	0.0	0.0	1	1.3	0	0.0	0.4	0	0.0	0	0.0	0.0
FATA Khyber Agency	0	0.0	0	0.0	1	1.3	1	2.3	11	8.1	6.7	2	2.7	6	3.4	3.2	1	1.5	6	4.0	3.2

District/Province/Country	A levels 2007–9		A levels 2008–10		A levels 2009–11		Degree 2007–9						Degree 2008–10						Degree 2009–11					
							B.Sc.		B.A.		C		B.Sc.		B.A.		C		B.Sc.		B.A.		C	
	Nos.	%age	Nos.	%age	Nos.	%age	Nos.	%age	Nos.	%age	Nos.	%age	Nos.	%age	Nos.	%age	Nos.	%age	Nos.	%age	Nos.	%age	Nos.	%age
Kohat	3	6.5	0	0.0	1	1.3	4	9.1	7	5.2		6.1	0	0.0	1	0.6		0.4	1	1.5	2	1.3		1.4
FATA Kurram Agency	0	0.0	0	0.0	0	0.0	0	0.0	6	4.4		3.4	0	0.0	2	1.1		0.8	1	1.5	2	1.3		1.4
Lakki Marwat	0	0.0	0	0.0	0	0.0	0	0.0	0	0.0		0.0	2	2.7	1	0.6		1.2	1	1.5	6	4.0		3.2
Malakand Agency	0	0.0	0	0.0	4	5.3	2	4.5	2	1.5		2.2	0	0.0	3	1.7		1.2	0	0.0	1	0.7		0.5
Mansehra	1	2.2	2	3.0	0	0.0	0	0.0	1	0.7		0.6	0	0.0	0	0.0		0.0	1	1.5	1	0.7		0.9
FATA Mohmand Agency	1	2.2	1	1.5	2	2.7	2	4.5	3	2.2		2.8	0	0.0	2	1.1		0.8	0	0.0	1	0.7		0.5
FATA North Waziristan	0	0.0	1	1.5	0	0.0	0	0.0	1	0.7,		0.6	0	0.0	2	1.1		0.8	0	0.0	2	1.3		0.9
FATA Orakzai Agency	0	0.0	0	0.0	0	0.0	1	2.3	1	0.7		1.1	0	0.0	0	0.0		0.0	0	0.0	0	0.0		0.0
Punjab	2	4.3	0	0.0	0	0.0	0	0.0	0	0.0		0.0	3	4.0	0	0.0		1.2	0	0.0	0	0.0		0.0
Riaz	1	2.2	0	0.0	0	0.0	0	0.0	0	0.0		0.0	0	0.0	0	0.0		0.0	0	0.0	0	0.0		0.0
Shangla	1	2.2	0	0.0	2	2.7	0	0.0	0	0.0		0.0	0	0.0	0	0.0		0.0	0	0.0	1	0.7		0.5
FATA South Waziristan	1	2.2	0	0.0	1	1.3	1	2.3	0	0.0		0.6	1	1.3	3	1.7		1.6	0	0.0	0	0.0		0.0
Sukhar	0	0.0	1	1.5	0	0.0	0	0.0	0	0.0		0.0	0	0.0	1	0.6		0.4	0	0.0	0	0.0		0.0
Swabi	3	6.5	1	1.5	1	1.3	4	9.1	6	4.4		5.6	2	2.7	3	1.7		2.0	0	0.0	7	4.7		3.2
Swat	1	2.2	1	1.5	0	0.0	0	0.0	0	0.0		0.0	1	1.3	4	2.3		2.0	0	0.0	1	0.7		0.5
Tank	0	0.0	0	0.0	0	0.0	0	0.0	0	0.0		0.0	1	1.3	0	0.0		0.4	0	0.0	2	1.3		0.9
USA	0	0.0	0	0.0	1	1.3	0	0.0	0	0.0,		0.0	0	0.0	0	0.0		0.0	0	0.0	0	0.0		0.0
Total/overall %age	16	34.8	22	32.8	22	29.3	21	47.7	57	42.2		43.6	26	34.7	57	32.8		33.3	19	27.9	55	36.9		34.1
Peshawar/Nowshera/Charsadda/Mardan	30	65.2	45	67.2	53	70.7	23	52.3	78	57.8		56.4	49	65.3	117	67.2		66.7	49	72.1	94	63.1		65.9
Total	46	100.0	67	100.0	75	100.0	44	100.0	135	100.0		100.0	75	100.0	174	100.0		100.0	68	100.0	149	100.0		100.0
Total FATA	2	4.3	3	4.5	6	8.0	5	11.4	25	18.5		16.8	3	4.0	18	10.3		8.4	5	7.4	18	12.1		10.6

Annex A: Distribution of student homes according to course: bachelor of computer science (BCS), higher national diploma (HND) and management (MBA)

District/Province/Country	HND 2007-9 Nos.	%age	HND 2008-10 Nos.	%age	HND 2009-11 Nos.	%age	BCS 2005-9 Nos.	%age	BCS 2006-10 Nos.	%age	BCS 2007-11 Nos.	%age	BCS 2008-12 Nos.	%age	BCS 2009-13 Nos.	%age	MBA 2008-10 Nos.	%age
Abbottabad	0	0.0	0	0.0	1	1.6.	0	0.0	0	0.0	0	0.0	0	0.0	0	0.0	0	0.0
Afghanistan	0	0.0	4	4.2	0	0.0	0	0.0	0	0.0	1	2.9	2	4.8	0	0.0	0	0.0
FATA Bajaur	1	1.3	1	1.1	1	1.6	1	3.0	1	3.6	0	0.0	0	0.0	0	0.0	3	5.9
Balochistan	0	0.0	0	0.0	0	0.0	0	0.0	1	3.6	0	0.0	0	0.0	0	0.0	0	0.0
Bannu	0	0.0	1	1.1	2	3.1	1	3.0	0	0.0	0	0.0	0	0.0	0	0.0	0	0.0
Battagram	0	0.0	0	0.0	0	0.0	0	0.0	1	3.6	0	0.0	0	0.0	0	0.0	0	0.0
Buner	0	0.0	0	0.0	0	0.0	0	0.0	0	0.0	0	0.0	1	2.4	0	0.0	1	2.0
Chitral	0	0.0	2	2.1	0	0.0	1	3.0	0	0.0	1	2.9	0	0.0	0	0.0	0	0.0
Chirat	0	0.0	0	0.0	0	0.0	0	0.0	0	0.0	0	0.0	0	0.0	0	0.0	0	0.0
Dera Ismail Khan	1	1.3	0	0.0	1	1.6	0	0.0	0	0.0	0	0.0	0	0.0	0	0.0	0	0.0
Dir	0	0.0	2	2.1	0	0.0	0	0.0	0	0.0	0	0.0	2	4.8	0	0.0	1	2.0
FATA (unspecified)	0	0.0	0	0.0	0	0.0	0	0.0	0	0.0	2	5.7	0	0.0	0	0.0	0	0.0
Faysalabad	0	0.0	1	1.	0	0.0	0	0.0	0	0.0	0	0.0	0	0.0	0	0.0	0	0.0
Ghanch Northern Area	0	0.0	0	0.0	0	0.0	0	0.0	0	0.0	0	0.0	0	0.0	0	0.0	0	0.0
Hangu	4	5.1	2	2.1	0	0.0	1	3.0	0	0.0	1	2.9	1	2.4	1	2.4	0	0.0
Karak	0	0.0	2	2.1	0	0.0	0	0.0	1	3.6	0	0.0	2	4.8	0	0.0	0	0.0
FATA Khyber Agency	2	2.6	3	3.2	2	3.1	0	0.0	2	7.1	1	2.9	2	4.8	0	0.0	1	2.0
Kohat	0	0.0	1	1.1	1	1.6	1	3.0	2	7.1	1	2.9	2	4.8	0	0.0	0	0.0

District/Province/Country	HND 2007-9		HND 2008-10		HND 2009-11		BCS 2005-9		BCS 2006-10		BCS 2007-11		BCS 2008-12		BCS 2009-13		MBA 2008-10	
	Nos.	%age	Nos.	%age	Nos.	%age	Nos.	%age	Nos.	%age	Nos.	%age	Nos.	%age	Nos.	%age	Nos.	%age
FATA Kurram Agency	5	6.4	4	4.2	0	0.0	0	0.0	0	0.0	1	2.9	0	0.0	0	0.0	2	3.9
Lakki Marwat	0	0.0	0	0.0	0	0.0	0	0.0	1	3.6	0	0.0	0	0.0	0	0.0	0	0.0
Malakand Agency	0	0.0	1	1.1	1	1.6	0	0.0	1	3.6	0	0.0	0	0.0	0	0.0	1	2.0
FATA Mohmand Agency	0	0.0	3	3.2	0	0.0	1	3.0	2	7.1	2	5.7	0	0.0	0	0.0	0	0.0
FATA North Waziristan	0	0.0	0	0.0	0	0.0	0	0.0	0	0.0	0	0.0	0	0.0	0	0.0	0	0.0
FATA Orakzai Agency	0	0.0	1	1.1	1	1.6	0	0.0	1	3.6	2	5.7	0	0.0	0	0.0	1	2.0
Punjab	0	0.0	0	0.0	0	0.0	0	0.0	0	0.0	0	0.0	0	0.0	0	0.0	0	0.0
Skardu	1	1.3	0	0.0	0	0.0	0	0.0	0	0.0	0	0.0	0	0.0	0	0.0	0	0.0
FATA South Waziristan	1	1.3	2	2.1	0	0.0	0	0.0	0	0.0	0	0.0	0	0.0	0	0.0	0	0.0
Swabi	4	5.1	12	12.6	3	4.7	3	9.1	3	10.7	1	2.9	1	2.4	0	0.0	2	3.9
Swat	0	0.0	9	9.5	2	3.1	1	3.0	1	3.6	0	0.0	1	2.4	0	0.0	0	0.0
Wana	0	0.0	1	1.1	0	0.0	0	0.0	0	0.0	0	0.0	0	0.0	0	0.0	0	0.0
Total/overall %age	19	24.4	62	54.7	15	23.4	10	30.3	17	60.7	13	37.1	14	33.3	1	2.4	12	23.5
Peshawar/Nowshera/Charsadda/Mardan	59	75.6	43	45.3	49	76.6	23	69.7	11	39.3	22	62.9	28	66.7	40	97.8	39	76.5
Total	78	100.0	95	100.0	64	100.0	33	100.0	28	100.0	35	100.0	42	100.0	41	100.0	51	100.0
Total FATA	9	11.5	14	14.7	4	6.3	2	6.1	6	21.4	8	22.9	2	4.8	0	0.0	7	13.7

Annex A: Distribution of student homes according to course: intermediate courses

The Computer Science and Arts are signified together as Gen.Sc./Arts in the table.

District/Province/Country	Intermediate 2007-9							Intermediate 2008-10							Intermediate 2009-11						
	Pre-Medical		Pre-Eng.		Gen.Sc./Arts		c.	Pre-Medical		Pre-Eng.		Gen.Sc./Arts		C.	Pre-Medical		Pre-Eng.		Gen.Sc./Arts		c.
	Nos.	%age	Nos.	%age	Nos.	%age	%age	Nos.	%age	Nos.	%age	Nos.	%age	%age	Nos.	%age	Nos.	%age	Nos.	%age	%age
Abbottabad	1	0.5	1	0.5	1	0.7	0.6	0	0.0	0	0.0	0	0.0	0.0	1	0.5	1	0.5	0	0.0	0.4
Afghanistan	2	1.0	2	1.1	4	2.9	1.5	4	2.1	5	2.5	3	2.3	2.3	3	1.6	2	1.0	3	2.5	1.6
FATA Bajaur	1	0.5	1	0.5	0	0.0	0.4	2	1.1	0	0.0	0	0.0	0.4	1	0.5	0	0.0	0	0.0	0.2
Balochistan	0	0.0	0	0.0	1	0.7	0.2	0	0.0	0	0.0	1	0.8	0.2		0.0	0	0.0	1	0.8	0.2
Bannu	3	1.5	2	1.1	3	2.2	1.5	2	1.1	6	3.0	0	0.0	1.5	3	1.6	5	2.4	3	2.5	2.2
Battagram	0	0.0	0	0.0	0	0.0	0.0	0	0.0	0	0.0	0	0.0	0.0	0	0.0	0	0.0	0	0.0	0.0
Buner	11	5.6.	3	1.6	0	0.0	2.7	3	1.6	1	0.5	4	3.0	1.5	5	2.7	2	1.0	1	0.8	1.6
Chitral	2	1.0	0	0.0	1	0.7	0.6	0	0.0	0	0.0	0	0.0	0.0	2	1.1	0	0.0	2	1.7	0.8
Dera Ismail Khan	2	1.0	3	1.6	0	0.0	1.0	3	1.6	2	1.0	0	0.0	1.0	1	0.5	2	1.0	1	0.8	0.8
Dir	12	6.1	9	4.8	1	0.7	4.2	8	4.3	5	2.5	0	0.0	2.5	7	3.8	8	3.9	0	0.0	2.9
FATA (unspecified)	2	1.0	1	0.5	1	0.7	0.8	3	1.6	0	0.0	5	3.8	1.5	2	1.1	0	0.0	0	0.0	0.4
Ghanch Northern Area	0	0.0	1	0.5	0	0.0	0.2	0	0.0	0	0.0	0	0.0	0.0	0	0.0	0	0.0	0	0.0	0.0
Gilgit	0	0.0	0	0.0	0	0.0	0.0	0	0.0	0	0.0	0	0.0	0.0	0	0.0	0	0.0	0	0.0	0.0
Hangu	1	0.5	5	2.6	3	2.2	1.7	5	2.7	3	1.5	0	0.0	1.5	5	2.7	2	1.0	1	0.8	1.6
Haripur	0	0.0	0	0.0	0	0.0	0.0	0	0.0	2	1.0	1	0.8	0.6	0	0.0	0	0.0	0	0.0	0.0
Karak	6	3.0	3	1.6	0	0.0	1.7	8	4.3	7	3.5	0	0.0	2.9	1	0.5	3	1.5	2	1.7	1.2
FATA Khyber Agency	6	3.0	6	3.2	3	2.2	2.9	5	2.7	5	2.6	5	3.8	2.9	5	2.7	0	0.0	2	1.7	1.4
Kohat	2	1.0	5	2.6	4	2.9	2.1	4	2.1	6	3.0	4	3.0	2.7	5	2.7	5	2.4	1	0.8	2.2

FATA Kurram Agency	6	3.0	3	1.6	7	5.1	3.1	2	1.1	7	3.6	3	2.3	2.3	6	3.3	10	4.9	9	7.4	4.9
Lakki Marwat	1	0.5	2	1.1	0	0.0	0.6	4	2.1	1	0.5	0	0.0	1.0	2	1.1	3	1.5	1	0.8	1.2
Malakand Agency	2	1.0	6	3.2	1	0.7	1.7	3	1.6	7	3.5	0	0.0	1.9	5	2.7	7	3.4	1	0.8	2.5
Mansehra	0	0.0	0	0.0	1	0.7	0.2	1	0.5	2	1.0	0	0.0	0.6	1	0.5	0	0.0	1	0.8	0.4
FATA Mohmand Agency	5	2.5	7	3.7	3	2.2	2.9	5	2.7	1	0.5	2	1.5	1.5	3	1.6	3	1.5	3	2.5	1.8
FATA North Waziristan	2	1.0	1	0.5	0	0.0	0.6	5	2.7	3	1.6	0	0.0	1.5	6	2.7	0	0.0	0	0.0	1.0
FATA Orakzai Agency	3	1.5	2	1.1	0	0.0	1.0	2	1.1	0	0.0	0	0.0	0.4	2	1.1	1	0.5	0	0.0	0.6
Punjab	0	0.0	1	0.5	0	0.0	0.2	0	0.0	0	0.0	0	0.0	0.0	1	0.5	1	0.5	1	0.8	0.6
Shangla	0	0.0	2	1.1	0	0.0	0.4	1	0.5	1	0.5	0	0.0	0.2	4	2.2	1	0.5	0	0.0	1.0
FATA South Waziristan	0	0.0	0	0.0	0	0.0	0.0	1	0.5	0	0.0	0	0.0	0.2	2	1.1	0	0.0	1	0.8	0.6
Swabi	12	6.1	17	9.0	7	5.1	6.9	16	8.6	15	7.4	6	4.5	7.1	7	3.8	11	5.3	5	4.1	4.5
Swat	3	1.5	3	1.6	1	0.7	1.3	4	2.1	2	1.0	5	3.8	2.1	5	2.7	8	3.9	1	0.8	2.7
Tank	1	0.5	0	0.0	0	0.0	0.2	0	0.0	0	0.0	0	0.0	0.0	0	0.0	0	0.0	0	0.0	0.0
Total/overall %age	86	43.7	86	45.5	42	30.7	40.9	90	48.1	81	40.1	39	29.3	40.2	84	45.9	75	36.4	40	33.1	39.0
Peshawar/Nowshera/Charsadda/Mardan	111	56.3	103	54.5	95	69.3	59.1	97	51.9	121	59.9	94	70.7	59.8	99	54.1	131	63.6	81	66.9	61.0
Total	197	100.0	189	100.0	137	100.0	100.0	187	100.0	202	100.0	133	100.0	100.0	183	100.0	206	100.0	121	100.0	100.0
Total FATA	25	12.69	21.00	11.11	14.00	10.22	11.5	25	13.37	16.00	7.92	16.00	11.28	10.7	26	14.21	14.00	6.80	15.00	12.40	10.8

Annex B

MBA and HND

MBA (Third Semester)
Total students: 27
Total 1st divisions = 11

College no.	Name	Position	Percentage
3336	Heena Stephen	1st	74%
4559	Saira Riaz	2nd	72%
5538	Saira Anwar	3rd	68%

HND Business (Finalist)
Total students: 24
Total distinctions in various subjects = 10
Total merits in various subjects = 17

College no.	Name	Position	Total distinctions	Total merits
7199	Sarah Nasir	1st	5	4
7190	Meena Akbari	2nd	3	4
7191	Saad Mumtaz	3rd	3	3

HND Business (Fourth Semester)
Total students: 37
Total distinctions in various subjects = 25
Total merits in various subjects = 120

College no.	Name	Position	Total distinctions	Total merits
7199	Muhammad Uzair	1st	5	4
7190	Syed Muhammad Ali	2nd	3	4
7191	Rehan Khan	3rd	3	3

HND Computing (Fourth Semester)
Total students: 16
Total distinctions in various subjects = 6
Total merits in various subjects = 30

College no.	Name	Position	Total distinctions	Total merits
7210	Khurshed Alam Khan	1st	2	4
7213	Sardar Muhammad Hussain	2nd	2	2
7227	Syed Ashfaq Bukhari	3rd	2	5

BCS (Finalist)
Total students: 33
Students with more than 3.0 Cumulative Grade Point Average (CGPA) = 08
Highest Cumulative Grade Point Average (CGPA) = 3.8/4.0

Annex C: Publications by teaching staff according to subject

BIOLOGY

Donald S. Joseph, contribution to Abdul Waheed, ed., *Book of Model MCQs for Entrance Test Preparation*, NWFP Educational Testing and Evaluation Agency, Peshawar, 2005.

S. Nasim Haider Kazmi, contribution to Abdul Waheed, ed., *Book of Model MCQs for Entrance Test Preparation*, NWFP Educational Testing and Evaluation Agency, Peshawar, 2005; Biology Reference Books, Vol. 1, 2005, Zoology Reference Books Part II Intermediate, 2005.

Atta ur Rehman Anjum, 'Algae associated with alluvial gold in the Indus (Attock)'.

'The influence of *in vitro* culture conditions on the glucosinolate levels in the regenerates derived from Brassica juncea and Brassica napus L'.

Khan Niaz Khan, 'Goiter versus the use of iodised salt in the Surani District of Bannu NWFP'.

'The detection of mutations in ATP-binding domains of ABL-genes in Chronic Myeloid Leukemia in patients from Pakistan'.

CHEMISTRY

Naveed Attaullah, contribution to Abdul Waheed, ed., *Book of Model MCQs for Entrance Test Preparation*, NWFP Educational Testing and Evaluation Agency, Peshawar, 2005.

Rubna Zafar (née Masoud), *et al.*, 'Separation and determination of pesticides in samples of environmental importance', *The Journal of the Chemistry Society of Pakistan*, Vol. 12, No. 4, 1990, pp. 337–340.

'Investigation of a spectrophotometric method for the determination of organophosphorus pesticides', *The Journal of the Chemistry Society of Pakistan*, Vol. 13, No. 4, 1991, pp. 263–267.

COMPUTER SCIENCE

Muhammad Naveed Ali, 'Computational theory of short distance reflexive anaphoric devices in Urdu discourse for effective machine translation', *Frontier of Information Technology (FIT-ACM 2009)*, Pakistan, 2009.

'Corpus based mapping of Urdu characters for cell phones', *Proceedings of International Conference on Language and Technology*, Lahore, 2009.

'Design of Urdu virtual keyboard', *Proceedings of International Conference on Language and Technology*, Lahore, 2009.

'An optimal order of factors for the computational treatment of personal anaphoric devices in Urdu discourse', *Proceedings of International Conference on Processing of Low Privileged Languages*, Hyderabad, India, 2008.

'Resolution of relative anaphoric devices in Urdu discourse for effective machine translation', *Proceedings of International Conference on Language and Technology*, Bara Gali, Pakistan, 2007.

'Computational treatment of demonstrative pronouns in Urdu', *Proceedings of International Conference on Language and Technology*, Bara Gali, Pakistan, 2007.

'Algorithm for subject zero pronoun detection and restoration of Urdu discourse', *Proceedings of Computational Approaches to Arabic Script-based Languages*, Stanford University, USA, 2007.

'Zero pronoun detection and restoration of Urdu discourse', *South Asian Language Review: A Biannual Journal of Language and Linguistics*, Vol. XVI, No. 2, India, 2006.

'Treatment of pronominal anaphoric devices in Urdu discourse', *Proceedings of Second International Conference on Emerging Technologies*, Peshawar, 2006.

'Discrete mathematics', Peshawar, Discount Books, 1999.

ENGLISH

Muhammad Jehangir, *New Technology in Language and Arts Literature and its use in English Teaching Skills*, Peshawar, n.d.

Alwin Edwin, *Terminologies of the Handicapped*, Peshawar, FAMH/UNICEF Publishers, 1982.

Contribution to *Cobuild Dictionary*, UK, Cobuild, 1987.

English Grammar Lessons, Oregon, 2007.

Gulzar Ahmed, 'Vocabulary learning for the handicapped', in *Political Dynamics and the Muslim World*, Peshawar, n.d.

The History of Local Government in Pakistan, Pashto (translation from English), Peshawar, n.d. Winner of Abasin Gold Medal award for the best prose work of 1999-2000.

A Practical Approach to Vocabulary, Peshawar, n.d.

Teaching Language Skills, Peshawar, n.d.

Atteq ur Rehman, *A Synopsis of Text Books: Formal and Non Formal Education*. A research project of Basic Education for Afghan Refugees, BEFARE, GTZ, 2003.

Documentary Report on the Achievements of BEFARE Projects, 2004.

PASHTO AND ISLAMIAT

Dr Yar Muhammad Maghmoom Khattak, *Da Yurap Saensdanan* (The Scientists of Europe), Peshawar, 1982.

Da Khushal Farhang (Glossary of Khushhal), Vol. 1, *Kulliyat-e-Khushyhal*, Peshawar, 1985. (This book was awarded a prize by the Peshawar University Council.)

A Text Book of B. A. Pushto (Poetry Section), Peshawar University, 2003.

Da Khaist da lar Musafir (The Pilgrim of Beauty), translation from English, Peshawar, 2004.

Dastar Nama - a prose book of Khushhal Khan Khattak (editing and footnotes), Peshawar, 2005.

Da Khushal Farhang (Glossary of Khushhal), Vol. II, *Dastar Nama*, Peshawar, 2005. (This book was awarded a prize by the Abasin Arts Council.)

The Rowshanites and Pashto Literature, Peshawar, 2005.

Da Azadai Tehreek of Pashto Shayari (Freedom Movement and Pushto Poetry), Peshawar, 2007.

Sufi Poetry and the Reformation of Society (Pashto), Bayan Publications, Peshawar, 2010.

Sardar Sabir Hussain, *Islamic Education for Degree Classes* (text book), Peshawar, n.d.

MATHEMATICS

Fazl-e-Mabood, *Quid Mathematics Book*, Vols. 1 and 2, Peshawar, n.d.

How to Prepare Entry Test Mathematics, Vols. 1 and 2, Peshawar, n.d.

Maths M.C.Qs for Ninth and Tenth Class, Peshawar, n.d.

'Application of optimal homotrophy asymptotic method to boundary layer flow and convection heat transfer over a flat plate', Begell House, Peshawar, 2009.

Zafar Iqbal, *Al Hamra Mathematics M.C.Qs*, Peshawar, n.d.

SOCIAL WORK

Professor Dr Sarah Safdar, *Kinship and Marriage in Pukhtoon*, Pak Book Empire, Shahdab Centre, Lahore, 1997.

Introduction to Social Work, Wahdat Printing Press, Khyber Bazaar, Peshawar, 1998.

Training Manual on Research/Survey Methodology, Health International Office, Peshawar, 2000.

'Psycho-social problems of aging', *Journal of Law and Society*, Vols XII to XVI, Nos. 23–29, July 1994–January 1997.

'Role of women in national development', *Culture*, Vol. II, No. 1, Department of Social Work, Sociology and Anthropology, University of Peshawar, July 1995.

'Status of Pukhtoon tribal women', *Culture*, Vol. II, No. 1, Department of Social Work, Sociology and Anthropology, University of Peshawar, July 1995.

'Domestic violence in Pakistan', *Culture*, Vol. II, No. 1, Department of Social Work, Sociology and Anthropology, University of Peshawar, July 1995.

'Social empathy and drug demand reduction', The Colombo Plan Advisory Programme, Guidelines from the Workshop on Developing Family Response in Drug Prevention Programme, n.d., 1994.

'Women's privilege and influence in drug abuse prevention', *Proceedings of National Conference*, Government of Punjab, Punjab Social Board, Lahore, 1994.

'Women's employment pattern in NWFP', *Law and Society*, Vol. XI, No. 19, Faculty of Law, University of Peshawar, 1993.

'Women's participation in agriculture', Pak-German Project, Peshawar, 1991.

Status of Rural Women, Government of Pakistan Ministry of Women, Development, Social Welfare and Special Education, Islamabad, 1991.

'Role of women in community development', *Industrial Times*, Vol. IV, Nos. 3-4, 1989.

'Parent role in drug abuse prevention', *Proceedings of International Conference of NGOs*, held in Karachi by Pakistan Narcotics Control Board, Islamabad, 1988.

'Parent role in combating drug abuse', *Industrial Times*, Vol. III, Nos. 11-12, 1988.

'Moving forward as women', *Culture*, Vol. I, Department of Social Work, University of Peshawar, 1986.

'Status and role of females in the process of rehabilitation', *Culture*, Vol. I, Department of Social Work, University of Peshawar, 1986.

'Social set-up of Kafirism', *Pakistan*, Area Study Centre, University of Peshawar, 1980.

PHYSICS AND PHILOSOPHY

Dr David L. Gosling, *Science and the Indian Tradition: When Einstein met Tagore*, New York and London, Routledge, 2007; New Delhi, 2008.

Religion and Ecology in India and Southeast Asia, New York and London, Routledge, 2001; New Delhi, Oxford University Press, 2001.

Appendix 3

*Pakistan's role in securing a permanent Afghan peace**

ANALYSIS COMMISSIONED FOR SUBMISSION TO US
DEFENSE SECRETARY, MARCH 2011

1 Preamble
2 Pakistan's Islamic extremism
3 Encounters with Pakistan's extremists
4 The Afghan endgame
5 The Taliban
6 Regional relationships

David L. Gosling (Dr)
University of Cambridge (Clare Hall)

* This report has been published in Stefan Halper, ed., *The Afghan Endgame*, Washington, Office of the Secretary of Defense

The line that divides good and evil is not a line that divides good
[people] from bad, but a line that cuts through the middle of every
human heart.
Alexander Solzhenitsyn

Pakistan's role in securing a permanent Afghan peace

Following the proposed NATO withdrawal from Afghanistan, there is unlikely to be an enduring peace unless positive relationships are fomented between all the contributory actors in the region, especially Pakistan. We shall consider the implications of this claim in some detail presently, but the following highly simplistic preamble will illustrate the complexity of the situation.

1 Preamble

The government of Hamid Karzai is weak and already does not control large parts of the country. Following Western withdrawal, the Taliban will probably regain the south and east. It is not known whether or not they will want to dominate the north, west and Hazarajat areas, so there is the possibility of a non-Taliban broadly northern region. Internally this will require good local leadership, the devolution of certain powers from Kabul, and the sensitive and participative involvement of the tribes.

Pakistan's goodwill and cooperation will be especially important in negotiating with the Pashtun south and the tribes. They must not permit agents from their Inter-Services Intelligence (ISI) to assist Afghanistan's Pashtun south to undermine the north; on the other hand, they will not want Pashtuns inside their border to combine with Afghan Pashtuns to form an independent state. The ISI are unlikely to interfere in Afghan affairs if they can be certain that India's role in Afghanistan is purely developmental, and that some progress is being made in talks over Kashmir. Pakistan's armed forces – the seventh largest in the world – are close to the Taliban and helped to create it (together with the West) in order to drive the Russians out of Afghanistan in the 1980s. Pakistan's military leaders therefore continue to have a particular influence in relation to Afghan affairs, and should not be regarded as relics from Pakistan's pre-democratic past.

Iran may not wish for strong Taliban influence along its borders with Afghanistan, and will want to oppose the flow of narcotics. It could be a major positive influence on the Hazarajat area inside Afghanistan, where the population is predominantly Shi'i. Russia can be a strong positive influence among the Uzbeks and others in the north, and China will be supportive provided trade links and access to mineral resources continue.

NATO and the USA in particular will need to disengage in such a manner as to strengthen the positive influences in this complex regional and historical matrix. The Russians and Iran will not accept permanent US bases near their borders, and the Taliban is unlikely to enter into any discussions as long as they remain. And Pakistan will not accept the continuing and currently escalating violation of their borders by unmanned US drones.

This is a gross oversimplification, but it will give some idea of the complex relationships that must be encouraged if there is to be permanent peace in the Afghan–Pakistan region.

2 Pakistan's Islamic extremism

The birth of Pakistan as an Islamic Republic in 1947 eventually gave Muslim extremists a rationale to use Islam for political ends. The leaders at that time, including Muhammad Ali Jinnah (*Quaid-e-Azam*, 'Father of the Nation'), were a fairly liberal elite who wanted a small state where they could create an identity without interference from the assertive Hindu majority – the Nehrus and the Gandhis, in particular.

General Ayub Khan and Z. A. Bhutto were strong leaders who did much for national development. But Bhutto was cruelly executed, and General Zia-ul-Haq actively promoted a much more officially Islamic rule. The army and the mullahs worked together, and the West, especially the CIA, encouraged and financed the Pakistan/Afghan *jihād* against the Russians following their ill-considered intervention in Afghanistan in 1980.

The ISI became the chief intelligence agency of Pakistan's military, and is still independent of Parliament and the Prime Minister. Opposition to the Russians was spearheaded from camps where *talibs* (i.e. religious students often recruited from *madrasas*) were trained. These were located along the borders of Chaman in Balochistan, North Waziristan, Parachinar and Bajaur. They were well constructed in isolated locations and have subsequently become convenient places for anti-NATO militants to train (including some British citizens). Osama bin Laden initially took refuge in one of these mountain hideouts at Tora Bora before moving south along the Waziristan border.

Osama bin Laden was among a number of Arabs who were encouraged by the West to come to the Pakistan/Afghan area to oppose the Russians. From 1984 he lived in Peshawar, where his former associates have told me he was very close to Abdullah Yusuf Azzam, a Palestinian Sunni Islamic scholar who preached defensive *jihād*. Azzam was killed by a bomb in 1989, by which time the Russians were leaving Afghanistan, and bin Laden was on his way to the Sudan, having been refused re-entry into Saudi Arabia. In the Sudan, he used his enormous wealth to fund the construction of roads and a university; he remains very popular there and is believed to have returned, though some of his enemies prefer to perpetuate the myth that he remains near the Pakistan/Afghan border.

The *mujahideen* (i.e. 'those who fight in the name of Allah') contributed to the rise of the Taliban and ruled all but one of Afghanistan's 34 provinces from 1995 to 2000, and were led by mullah Muhammad Omar, a former *talib* from Hangu in Pakistan. Of the five Afghan leaders who were in the ascendancy when the Russians left, Ahmad Shah Massoud presided for some time over a single province, Gulbuddin Hekmatyar (leader of Hezb-e-Islami) went to Iran after temporarily becoming President (following Rabbani), Najibullah was killed by the Taliban, and Dostan and Rabbani were sent into exile.

Pakistan's ISI allowed Hekmatyar to live in Peshawar in 1993 as a puppet Afghan President in exile, but he lacked credibility within the tribal belt, which separates the settled areas of the then North-West

Frontier Province (now Khyber-Pakhtunkhwa) and the Afghan border. When the ISI realised their mistake, they took advantage of the presence of the Taliban in the tribal belt and gave themselves a strong Islamic tag that enabled them to overcome the traditional tribal mistrust of Pakistan's urban centres of power. It also made it easier for them to help the Taliban to capture Kabul in 1996. This is significant because the support of the tribal groups on both sides of the border (the nebulous Durand Line) is vital if there is to be any enduring peace in Afghanistan. And if this means that collaborating with religious leaders is an integral part of the peace process, then the NATO representatives must learn to work with them – even the USA, with its constitutional separation between Church and State!

Having said this, it must not be assumed that the Taliban, composed as it is of various splinter groups, is necessarily close to the villagers who currently make up the vast majority in the Pakistan/Afghan region. Afghanistan has no Muslim centres of learning and most Afghans understand Islam as a way of life rather than as a set of doctrinal options with political implications. Much the same is true in parts of Pakistan. In Bannu, for example, well-off householders may own *hijra*s (sometimes translated as 'transvestites'), who entertain at weddings, and in other ways. *Bacha bazi*, involving boys, is practised in Afghanistan. The Taliban may disapprove of such practices but find it hard to eliminate them.

But the fact remains that religion, whether as a way of life or a creed, needs to be taken seriously in the peace process, and the tribal groups, which are for the most part Sunni or Shi'i, must be enabled to participate fully in any genuine moves towards a lasting settlement in the region.

3   Encounters with Pakistan's extremists

I met the most senior Taliban leader in Pakistan, Sufi Muhammad of Timergara, during his incarceration in the Central Prison, Peshawar, in September 2009 after he was rearrested. He had been in prison from 2002 to 2008, following his *jihād* in Afghanistan. He was released as the result of an extraordinary deal between the leading provincial Awami National Party (ANP) and the Taliban. Although the ANP is secular and leftist, and the Pakistan People's Party (PPP), which backed them, is liberal (Benazir Bhutto having twice been elected from their ranks as prime minister), it was agreed that sharia law should be enforced among the 1.8 million people living in the Swat valley.

Following my brief but cordial meeting with the Sufi, with his two sons interpreting between us in the prison hospital, I went to the boys' section where some 150 boys aged between 11 and 18 were detained (some were unsuccessful suicide bombers). As soon as I said that I had been talking to Sufi Muhammad, a ripple of excitement went round the hall. They saw him as a great leader who in his younger days (he is now about 90 years old) had led 12,000 *jihādis* across the mountains to fight the foreign invaders.

Much the same admiration for Taliban leaders was expressed by other young people I met, and I saw no evidence for the popular Western view that 'mad mullahs' are brainwashing the youth of the region with extremist propaganda extolling suicide and martyrdom. Perhaps it is worth pointing out that wherever the Judaeo-Christian Hebrew Scriptures (Old Testament) and the Qur'ān include the same story, the latter is always extremely careful to remove any suggestion of suicide (references to adultery are similarly airbrushed out in the case of important religious figures, such as King David!).[1]

In mentioning the importance of charismatic leaders in the eyes of young people, it must not be forgotten that 45 per cent of Afghanistan's population of 28 million are under the age of 15. The first suicide bomber to blow herself up in Peshawar close to where I worked was 19. Two teenagers blew themselves up on a motorcycle on Christmas Eve, 2009 – the head of one was found in the grounds of a Roman Catholic Primary School. An Intelligence representative came to my office one day to tell me that an 11-year-old boy with a bomb was targeting our college; he never arrived, so presumably they caught him, or he changed his mind.

Other encounters with extremists between September 2006 (when I assumed the principalship of Edwardes College) and the summer of 2010 (when I left) were as follows. On 31 October 2006,

Prince Charles was scheduled to visit the College and deliver his longest speech during his official visit to Pakistan on Muslim/Christian dialogue. He never came because on the previous night an unmanned US drone killed 85 seminary students at a *madrasa* in Bajaur. The Prince received two death threats delivered in London, and Pervez Musharraf, then President, stated that the Pakistan army was to blame for the incident. But our students from Bajaur were categorical that this was done by an unmanned US missile. By the end of the week I had closed the college for fear of an attack by an extremist mob (this happened under my predecessor's principalship – he told me that most of the attackers who destroyed college buildings were schoolchildren bussed in from outside the city – more recently our assailants were extremist older students and others from University Town on the far side of Peshawar).

The College closed again following ill-judged remarks by the Pope in which he used the word *jihād* out of context, and by January 2007 there had been nine bomb blasts in the city, one of which killed a police deputy inspector general.[2] Rockets were fired on city targets from two neighbouring tribal districts. These were probably the work of Mangal Bagh, a former bus ticket collector who became a powerful 'warlord' with strong Taliban sympathies, though not recognised as Taliban by senior figures such as Sufi Muhammad. One of our college graduates, currently working at the Torkham Customs checkpoint, a Roman Catholic, has met Mangal Bagh and found him reasonably cordial.

By May 2007, *The News* reported that there had been 16 bomb blasts in Peshawar claiming 52 lives and seriously injuring many more.[3] The targets were mainly the police, public buildings such as the airport, and ANP officials. On 21 October three rockets from the tribal areas were fired at the US Consulate, one of which fell short and almost hit our College. On 8 November, leaflets in Urdu threatening to suicide bomb me personally were distributed around the College.[4] Peshawar's first woman suicide bomber blew herself up on 4 December, there was a threat to Elizabeth College and all similar (i.e. Christian) institutions on 13 December, and on 27 December Benazir Bhutto was killed – resulting in arbitrary violence and killings just about everywhere.

In 2008 the violence continued, the largest incident being the blowing up of the Marriott Hotel in Islamabad in August. Six hundred kilograms of explosives in a truck produced a crater six metres deep. The same month, the US consul in Peshawar had her car sprayed with bullets. In June 2009, the Pearl Continental Hotel in Peshawar was blown up; in the autumn a huge bomb estimated at 800 kilograms of explosives blew up the ISI building in Peshawar, and in March 2009 five bombs exploded at or near the US Consulate in Peshawar – militants jumped out of a vehicle and tried to storm the Consulate. There were also some huge bomb blasts in crowded bazaars, especially in Shi'i areas.

Major bomb incidents occurred in Lahore, Islamabad and Karachi, but Peshawar bore the brunt of the violence, possibly on account of its proximity to the Afghan border (the Khyber Pass), probably also because of the Taliban's hostility to the regional ANP Party once the sharia enforcement agreement in the Swat valley had fallen through and the army had started their operation to clear the valley of militants. Once the military operation in Waziristan got under way it was claimed that militant attacks on soft targets in the cities were intensified. Shi'i mosques and communities were particularly targeted, Christians less so, though church institutions in Peshawar received threats, the Director of Bannu Christian Hospital was kidnapped (but released after a few weeks without a ransom), and rockets were fired into the Pennell Memorial High School in Bannu in November 2008. The timing of this appeared to coincide with a US drone attack 70 kilometres inside the provincial border in a settled area (i.e. it had crossed completely over the tribal belt).

These events deserve careful analysis. What began with crowds of protesting extremist students became progressively more organised and focussed on government officials (e.g. the police), high-profile buildings (e.g. hotels and a bank used by members of the Combined Military Hospital), and Shi'i and other minority community centres. Officials and buildings belonging to the USA were very much targeted, but whenever this happened government commentators and the press were at great pains to deny that this was deliberate. Thus, when the Marriott Hotel was blown up, it was immediately announced that the President and Prime Minister had been due to dine there. Later, the hotel manager denied this, but by then the international press had lost interest (except in Scotland, where an acquaintance saw it!). When the car of the US Consul in Peshawar was sprayed with bullets, it was quickly explained that the miscreants were trying to kill a prominent politician who lived next door, but they had made a mistake. Very little publicity was given to the shooting of a US aid worker and his driver outside the American Club.

Students and academic staff at Edwardes College had no sympathy for Taliban and al-Qaeda killings; one student suffered incredibly when first, his father, a police superintendent in Lakki Marwat, was killed by a suicide bomb; when he went to the family village in Swat for the funeral, a second bomber killed half the rest of the family. Equally, though, some students had lost family members to the US drones. On one occasion I was showing the Bollywood movie *New York* to the hostel students. During the film, a terrorist bomb went off in a New York subway blasting potential passengers out of the escalator stairways. The students all cheered. 'Why?' I asked later. 'Because that is what the Americans are doing to us in Waziristan,' one answered.

4   The Afghan endgame

There is nothing really surprising about the WikiLeaks cables relating to Afghanistan. Everybody already knew that Hamid Karzai is little more than the 'Mayor of Kabul', and that he is corrupt and deeply suspicious of British military efforts in Helmand province, as are the US marines – or were, until they began to experience the difficulties of engaging the Taliban there themselves. The real problem is that for the average Pashtun, faced with a choice between the Taliban and the local narcotics bosses, there is nothing to look forward to in the long-term future.

Much hard thinking must take place on how to decentralise Afghanistan in a way that is consistent with the culture and also acceptable to the country's neighbours, especially Pakistan, Iran and Russia.

Various proposals are being made. Twenty per cent of Afghanistan's 28 million people live in cities. With a fertility rate of 6.6 children per woman, this figure will rise to 111 million by 2050, of which possibly half may be urban. It is therefore tempting to devolve administration to the largest regional cities; these are Herat in the west, Mazar-i-Sharif in the north, Kunduz in the north-east, Jalalabad in the east, Ghazni in the south-east, Kandahar in the south and Kabul in the centre. But such an apparently straightforward scheme would also need to take into account the regional ethnic mix. There has never been a census in Afghanistan, but most estimates of the major groupings are approximately as follows:

Pashtuns	~ 40%
Tajiks	25%
Hazara	19%
Uzbeks	6%

The Pashtuns are located in the south, with pockets elsewhere, including Kunduz in the north-east. They also extend across Pakistan's Federally Administered Tribal Areas (FATA) into the other non-FATA parts of the Khyber-Pakhtunkhwa Province. Russia and satellite states will support the Tajiks and Uzbeks (who will also be supported by Turkey). Tajiks traditionally dominate the central and northern bureaucracy and are strongly represented in the Afghan military. The Hazara are mainly Shi'i Muslims, which gives them much in common with Iran; they speak Dari, as do many Tajiks and Uzbeks in the north-west.

To complicate matters further, the various tribes operate a complex web of patronage networks from which the administrative centres lease power. The tribe and the family are the building blocks of Afghan society, the FATA and Balochi areas of Pakistan, and beyond. At this level the future of Afghanistan lies in the empowerment of local communities, for example a confederation of cantons (possibly as in Switzerland), which are strong enough to resist undesirable external influences – such as radical Islamists, narcotics operatives and warlords like Mangal Bagh – who are not true tribal leaders, but spring up when there is a vacuum in local politics. But Taliban leaders and local mullahs, who are often very close to the tribals, will have to be involved in whatever pattern of decentralised regions eventually emerges.

Tribal autonomy in Afghanistan has always resisted centralisation based on Kabul. This was the case in 1880 following the second Anglo-Afghan war, and also in the 1920s. But although much of the work of the present government's 25 ministries can be devolved, Kabul must retain certain functions, and these will need to be carefully and participatively negotiated.

One would expect any central government to retain control of the army, the judiciary, foreign affairs and a national bank – probably also revenue collection. But each of these will need regional and/or provincial representatives, and in choosing them a combination of shrewd judgement and tactical wisdom will be essential. In Pakistan, for example, it was a wise move for President Pervez Musharraf to appoint a retired General from the Orakzai tribe as Governor of the North-West Frontier Province (he was also the Chair of our College Board). It was also shrewd of India's BJP government to appoint a distinguished Christian theologian from south India (M. M. Thomas from Kerala) as Governor of the tribal state of Nagaland, consisting mostly of Baptists and Roman Catholics. Sensitivity, participation in decision-making (*jirgas*), and attention to detail will reap dividends at the regional level in the long run.

The central government could retain regulatory control of certain ministerial areas such as the customs, finance, the environment, transport and education – it will need to monitor the standards of education boards and university degrees, for example. But local participation is essential if people are to be given a stake in their future, and it is, ironically, only when national centres hand over power to local populations that a genuine sense of national identity begins to emerge.

The Western Coalition countries can encourage the process of participatory devolution in various ways, but education is the most important. Between them they might usefully emulate a model of university and technological development that was originally proposed by Pervez Musharraf and others between Pakistan and six European countries, but abandoned when Musharraf left office. Each country was to have funded and sent academic staff to set up six universities of science and technology in Pakistan. Once students had graduated they would do postgraduate research in the parent European country, returning home eventually to replace the expatriate staff. The entire scheme was to have been masterminded by the distinguished Cambridge nanotechnologist Professor Haroon Ahmed. It could easily be taken up now in Afghanistan with several Coalition nations participating. Pakistan could supply some of its excellent physicists, who were marginalised following Pervez Musharraf's resignation as president, and the Chinese, who are interested in Afghanistan's natural resources, could set up faculties of Earth Sciences to train young Afghans in mineralogy and petrology. And why shouldn't the religious and cultural centres of learning in Iran and Turkey set up joint programmes with Afghanistan to train the country's mullahs and imams?

5   The Taliban

In Pakistan, the Taliban consists of several branches and groupings, some more significant and visible than others. We have mentioned Sufi Muhammad, who leads the Tehreek-e-Nifaz-e-Shariat-e-Muhammadi, and is currently in the Central Prison, Peshawar, where he has become a recluse. During the brief period of sharia-enforced rule in the Malakand/Swat area the administration worked reasonably well, and the sharia courts were reckoned to be more efficient than government ones. The closure of hotels in the valley resulted in purer water in the rivers, and anyone who cut down trees without prior approval was publicly flogged. When approached by local Christians to ask if they could worship as usual at Easter, the Taliban agreed, adding that they should receive a list of any who missed the services![5]

Rule by the Taliban began to cause discontent when the more extremist son-in-law of Sufi Muhammad, Maulana Fazlullah, began to close girls' schools and executed people for trivial offences.

The army were eventually ordered to remove the Taliban, and were able to do so successfully by converging from the hills, which have no common border with Afghanistan. When they mounted a similar operation in Waziristan the militants escaped across the border, and the US forces did nothing to stop them. This has caused much bad feeling among the Pakistan military, which has suffered considerable casualties in these two operations (more than 2,500 troops dead, and many more civilians).

Baitullah Mehsud was for several years the leader of the Waziristan Taliban. He died – allegedly in a US drone attack – and his son Hakimullah took over. US reports claim that he has also been killed by a US drone, but students in Peshawar from Wana say that Hakimullah likes people to think that he is dead. They also point out that there is no clear way of deciding who is and who is not a Taliban militant. One student's brother joined the local Taliban in Waziristan for a few months – since he was a paramedic, his jobs included anaesthetising captives before they were beheaded. Another, from Hangu, said that the local dry cleaner joined the Taliban after his brother was killed.

According to the recent WikiLeaks disclosures, the USA believes that the ISI maintains links with the Afghan Taliban (led by Mullah Omar) and its allied Haqqani and Hekmatyar networks on the western front (Hekmatyar himself is dead), and also with *Lashkar-e-Taiba* on the Punjab border. They also believe that the Quetta Shura in Balochistan supports the Waziristan branch of the Haqqani network, and they have concentrated their drones there accordingly. While it is not clear what the current army chief, General Ashfaq Kayani, who was head of the ISI from 2004 to 2007, thinks of all this, his ISI successor, General Shuja Pasha, has stated that he wants an end to the ISI's support for 'proxy forces'.[6]

The USA maintains that their drone strikes in the tribal belt (which includes Waziristan) have killed ten of the top 20 al-Qaeda leaders. There is no way of verifying this, but according to Pakistan sources out of 44 Predator drone strikes in 2009 only five targets were correctly identified and 700 non-militant civilians were killed.[7] The New America Institute puts the number of civilian casualties slightly lower at 400–700 during the same period.

According to Anne Patterson, until recently US Ambassador to Pakistan, the unmanned drones run the risk of 'destabilising the Pakistani state, alienating both the civilian government and the military leadership, and provoking a broader governance crisis without finally achieving the goal [of eliminating the al-Qaeda leadership in the tribal belt]'.[8] Much the same has been said by Lt General Aurakzai, former Governor of Khyber-Pakhtunkhwa and himself a Pashtun from the tribal belt, who was forced to resign after brokering a controversial peace agreement via a tribal *jirga* in North Waziristan. He claims that the threat posed by al-Qaeda in the tribal areas has been 'greatly exaggerated' by the West, and that the drone strikes have caused many innocent deaths and a lot of collateral damage:

> Nobody has said don't fight terrorism. But if the US keeps asking us to do more, Pakistan will be in a critical position. So leave us alone for some time and let us give a political solution a chance.[9]

Al-Qaeda lost its Afghan base following the initial Coalition attack in 2001, but during the subsequent months its members were able to regroup and forge links with the Taliban. While the Coalition allies have never offered a clear justification for their continuing presence, the rejuvenated Taliban based their appeal and rationale on the following basic tenets:

1 The Coalition forces represent a foreign occupation.
2 Hamid Karzai is an illegitimate Western puppet (he is, in fact, a US citizen holding a US passport).
3 Historically, the Afghans have always won their wars (which more than anything reflects the treacherous nature of the mountainous terrain).
4 Whether or not the ISAF forces leave, the Afghans, and therefore the Taliban, will remain.

Talking to the Taliban about an Afghan endgame is, of course, always a good idea. But their prerequisite will almost certainly be that all Coalition forces must leave and that no US bases or drone facilities remain. But at a more local level the Taliban has already proved willing to negotiate on specific issues. In Wardak, for example, they were prepared to approve of women's education provided the girls were taught by women teachers. A similar plan was envisaged at Edwardes College in Peshawar when it looked as though the Taliban were about to take over the city.

We conclude this section with a quote by a distinguished Muslim scholar on the reasons why young Muslims are attracted by Islamic radicalism:

> What attracts young Muslims to this type of ephemeral but ferocious activism? One does not have to subscribe to determinist social theories to realise the importance of the almost universal condition of insecurity which Muslim societies are now experiencing. The Islamic world is passing through a most devastating period of transition. A history of economic and scientific change which in Europe took five hundred years, is, in the Muslim world, being squeezed into a couple of generations.[10]

Primary, secondary and higher education, with a strong emphasis on science and vocational technological studies, within the context of a more devolved and regionally based society, must be a high priority for Afghanistan's future.

6   Regional relationships

The cooperation of Afghanistan's neighbours will be crucial in achieving a peaceful and sustainable future, especially Pakistan and India, and to a lesser extent Iran and Russia. The United Nations should become a forum for discussion.

First, however, there needs to be a consensus about objectives and timescales. The USA currently plans to withdraw troops from mid-2011, and it is hoped that all Coalition forces will have left by an agreed date. Hamid Karzai's current constitutional term of office will continue until 2014.

The removal of an Afghan base for al-Qaeda was achieved in 2001. Building Afghanistan into a regionally devolved and democratic state with respect for a range of human rights, especially for women, could take more than 20 years. It is facile to imagine that if the Coalition forces, al-Qaeda and the Taliban were suddenly, as if by magic, to disappear, then Afghan women would instantly assume the freedoms of their Western counterparts. The key to women's rights is education – on both sides of the border – which is what we have been doing at Edwardes College in Peshawar, and what is being set up at Durham University where funds have been raised to enable Afghan women to study for degrees.

Realistically, the Coalition forces might hope to leave a relatively peaceful and stable Afghanistan, characterised by devolved and more participatory governance, the beginnings of democracy, and some basic human freedoms such as access to health care and education. It must not become a base for internal or international terrorism.

If devolved federalism is to work, then neighbouring countries must cooperate. Iran can influence the Shi'i communities in and around Herat and may be able to offer religious training to imams and mullahs. Iran will want an end to the narcotics trade and will not accept the continued presence of the US Shindand base near its border. The US must stop their one-sided rhetoric against Iran's nuclear programme to please Israel.

The Russians also will not want US bases near their borders. But they will be able to exert a positive influence on the Uzbeks and Tajiks. Turkey may also support the Uzbeks. China will want to continue its economic interests, such as copper mining, and will support ethnic Uighurs. Neither Uzbekistan nor Iran will want to be bordered by the Taliban, but the latter may have little choice if the southern Afghan Pashtuns opt for Taliban rule.

It is vital that India be persuaded to stop using Afghanistan as a proxy battle space against Pakistan. For this and other reasons, it is essential for peace talks between India and Pakistan to make progress. Kashmir is only part of the problem. Traditionally, India has enjoyed good economic and trading relationships with Afghanistan and with Hamid Karzai, who was educated in India.

India has not sent troops to Afghanistan and since the military defeat of the Taliban has become the sixth largest aid donor – funds are distributed within sectors chosen by the Afghans.

The West is concerned that since 1998 India and Pakistan have both acquired viable nuclear weapons. But each knows that the other will not use them; there should be much more cause for concern at the quantities of fissile nuclear material that went missing when the former Soviet Union collapsed. In the opinion of this author, who trained as a nuclear physicist, biological and chemical weapons pose a much more serious terrorist threat than nuclear ones.

Pakistan will only reduce its alliances with Taliban groups if it believes that the Indian threat on all sides is diminishing. US former Ambassador Anne Patterson has pointed out that no amount of US aid to Pakistan will ever change this situation.[11] Hamid Karzai was therefore wise recently to invite General A. P. Kayani, Pakistan's military chief and former ISI head, to Kabul for talks at the same time as he sacked his own pro-Indian security chief (A. Saleh).

Pakistan must be persuaded that a federal system in Afghanistan gives it a security belt and an area of influence. This will militate against the emergence of a cross-border 'Pashtunistan', and offers the possibility of peace among the restless tribal populations along the border, thereby reducing the pressures on an overburdened military. The Kashmir earthquake and recent floods have left more than enough of a legacy of major problems for any government. It would also be helpful to Pakistan if, to echo the words of former Governor Aurakzai, the USA were to stop demanding 'more, more!' of Pakistan's military, and stop killing civilians in their already restless border areas with their drones!

* * * * *

In conclusion, a satisfactory outcome in Afghanistan is achievable following the complete withdrawal of Coalition troops. But the nature of that outcome must be realistically and participatorily defined, and steps towards it must be taken as soon as feasible.

- *Internally*, there should be a progressive devolution of governance, which takes into account ethnic and urban factors and the cultural mores of the tribes. Careful consideration will need to be given to the distribution of ministerial responsibilities between central, regional and district governments and the implications at these different levels if parts of the south want to implement sharia law. Local leaders should be identified and encouraged to participate in this process, and they need to include Taliban representatives and religious leaders. Primary, secondary and higher education, with a bias towards vocational subjects, science and technology, must be funded adequately.

- *Externally*, we have indicated the importance of the collaboration of *all* Afghanistan's regional neighbours. The US-led Coalition must keep its agreement to withdraw all military forces (including military bases) and should immediately stop using unmanned drones. Pakistan and India must be discouraged from fighting a proxy war in Afghanistan and brought together to try to resolve a whole range of problems, of which the Kashmir issue is the most pressing.

In all of these measures, most of which can start now and proceed simultaneously, the one which is most frequently omitted from official discussions is underlined here as being of the utmost importance, namely education.

Notes

1 Abdal-Hakim Murad, *Islamic Spirituality: the Forgotten Revolution*, 2009, http://www.masud.co.uk/ISLAM/ahm/fgtnrevo.htm. But see also the same author's critique of ill-informed publications relating to suicide bombings and Islam emanating from, of all places, Ivy League university presses:

> A substantial literature now exists seeking to identify suicide bombing as a paradigmatically Muslim act. See, for instance, Shaul Shay, *The Shahids: Islam and Suicide Attacks* (Transaction, 2003); also Christoph Reuter, *My Life is a Weapon: A Modern*

History of Suicide Bombing (Princeton, 2004). This forms part of a larger determination to show the radicals as authentic expressions of Islamic tradition (see, for instance, the works of Emmanuel Sivan). The level of Islamic knowledge present in this literature is usually poor; see for instance Reuter's belief (p. 22) that the Mu'tazilites were founded by Ibn Sina and Ibn Rushd! Reuter is a *Stern* journalist, whose patronage by Princeton University Press shows the fragility of the standards of American academic institutions in times of international crisis.

> (Abdal-Hakim Murad, *Bombing without Moonlight:*
> *The Origins of Suicidal Terrorism*, October 2004,
> www.masud.co.uk, footnote 33)

2 Javed Aziz Khan, 'Insecurity haunts Peshawar', in *The News*, 11 January 2007.

3 Javed Aziz Khan, '16 blasts rocked Peshawar in less than eight months', in *The News*, 17 May 2007.

4 The two-page death threat was from Captain Halifah. He accused me of promoting co-education, being a non-Muslim (using the term *kafir*, which is incorrect) and of not letting students out of lectures on Fridays in time for the *jum'a* prayers, which we do. For these 'crimes' against Islam, I was to be suicide bombed. Nothing happened.

5 *Church Times*, 17 April 2009.

6 Much of this information has been published in the *Guardian* of 1 December 2010 following the WikiLeaks disclosures. It may not be new, but it has been conveniently classified.

7 *The Guardian Weekly* (editorial by Asim Qureshi), 16 April 2010, p. 20.

8 Anne Patterson, quoted in the *Guardian*, 1 December 2010, p. 6.

9 'Orakzai blames US, UK for violence in Pakistan', *The Statesman*, 27 March 2008.

10 Abdal-Hakim Murad, *Islamic Spirituality: the Forgotten Revolution*, 2009, www.masud.co.uk.

11 Anne Patterson's views on the importance of reducing Indo-Pakistan tensions are extensively quoted in the WikiLeaks documents.

Glossary of terms

burqa	the enveloping outer garment worn by women to cover their bodies when in public
chowkidar	night watchman
frangipani	flowering night-scented bush
ḥadīth	the words and deeds of Muhammad and other early Muslims and second only to the Qur'ān
hafiz-e-Qur'ān	one who recites the Qur'ān
jihād	a struggle or exertion, the only legal warfare in Islam
jum'a	Friday midday prayers
kharee	reciter of the Qur'ān during Ramazan
khatam-ul-Qur'ān	the final night of the recitation of the Qur'ān
madrasa	Islamic centre of learning
maghrib	prayer given at sunset
mali	gardener
masjid	mosque, a place for ritual prostration
muezzin	person who gives call to prayer
mujahideen	those who engage in *jihād*
mushaira	poetic symposium
Ramazan	the Urdu for Ramadan (Arabic), the ninth month of the lunar calendar, when fasting is required
shamianah	tent

talib	a person who searches for knowledge in accordance with Islam; Taliban is the plural of *talib*
tehsil	unit of government similar to a county, typically consisting of one or more towns and a few villages
zakāt	the giving of alms

Notes:

1 Arabic and other technical terms are given initially in italics with the appropriate diacritical marks (e.g. *imām*). Later, and if the term is familiar, a more standard form may be used (e.g. imam).

2 We have standardised the spelling of Muhammad when the prophet's name occurs inside Pakistan (as directed by the federal government). Elsewhere, as in quotes or in the case of an author based elsewhere, we may use Mohammed.

Notes

Chapter 1 The Prince Who Never Came

1 Arabic, Persian and Urdu words resemble one another, and the differences are often difficult to render in English. *Dervish* is a Persian word, usually spelled *darwish* in Pakistan, where the national language is Urdu. Our usage will be according to context. See also the glossary of terms.

2 Ramazan is the Urdu version of Ramadan.

3 David L. Gosling, *Science and the Indian Tradition: When Einstein met Tagore*, Abingdon, and New York, Routledge, 2007, p. 26.

4 Email from Alice Ross, Bureau of Investigative Journalism, to the author, 17 October 2012: 'The Bajaur strike of October 30 2006 remains one of the most shocking incidents in the entire series [of US drone attacks].' A report in *The News* (Pakistan) on 31 October 2006 states that 80-3 civilians were killed, including 69 children. A report in the *Independent* on 25 September 2012 based on US sources claiming to cover all US drone strikes between 2004 and 2012 makes no mention of it and does not show it anywhere on their map.

Chapter 2 Brave New World

1 On 7 November 2007, leaflets were distributed around the college containing a threat to kill the principal. Co-education was stated to be the main justification for this threat, but it was also claimed to be because the college did not close on Fridays in time for the *jum'a* prayers. This is not true. The two-page leaflet in Urdu was signed by an unknown person calling himself Captain Halifah.

263

2 This was originally the Royal Artillery (RA) Bazaar. Many locals call it *Toph Khana* (gun house) in Urdu.

3 According to Wikipedia and other sites, Shah Rukh Khan was born in Delhi. This is not true, though he may have acquired Indian citizenship by living in India for much of his life. There may be political reasons why he prefers to conceal his Pakistani past, though in a press interview he did once describe himself as a 'demented Pathan'!

Chapter 4 Enter the Taliban

1 The original Hezb-e-Islami was founded in 1977 by Gulbuddin Hekmatyar. It was not strictly Taliban but formed part of the 'Peshawar Seven' alliance of the Sunni *mujahideen* forces during and following the Soviet intervention in Afghanistan.

2 John L. Esposito, *Oxford Dictionary of Islam*, Oxford and New York, Oxford University Press, 2003, p. 313.

3 Ahmed Rashid, *Taliban*, London and New York, I.B.Tauris and Co. Ltd, 2000, revised 2010–13, p. 10.

4 Nicholas Barrington, *Envoy*, London and New York, I.B.Tauris and Co. Ltd (Radcliffe Press), 2014, p. 334. He cites Christopher Andrew and Vasili Mitrokhin, *The Mitrokin Archive II: The KGB and the World*, London, Allen Lane, 2005.

5 Stefan Halper, ed., *The Afghan Endgame*, Washington, Office of the Secretary of Defense, 2011.

6 Mohammed Hanif, *A Case of Exploding Mangoes*, London, Vintage Books, 2009.

7 Ahmed Rashid, *Taliban*, p. 89.

8 *Ibid.*, p. 130.

9 *Ibid.*, p. 135.

10 Peter Bergen's edited *Talibanistan: Negotiating the Borders between Terror, Politics, and Religion*, Oxford, Oxford University Press, 2013, p. 166, places his age as a Taliban fighter at 18; Ahmed Rashid more realistically at 27 (*Taliban*, p. 238).

11 Ashfaq Yusufzai, 'Impotence fears hit polio drive', 25 January 2007, http://news.bbc.co.uk/2/hi/south_asia/6299325.stm.

12 Daud Khan Khattak, 'The Taliban in Swat', in Bergen, ed., *Talibanistan*, p. 297.

13 Carey Schofield, *Inside the Pakistan Army*, London, Biteback Publishing Ltd, 2011, p. 1.

14 Robin Brooke-Smith, *Storm Warning*, London and New York, I.B.Tauris and Co. Ltd (Radcliffe Press), 2013, p. 201.

15 Schofield, *Inside the Pakistan Army*, p. 105.
16 *Ibid.*, p. 209.
17 Aqil Shah, *The Army and Democracy: Military Politics in Pakistan*, Harvard, Harvard University Press, 2014.
18 Grégoire Chamayou, *Drone Theory*, London, Penguin, 2015.
19 'Human face of hellfire – hidden cost of America's remote-controlled missiles', *Guardian*, 18 July 2011, p. 16.
20 *Ibid.*
21 *Ibid.*
22 'Outrage at CIA's deadly "double tap" drone attacks', *The Independent*, 22 September 2012.
23 Alice Ross, email to the author, 17 October 2012. For a full account of this incident see https://www.thebureauinvestigates.com/category/projects/drones/drones-graphs/.

Chapter 5 In the Eye of the Storm

1 Nicholas Barrington, *Envoy: a Diplomatic Journey*, London, New York, I.B.Tauris and Co. Ltd (Radcliffe Press), 2014, pp. 326–7.
2 Anatol Lieven, *Pakistan: A Hard Country*, London, Allen Lane, 2011, p. 254.
3 Saeed Shah, *Guardian*, 27 August 2008.
4 Ahmed Rashid, *Taliban*, London and New York, I.B.Tauris and Co. Ltd, 2000, p. 240.
5 'Easter with Taliban blessing', *Church Times*, 17 April 2009.
6 'Diocese tries to help Swat refugees', *Church Times*, 22 May 2009.
7 'Eleven killed and 70 injured in suicide bomb blast at luxury hotel in Pakistan', *Guardian*, 10 June 2009.

Chapter 6 Islam in Context

1 John L. Esposito, *Oxford Dictionary of Islam*, Oxford and New York, Oxford University Press, 2003, p. 326.
2 Olaf Caroe, *The Pathans*, Oxford, Oxford University Press, 1958, p. 100.
3 *Ibid.*, p. 101.
4 This incident is recorded in 1 Samuel 31.4 and slightly differently in 2 Samuel 1.6.
5 Shaikh Abdal-Hakim Murad, 'Bombing without Moonlight', October 2004; see www.masud.co.uk.

6 Mohammed Hanif, *A Case of Exploding Mangoes*, London, Vintage, 2009, p. 164.

Chapter 7 Educational Renaissance

1 Pervez Hoodbhoy, 'Pakistan's Higher Education System. What Went Wrong and How to Fix It', *The Pakistan Development Review* 48: 4 Part II, Winter 2009, pp. 581-94 (p. 585).

2 *Ibid.*, p. 581.

3 James Prinsep's unpublished report is quoted in Charles E. Trevelyan, *On the Education of the People of India*, London, Longman and Orme, 1838, p. 31.

4 Thomas B. Macaulay, Minute dated 2 February 1835, quoted in Bureau of Education, *Selections from Educational Records, part I (1781-1839)*, pp. 107-17. A reprint can be obtained from the National Archives of Delhi, 1965.

5 Keshub Sen, *Epistle to Indian Brethren*, quoted in David L. Gosling, *Science and the Indian Tradition: When Einstein met Tagore*, Abingdon and New York, Routledge, 2007, p. 17.

6 David L. Gosling, 'India's response to Darwin', in Yiftach J. H. Fehige, ed., *Science and Religion: East and West*, Routledge India, forthcoming 2016.

7 Gosling, *Science and the Indian Tradition*, p. 22.

8 C. F. Andrews, *Zaka Ullah of Delhi*, Cambridge, Heffner & Sons, 1929, p. 91.

9 R. C. Majumdar, *British Paramountcy and Indian Renaissance*, Vol. II, Bombay, Bharatiya Vidya Bhavan, 1965, p. 76.

10 Ramchandra's *Memoirs* are in Urdu and are available in the Library of the Brotherhood of the Ascension in Delhi. These quotations are taken from E. Jacob, *Life of Professor Yesudas Ramchandra of Delhi*, Vol. I, Cawnpore, Christ Church Mission Press, 1902. In some cases, extracts from the *Memoirs* that appear in Jacob's work were retranslated by Dr K. A. Farqui of Delhi University.

11 Jacob, *Life*, p. 11. Jacob renders 'Maulvīs' incorrectly as 'Maulavies'.

12 *Ibid.*, pp. 11-12.

13 According to Taylor's Theorem: $f(x+h) = f(x) + f'(x+0.h)$. $h+ \ldots$ where $f(x)$ is a variable function of x, h is a constant, and f' represents the first order differential with respect to x. *A priori* it would seem that '0' should be a complicated function of x and h, but in actual fact it is constant. Ramchandra proved why this should be so.

14 S. M. Ikram, *Muslim Civilization in India*, New York, Columbia University Press, 1964, p. 280.

15 T. E. Slater, *Proceedings of the Third Decennial Missionary Conference*, Vol. I, Bombay, 1892–93, p. 282. These original books are without a publisher and appear to have been produced by the conference participants.

16 Syed Ahmad Khan, in W. T. de Bary *et al.*, eds, *Sources of Indian Tradition*, New York, Columbia University Press, 1958, reprinted in two volumes, 1966, Vol. 2, p. 192.

17 *Ibid.*, p. 291.

18 M. Iqbāl, 'Man and nature', in *Poems from Iqbāl*, London, John Murray, 1955, p. 3.

19 M. Iqbāl, *Lectures on Metaphysics*, in V. S. Naravane, *Modern Indian Thought*, New York, Asia Publishing House, 1964, p. 290.

20 M. Iqbāl, *Reconstruction of Religious Thought in Islam*, in de Bary, *Sources of Indian Tradition*, p. 207.

21 M. Iqbāl, *The Secrets of the Self*, in de Bary, *Sources of Indian Tradition*, p. 203. Iqbāl also wrote a poem 'Time', *Poems from Iqbāl*, p. 50.

22 M. Iqbāl, in Naravane, *Modern Indian Thought*, p. 293.

23 M. Iqbāl, in de Bary, *Sources of Indian Tradition*, p. 209.

Chapter 8 The Dominant Minority

1 The USPG changed its name in 2012 to United Society or Us.

Chapter 9 Trials and Tribulations

1 Robin Brooke-Smith, *Storm Warning*, London and New York, I.B.Tauris and Co. Ltd (Radcliffe Press), 2013, pp. 281-8.

Chapter 10 Finally – A New Beginning?

1 David L. Gosling, *Science and the Indian Tradition: When Einstein met Tagore*, New York and London, Routledge, 2007; New Delhi, 2008.

2 'Christian groups fight over church funds in Mardan', *Dawn*, 27 September 2012.

3 'Corruption of the Diocese of Peshawar', Shoebat Foundation, 17 October 2013.

4 'Bishop of Peshawar wants to usurp Edwardes College: Shirazi', *The News*, 3 April 2014.
5 'Peshawar High Court seeks comments in Edwardes College principal appointments case', *The News*, 6 March 2015.

Chapter 11 Afterword

1 Robin Brooke-Smith, *Storm Warning*, London and New York, I.B.Tauris and Co. Ltd (Radcliffe Press), 2013.
2 Holly Williams, 'Islamic tale preaches to the converted', *The Independent*, 4 February 2015, p. 40.
3 David L. Gosling, *Science and the Indian Tradition: When Einstein met Tagore*, Abingdon & New York, Routledge, 2007, p. 40.
4 Brooke-Smith, *Storm Warning*, pp. 169-71.

Recommended reading

Banerjee, Mukulika, *The Pathan Unarmed: Opposition and Memory in the North West Frontier*, Santa Fe, New Mexico, School of American Research Press, 2000.

Barrington, Nicholas, *Envoy: A Diplomatic Journey*, London and New York, I.B.Tauris & Co. Ltd (Radcliffe Press), 2014.

Bergen, Peter, ed., *Talibanistan: Negotiating the Borders between Terror, Politics, and Religion*, Oxford, Oxford University Press, 2013.

Brooke-Smith, Robin, *Storm Warning: Riding the Crosswinds in the Pakistan-Afghan Borderlands*, London and New York, I.B.Tauris & Co. Ltd (Radcliffe Press), 2013.

Caroe, Olaf, *The Pathans*, Oxford, Oxford University Press, 1958.

Fraser, Gordon, *Cosmic Anger: Abdus Salam – The First Muslim Nobel Scientist*, Oxford, Oxford University Press, 2008.

Gandhi, Rajmohan, *Ghaffar Khan, Nonviolent Badshah of the Pakhtuns*, New Delhi, Viking, 2004.

Gosling, David L., *Science and the Indian Tradition: When Einstein met Tagore*, Abingdon & New York, Routledge, 2007.

Hanif, Mohammed, *A Case of Exploding Mangoes*, London, Vintage Books, 2009.

Hoodbhoy, Pervez, 'Pakistan's higher education. What went wrong and how to fix it', *The Pakistan Development Review*, 48:4, Part II, Winter 2009, pp. 581-594.

Lieven, Anatol, *Pakistan: A Hard Country*, London, Allen Lane, 2012.

Mujtaba, Tamjid & Reiss, Michael, 'The millennium development goals agenda: Constraints of culture, economy and empowerment in influencing the social mobility of Pakistani girls on mathematics and science related higher education course in Universities in Pakistan', *Canadian Journal of Science, Mathematics and Technology Education*, 15:1, 2015, pp. 51–68. DOI:10.1080/14926156.2014.992556.

O'Connor, Daniel, *Interesting Times in India: A Short Decade at St Stephen's College*, New Delhi, Penguin (India), 2005.

Rashid, Ahmed, *Taliban*, London and New York, I.B.Tauris & Co. Ltd, 2000.

Schofield, Carey, *Inside the Pakistan Army*, London, Biteback Publishing Ltd, 2011.

Sheikh, Farzana, *Making Sense of Pakistan*, London, C. Hurst and Co Ltd, 2009.

Siddiqui, Mona, *Christians, Muslims and Jesus*, New Haven and London, Yale University Press, 2013.

Index

INDEX